UNDER A DARK MOON

TRUE MURDERS & MYSTERIES FROM NORTH QUEENSLAND

by

ROBERT REID

Copyright© 2003

UNDER A DARK MOON: True Murders and Mysteries from North Queensland

First published in Australia in 2003 by Blue Heeler Books

Copyright© Robert Reid 2003

All rights reserved. No part of this publication may be reproduced, stored in a retrieval system, transmitted in any form or by any means, electronic, mechanical, photocopying, recording or otherwise, without prior written permission of the publisher.

National Library of Australia

Cataloguing-in-Publication data

Reid, Robert, 1939-

Under a Dark Moon: True Murders and Mysteries from North Queensland

ISBN 0 9751119 0 6.

1. Crime - Queensland, Northern - Case studies.
2. Murder - Queensland, Northern - Case studies. 1. Title.

364.9943

Cover design by Sheldrake Creative

Typesetting by K & A Collier

Printed in Australia by Griffin Press Pty Ltd

CONTENTS

CHAPTER ONE	**The Fatal Voyage**	1
CHAPTER TWO	**The Wheelie Bin Murder**	18
CHAPTER THREE	**Death in the Hinchinbrook Channel**	37
CHAPTER FOUR	**Where is Patanela?**	55
CHAPTER FIVE	**Dark Justice**	80
CHAPTER SIX	**"Trial by Television Framed Me for Murder"**	101
CHAPTER SEVEN	**The Killing of Jason Tyler**	124
CHAPTER EIGHT	**Missing on Mt Sorrow**	148
CHAPTER NINE	**A Lonely Place to Die**	164
CHAPTER TEN	**The Last Dive of Tom and Eileen Lonergan**	185
CHAPTER ELEVEN	**Who Killed Rachel Antonio?**	223
CHAPTER TWELVE	**Natasha Ryan and the Monster of Rockhampton**	236
CHAPTER THIRTEEN	**No Justice for the Mackay Sisters**	256

UNDER A DARK MOON

this book is dedicated to
the families who can never forget

INTRODUCTION

Strange things happen in the tropics of North Queensland.

It's a moody place, a canvas of wild beauty and drama, where exotic landscapes huddle together, juxtaposed in strange patterns as if they don't belong, yet exist for some mysterious, unknown purpose. There are towering mountain ranges, cloaked in mantles of lush, impenetrable rainforests, where ancient plants and animals live untouched by the passage of time. There are vast savannah grasslands, big-sky plains, and mangrove-lined rivers that wind in great looping curves through delta wetlands and out to sea. There are hardy forests of eucalypt, bloodwood and ironbark trees that have survived cycles of fire and drought for millennia. There are hills of giant black boulders tumbled upon each other where no vegetation grows and humans dare not tread. There are coastal swamps, and mangrove thickets, and white-sand beaches that stretch for thousands of kilometres around Cape York Peninsula. There are underground tubes of stone where rivers of molten fire once rampaged. And there are places that sit alone, isolated remnants of great continents now gone, brooding on their lost past.

Then there are the destructive forces of nature that bear down on the beauty. When the monsoon rains arrive at the beginning of summer they bring with them high seas, floods and terrifying cyclonic winds. This is the season of drama and danger, when only the foolhardy fail to prepare themselves and their homes against the threat of unleashed natural power. This is the time when muddy rivers quickly rise and estaurine crocodiles are ready to mate and fiercely protect their territory. These kings of the rivers and tidal lands, unchanged since time began, remain absolute masters of their environment. One error in judgement can quickly turn to tragedy. A steady roll-call of people have fallen victim to these lethal beasts, yet crocodiles belong in this land, magnificent creatures patrolling the domain they have always ruled.

Many human lives are lost in the steamy, restless tropics of north Queensland. People wander too far and die. Others die in waterholes and fall from cliffs. Still others die in the placid waters of the Great Barrier Reef. Some simply disappear and are never seen again. And some are murdered.

For a place with so few people, far from the mean streets of Australia's big cities, macabre killings happen too often. Murders that sometime defy reason and can only be described as mutations of the human condition. But why so many in the tropics? Is it just chance, a bad roll of the dice, and nothing more? Or people in the wrong place at the wrong time?

But perhaps it is something deeper than that, something to do with the primeval nature of the tropics, where life blooms large and vibrant, but death strikes quickly, returning physical existence to the earth with savage finality. Perhaps the monsoon has an influence on the human psyche that leads rational minds into unknown realms of madness.

Perhaps murder and mystery share a common bond with those unknown forces.

Perhaps it has something to do with living under a dark moon.

THE AUTHOR

Robert Reid is an award-winning investigative journalist and author who has published a wide range of articles and stories in newspapers and magazines both nationally and overseas.

Robert began his career as a fiction writer and has had short stories published in several Australian magazines and in an anthology of Queensland authors.

In 1993 Robert co-authored (with journalist Paul Whittaker) *Patanela is Missing*, an investigative account of Australia's greatest sea mystery. Sightings of the mystery vessel were subsequently reported in north Queensland and these have been documented in a chapter included in this book.

In 1997 Robert published *Third Party to Murder*, the result of a four-year investigation into the strange deaths of Atherton women, Vicki Arnold and Julie-Anne Leahy in 1991. A coroner found that Arnold had murdered her best friend and then committed suicide. Robert believed both women had been murdered and after the publication of *Third Party to Murder* the Queensland Government ordered a new investigation into the case. This was followed by a second inquest that heard fresh evidence. To the dismay of most observers of the case, including the community of north Queensland, many lawyers and journalists, and some police, the tragedy was again officially found to be a murder-suicide.

Robert recently spent three years as Cairns Bureau Chief reporting daily news for The Courier-Mail.

CHAPTER ONE

THE FATAL VOYAGE

Three people sailed out of Cairns Harbour on board the yacht Immanuel. Manfred Weissensteiner was later arrested on a South Pacific island. What happened to his companions?

At exactly 3.40pm on Wednesday 25 September 1991, Johann Manfred Weissensteiner stood impassively in the Cairns Circuit Court as a jury of nine men and three women pronounced him guilty of murdering fellow Austrian Hartwig Reudiger Bayerl and Bayerl's pregnant English girlfriend, Susan Avril Zack. Weissensteiner neither flinched nor showed any emotion when Justice Martin Moynihan sentenced him to life imprisonment, plus five years for the theft of Bayerl's 11-metre yacht, the *Immanuel*. The 26-year-old carpenter stood calmy in the dock as an interpreter translated the jury's verdict and the court's penalty. He then smiled faintly and repeated the only words he had uttered throughout the 12-day trial: "I am not guilty."

As he was escorted from the courtroom to begin his sentence, Weissensteiner paused to smile for the battery of press cameras. The smile was like the man himself - a carefully-controlled mask that, for reasons only he knew, concealed the secrets of the *Immanuel* and the fate of his two friends.

On Wednesday 18 November 1993, the High Court of Australia rejected Weissensteiner's appeal against his conviction by a 5-2 majority. The last door to freedom had slammed shut behind the enigmatic prisoner. When he was first told the news in north Queensland's Lotus Glen Correctional Centre, Weissensteiner smiled ironically and quietly declared once again that he was innocent.

Some observers of the case, including a number of journalists and lawyers, thought so too. Weissensteiner had been arrested and convicted entirely on circumstantial evidence in one of Australia's most bizarre and intriguing criminal cases. Although he had been arrested in sole possession of the *Immanuel*, no bodies or weapons were ever found, nor were there any signs of bloodshed. And there were no witnesses to murder. Despite this, the jury took only five hours to find him guilty.

During the trial, as with committal proceedings four months earlier, Weissensteiner, from the town of Bad Gams in Austria, showed no emotion, except for an occasional smile, as if he had deliberately decided not to take part in the proceedings. Incredibly, he did not to take the stand and give evidence on his own behalf, prompting the trial judge to inform the jury that inference could be drawn from the defendant's silence.When they rejected Weissensteiner's appeal two years later the High Court judges agreed, stating Weissensteiner had failed to explain his possession of the yacht in the absence of its owner, and the jury was right to conclude that he had not only stolen the vessel but had been involved in the deaths of Bayerl and Zack.

By his choice of silence, Weissensteiner shut the cell door in his own face, effectively locking himself away for life.

The strange and chilling saga of Weissensteiner, Bayerl and Zack began on the Cairns waterfront in early 1989 when Hartwig Bayerl arrived from Adelaide after living there since 1983 and becoming an Australian citizen. It wasn't long before he began to attract attention as a strange and fanatical prophet of doom. The 36-year-old drifter - formerly a toolmaker and merchant seaman from Salzburg - was obsessed with a bizarre theory that the international Freemason organisation was controlled by the world's police, legal and justice systems, and was plotting a nuclear holocaust in order to reduce the world's population by 80 per cent. Bayerl also believed that passages in the Bible relating to Armageddon proved his theory. Further, he claimed that extra-terrestrial aliens in the shape of lizards were involved in the Freemason conspiracy and were gradually taking over the planet by living in human bodies.

Machi Kondos, a former girlfriend who lived with Bayerl for two years, gave evidence in court that Bayerl had prepared himself to survive under harsh conditions by living off the land. She said the pair had camped near Kununurra in the Kimberley region of Western Australia for several months while Bayerl practised his bushcraft skills.

Another former girlfriend, Margarita Luka, said Bayerl started work on a bomb shelter beneath his Adelaide house in 1984 which he intended to stock with gas masks, protective clothes and food supplies, because he feared a nuclear war was imminent in the early 1990s.

Soon after arriving in Cairns, Bayerl became a familiar figure among the boating fraternity - a wild-eyed, marijuana-smoking character who constantly harangued anyone who would listen to his visions of doomsday. Eventually, however, few wanted to listen, and Bayerl was avoided by the local boaties who saw him as an arrogant nuisance.

Except for Weissensteiner - who liked to be called Manfred instead of Johann - and attractive 31-year-old Susan Zack from Chigwell, England. Both became willing victims of Bayerl's intense charm and soon fell under the spell of his relentless prophecies.

In October 1988, after buying the steel-hulled yacht, the *Elizabeth M*, for $45,000 - the proceeds from the sale of his Adelaide house - the brooding, darkly handsome Bayerl immediately renamed the vessel *Immanuel*, which means "God is with us" in the Old Testament.

For a time Machi Kondos lived with Bayerl on board the yacht, but grew fearful of his fanatical dream of escaping to some some distant South Pacific haven where he would be safe from the coming holocaust. She gave evidence in court that Bayerl "lived in a lot of religious fear" and offended everybody with his "end of the world" theories.

"He became violent at that stage and if anyone tried to take his boat away I don't know what would have happened," Kondos told the court. "I was afraid to sail off with him because he couldn't sail and I couldn't sail."

Kondos said Bayerl became influenced by a religious sect leader they met on an island during a 1987 visit to the Phillipines, who preached that "we were living in the last days of the world". She said the "missionary" talked about the Bible and "Satanic groups", such as the Freemasons, whom Bayerl believed were linked to the number 666, referred to in the Bible as the Devil's number. After that he became obsessed with warning others of approaching Armageddon.

"He wanted a base on an island for when the world blew up," Kondos said in evidence. In a further statement to the court, she said Bayerl had told her parents: "If you don't hear from us when things turn bad, don't worry, we will be all right."

Bayerl told his mother almost the same thing in late November 1989 when he telephoned her in Austria to say he was leaving Cairns soon on his yacht and taking Susan Zack with him. Elfriede Baylerl wept in court as she recalled the last words from her son: "Don't worry, you will never cry for me."

In April 1989, two weeks after Bayerl met Zack, Machi Kondos walked off the yacht and away from their relationship. "He paid me $7,000 in cash for the time we'd been together. It came from Susan Zack," she said.

Weissensteiner met Hartwig Bayerl for the first time in August 1989 when he answered an advertisement on a hostel noticeboard for a cabinetmaker, and agreed to help refit Bayerl's yacht. Working on the interior of the *Immanuel*, the quiet, introspective loner easily fell under the dominance of Bayerl's forceful personality. In a prison interview, Weissensteiner compared Bayerl with David Koresh - the self-styled Son of God who died with his followers in the bloody Waco, Texas, seige of 1993. "The more I read about Koresh, the more I think of Hartwig," Weissensteiner said.

But Zack, a university-educated world traveller and qualified pharmacist, was a rational, strong-willed individual, unlikely to be influenced by a person such as Bayerl. Strangely, though, she was. Her friends watched helplessly as she changed from a well-groomed, outgoing young woman into a "dishevelled stranger with a different personality".

The three were seen constantly working together on board the *Immanuel*, moored in Trinity Inlet adjacent to the Cairns wharf. Bayerl made no secret of the fact that he was fortifying the hull and bullet-proofing portholes in readiness for his long voyage into the South Pacific to escape the impending holocaust. Zack sold all she owned, including a $45,000 marina berth, to refit the vessel - amounting to an estimated total of $100,000. According to Weissensteiner, *Immanuel* was a "floating fortress".

Cairns yachtsman Patrick Francis Diver told the court he had known Susan Zack for five years and was shocked to learn she had been drawn into Bayerl's web of holocaust obsessions and drained of all her money.

"Sue was spending money like it was going out of fashion," Diver said. "She said if they had any money left they would take it on the boat and use it for toilet paper. She said it wouldn't be worth anything after the war."

Diver said Zack had tried to convince him of Bayerl's "truth" and wanted Diver to escape the impending world war before it was too late. She told him they intended to slip out of Cairns harbour under cover of night without telling the authorities, so the Freemasons wouldn't know where they'd gone.

In July 1989 Susan Zack became pregnant to Bayerl. The couple was last seen in November on board the *Immanuel* at Fitzroy Island, near Cairns. With them was Weissensteiner.

Zack's parents became alarmed when they hadn't heard from their daughter by 4 January 1990, and contacted the Cairns Port Authority expressing their concerns. As a result, port officer Angelo Nucifora visited the *Immanuel* to deliver a message to Susan. Nucifora testified in court that Weissensteiner appeared to be the only person on board the vessel. Weissensteiner told him that Zack and Bayerl had "gone to the Tablelands and would be back next week." Five days later Nucifora went out to the yacht again, but nobody was on board.

On 17 January Weissensteiner apparently sailed alone out of Trinity Inlet, heading for his officially declared destination of Papua New Guinea. Initially, customs and immigration officers had requested a written statement from Bayerl, as owner of the vessel, giving Weissensteiner permission to leave Cairns. Weissensteiner told customs officer Michael Golding that Bayerl had asked him to sail the *Immanuel* to Port Moresby, where he would meet him in six days time. However, Cairns immigration officer David Yeomans claimed Weissensteiner told him Bayerl was visiting friends in Kuranda and intended to wait for him there until he reurned from Papua New Guinea. Yeomans cancelled Weissensteiner's visa to return to Australia, because the Austrian's habit of leaving the country briefly each time his visa ran out, so he could return for another six months, were "actions not in the spirit of the visa". Nevertheless, Weissensteiner was somehow allowed to leave unhindered - even though, as Golding stated in court: "No written or verbal advice was ever received from the owner of the vessel". Weissensteiner later told police that, apart from their initial request for written permission, port officials didn't mention the subject again.

In August 1990, eight months after Susan Zack's parents in London had declared their daughter missing, Australian police were alerted by Interpol that the yacht *Immanuel* was anchored off Majuro, a tiny atoll in the Marshall Islands. Cairns police officers Detective Sergeant Bruce Gray and Detective Edwin Norris immediately flew to Majuro and arrested a surprised Weissensteiner. When he realised he was to be extradited to Australia, the fugitive feigned sickness, ran from the hospital and made a desperate but futile attempt to escape by swimming out to sea. When he swam back to shore, exhausted, Gray and Norris were patiently waiting for him. Weissensteiner later told an Austrian journalist the swim hadn't been an escape attempt at all, but merely a ploy to "gain time, hide for a while, write a letter to Bayerl and throw it in the letter box - this way nobody would have found out where he (Hartwig Bayerl) went." Weissensteiner said it would have been "silly" to try and escape and that wasn't his intention.

Police discovered the name *Immanuel* had almost faded from the hull of the vessel and a tarpaulin with the word "Mani" crudely painted across it was hanging over the rail, covering the original name. During a taped interview with police in Majuro, Weissensteiner said the word was a shortened version of his own Christian name and he had painted it because "Hartwig doesn't want it (the name *Immanuel*) on the boat." But in a book entitled "Mystery 666" found on the yacht, a highlighted passage reads: "Mani - Born in Baghdad in the third century AD - claimed to be the Apostle of Jesus".

Police found personal items belonging to Bayerl and Zack on board the vessel, including clothing, Bayerl's Bible - which his parents said he always carried with him and would never leave behind - and Zack's jewellery. Two rifles were also discovered on board.

A specialist police crew flown to Majuro to sail *Immanuel* back to Cairns endured an experience they'll never forget. They found the vessel "uninhabitable" due to an unbearable bilge stench and an infestation of cockroaches. As well, the yacht was dangerously overloaded and the engine had seized. The crew - three police officers and a Gold Coast sailmaker - spent several days repairing the yacht before putting to sea. It wasn't long before they wished they hadn't. After five days limping across the ocean at four knots, a fuel leak forced the crew to shut down the engine and backtrack 250 kilometres against the wind to Ebon, a tiny atoll almost completely isolated from the rest of the world.

After repairing the leak in front of an audience of astonished islanders, the crew put to sea again in what became a nightmare 13-day southward journey to Nauru. The vessel was becalmed for long periods in extreme heat that turned the interior into an oven and the deck a hotplate that melted the crew's shoes. It was, as crewman Sergeant Allan Manteit of the Brisbane Water Police put it, a "great adventure that turned into a nightmare".

At Nauru, after the engine seized up once more, the voyage was abandoned and the disabled *Immanuel* completed the rest of its journey to Cairns lashed to the deck of a phosphate freighter.

Weissensteiner told police that Bayerl and Zack had left him in charge of the *Immanuel* in Cairns while they went off to Kununurra in Western Australia where they intended to disappear into the wilderness and live off the land. "We went ashore, had a beer, and that's it - they went to Western Australia," he said. Weissensteiner said he had lied to authorities about Bayerl and Zack being on the Atherton Tableland because Bayerl ordered him not to reveal their true destination. "Hartwig told me to say anything, any story at all, it doesn't matter what."

But Gray and Norris were sceptical and found plenty of holes in the fugitive's story. In fact, Weissensteiner had told Joe Murphy, an American who had spent 25 years in the Marshall Islands and published Majuro's only newspaper, another version of events that sounded more like a Hollywood movie script.

Murphy said Weissensteiner told him he had left Cairns alone and picked up Bayerl and Zack at an isolated part of Cape York

Peninsula where they loaded a shipment of weapons onto the *Immanuel*. From there the trio sailed to Bougainville where the crates of arms were unloaded and delivered to rebels fighting for the island's independence from Papua New Guinea. Weissensteiner was then instructed to sail on alone to Port Moresby to clear customs. From there he was told to sail the yacht to Majuro, and wait there for Bayerl to contact him.

Weissensteiner later told Austrian journalist Werner Kopacka the same story during an interview in prison, referring to the weapons operation as the "Bougainville deal". Kopacka asked if the rebels paid for the guns in gold or marijuana. At the mention of marijuana, Weissensteiner smiled but said nothing.

Joe Murphy testified in court that Weissensteiner had turned up in Majuro in April 1990 and worked for him as a carpenter. He said the mild-mannered Austrian was well liked and locals were shocked when he was arrested. In fact, Murphy retained lawyers on his behalf until he realised the Austrian was to be charged with murder. "We advised him not to fight extradition." Murphy said. At one stage Weissensteiner had protested: "But they have nothing, they have no bodies, no proof."

Murphy allegedly told Werner Kopacka in a telephone conversation that Weissensteiner was seen as "a nice chap who was interested in the island girls and drank beer with us".

Defence counsel, Michael Sumner-Potts, asked Murphy if he had any reason to doubt Weissensteiner's Bougainville story.

"Yes, because I'd heard several variations of this story and got the impression Bayerl was a kind of nut, and this guy (Weissensteiner) had been stumbling from one island to another looking for Majuro."

Weissensteiner had, in fact, first turned up on the island of Kosrae - 1,000 kilometres west of Majuro - and then Kiribati, several days sailing to the southeast of Kosrae, before managing to make his way northwest to Majuro without apparent incident.

Ingomar Carlsson gave evidence at the trial that he met Weissensteiner in Kosrae and the Austrian told him he had bought the yacht from an old man in Cairns and he was sailing it to Hawaii. But Antony Dujmovic, an Australian citizen who worked with Weissensteiner in Majuro, testified the defendant told him he had worked as a gigolo in Australia to pay for the yacht. Weissensteiner had also mentioned he'd had a relationship with an older woman who suffered from a terminal disease.

It was well known on the Cairns waterfront that neither Bayerl, Zack nor Weissensteiner were competent sailors. Once, attempting to manoeuvre the *Immanuel* into position for repair work in dry dock, Bayerl crashed into the wharf. On another occasion a Cairns yachtsman sailed with the three to nearby Green Island but "couldn't wait to get off".

"It was a hair-raising trip and it was obvious to me none of them could sail," he said.

Cairns resident Herbert Hofmann sailed on the renamed and fortified yacht's "maiden" voyage and was also relieved to survive the trip. "Hartwig had no idea about sailing. We were almost stranded on a reef that time," he said.

A dry dock crane driver had this to say: "Hartwig was a madman, whom people avoided. I would not have sailed with him even to the entrance of the harbour. You hardly ever saw him without a joint. He smoked marijuana like others smoke cigarettes."

Weissensteiner admitted to detectives Gray and Norris in Majuro that he "knew nothing, nothing at all" about sailing before he left Cairns, but relied upon electronic satellite navigational equipment and "learned as (he) went" to complete the journey.

Weissensteiner's incredible claim that, without any ocean sailing knowledge whatsoever, he sailed 3,500 kilometres single-handed across the Pacific from Cairns to Majuro without incident raised plenty of eyebrows among police investigators. They simply didn't buy it at all. Bayerl and Zack must have been on board for at least most of the journey, they reasoned, or Weissensteiner couldn't have made it to Majuro.

Experienced seafarers told the court that Hartwig Bayerl's obsession with fortifying the *Immanuel* had made it extremely unseaworthy and not fit for ocean voyages. Richard Schaeffer, a professional boat builder, had advised Bayerl his modifications were making the vessel too heavy, but his advice was ignored. "I was surprised the boat was found so far north - I didn't think it would make it that far," Schaeffer said.

Engineer Daniel Croucher gave evidence that Bayerl added too much steel to the *Immanuel's* rudder, making it so heavy that four men could hardly lift it. "The rudder was perfectly fine as it was and nobody with any experience would have added those steel plates," he said. Croucher said when he joked about Bayerl "getting ready for World War Three," the Austrian flew into a rage. "He started raving like a madman in a mixture of both languages and I couldn't understand what he was saying. I backed off and decided to stay well away from him."

Hartwig Bayerl anecdotes were common around the Cairns waterfront. Stories like the marijuana-smoking prophet shooting wildly at the *Immanuel's* supposedly bullet-proof portholes and ordering the whole lot replaced when one cracked. And stories of a visibly pregnant and depressed Susan Zack sobbing for hours on end in Bayerl's car.

German-born electronics engineer Karl Dieter Oelrichs, who lived on his yacht anchored near the *Immanuel*, said he was eventually "the only living person left who would listen to Hartwig's ravings without telling him to get lost". That is until Bayerl threatened to blow Oelrichs' head off during a dispute over money.

"Before that he asked me to sail my boat with the *Immanuel* to the South Pacific ocean because two boats were better than one. He said we would pick up some black girls along the way because they were good at surviving."

Bayerl told Oelrichs he had guns and explosives on board and would use them to defend himself when society broke down and he was forced to live as a pirate by raiding other boats to stay alive. Oelrichs spent hours listening to stories of doom and the ultimate destruction of civilisation. He heard that the Freemasons had recruited other groups such as the Rosicrucians and they were using subliminal television messages to brainwash whole populations into civil war. Bayerl also believed that a force known as "pyramid power" ordered the destruction of the world every 2,000 years and it was time for it to happen again.

Oelrichs said it was obvious Bayerl was mentally unbalanced as his stories became even more bizarre, such as his belief that aliens were turning people into lizards and that television was an experiment by the aliens to induce people to kill themselves under the shower in mass suicides. Bayerl also told him the Bible said Jesus was the Devil.

Bayerl planned to sail from Cairns in the dead of night to avoid customs. Once safely on his tropical island he intended to scuttle the *Immanuel*.

Susan Zack's mother, Kate Marie Zack, gave evidence that her daughter was a dominant personality who "didn't suffer fools gladly" and it was out of character for her to associate with an "arrogant and self-opinionated" person like Bayerl. She said Susan was a prolific letter writer who always kept in touch with her parents, but she hadn't been heard from since 22 November 1989. "If my daughter was alive she'd be in touch with me now," Zack tearfully told a hushed court.

Evidence was given that as well as paying for extensive modifications to the yacht, Susan Zack had purchased $50,000 worth of sophisticated navigational equipment, a salt water conversion unit and 150 detailed ocean charts. Zack was regarded in boating circles as a naive young woman with too much money, hanging out with "yachtie bums".

Medical practitioner, Dr Saluay Kidson, testified that she attended Zack during her early pregnancy. Zack, who worked in a pharmacy next door to Kidson's surgery, was "very surprised" at being pregnant and at that stage was considering an abortion. The doctor was concerned that the unplanned pregnancy might cause Zack undue stress and "place her in jeopardy".

"I felt that if she didn't come to terms with the pregnancy she could inflict self-harm - suicidal tendencies are always possible with pregnancies," Kidson said. However, shortly afterwards, Zack suddenly announced she was looking forward to the birth and had "resolved all her conflicts". Kidson said Zack gave the distinct impression she intended to have the baby in a hospital when it was due at the end of April 1990.

While Hartwig Reudiger Bayerl prepared his bullet-proof floating fortress for that great, final voyage into the unknown, Johann Manfred Weissensteiner went almost unnoticed in the bustle of boating activity in Cairns Harbour. Quiet, with only a basic grasp of English, he worked with his new friends long into the night, seemingly content to play a back-stage part in Bayerl's grand plan to escape Armageddon.

But nobody knows what Weissensteiner was thinking as

departure day approached. Was he looking forward to sharing Bayerl's vision of discovering a brave new world where only the chosen ones would survive? Or was he nurturing secret plans of his own - a dark vision of betrayal and murder that would leave him free to sail the South Seas alone on board the *Immanuel*?

Manfred Weissensteiner was confident he would never be convicted of murder. He was innocent, he maintained, therefore the court must set him free. There were no bodies and no witnesses to murder - and how could he be sent to jail for something he didn't do? But his failure to explain to the jury what happened on that fateful voyage to the Marshall Islands sank him like a stone.

But Weissensteiner blamed his defence team, claiming barrister Michael Sumner-Potts and solicitor Danny Towne advised him not to give evidence and says, in spite of an interpreter being present, he couldn't follow court proceedings, except to "sometimes catch the beginning or end of a sentence".

"It's not true that I refused to give evidence - I was advised not to," he said during a prison interview.

Sumner-Potts, however, denies any suggestions that he and Towne were to blame for their client's silence, insisting every effort was made to persuade Weissensteiner to give evidence on his own behalf.

"Manfred was always his own worst enemy. He was very difficult to talk to and it was his sole decision to stay silent. We tried to convince him but our hands were tied. In the end I threw up my hands in despair. It wasn't until the death knock that he showed any interest in giving evidence, but by that time it was too late."

During his summing up to the jury, Sumner-Potts referred to the case as "a tropical Agatha Christie scenario", and drew attention to evidence that Weissensteiner and Zack were heavily influenced by Bayerl who was intent on planning, "with meticulous detail" his escape from the coming holocaust on board the *Immanuel*. "This vessel was his salvation, his key to Eden in the South Pacific, his paradise," Sumner-Potts told the jury.

The barrister also suggested that clothing and other possessions of the missing couple found by police on the yacht could only mean they would be needed in the future and that, indeed, Bayerl and Zack intended to return. "Wouldn't the female clothing go overboard with the bodies if there had been a wicked murder?" he asked.

Sumner-Potts suggested the missing couple had succeeded in their "Adam and Eve sojourn" and were still alive on Bougainville or another Pacific island awaiting the birth of their child.

"When you look through the eyes of Zack and Bayerl, this all falls into place," Sumner-Potts said. "The reality is Susan and Hartwig are alive. They were certainly alive the last time Manfred Weissensteiner saw them. Hartwig Bayerl has led the authorities on a merry dance. His plan has come off."

After the guilty verdict, Weissensteiner's appeal was lodged on the basis it was "unsafe and unsatisfactory". It was claimed the trial judge did not fairly direct the jury on the significance of the accused man's refusal to give evidence, and because of this the jury could have inferred guilt.

Sumner-Potts also raised the argument that if something had happened to Bayerl and Zack it did not happen in Queensland and the court therefore had no jurisdiction over the matter.

After the High Court rejected Weissensteiner's appeal, Sumner-Potts confirmed his faith in Weissensteiner's innocence, maintaining the convicted Austrian "still had some belief in what Bayerl had told him, and he was afraid of the consequences from Bayerl if he spoke the truth".

"It's a most unusual case and the High Court's decision is disappointing, but I'm sure that in the fullness of time more will be heard about this," he said.

Tapes of police interviews with Weissensteiner reveal investigators' frustration after endless questions and pleas to tell the truth are met with stony silences and mumbled replies of: "I don't know" and "I didn't kill anyone". Weissensteiner later went cold on the gun-running story, insisting instead Bayerl and Zack were hiding out near Kununurra in Western Australia and didn't care about the yacht because "Hartwig wanted to disappear and money wouldn't matter anymore." Weissensteiner remained adamant that Bayerl was to contact him by letter at the Majuro post office. Witnesses have added some credence to Weissensteiner's story by confirming he checked the post office every day while in Majuro.

But according to police, search parties had scoured the Kimberley area of Western Australia and failed to find any trace of the missing pair. Detective Sergeant James Cave of Kununurra testified that it was almost impossible for two people to live in his district of 22,000 square kilometres undetected for more than a few weeks without locals knowing they were there.

However, Kununurra cattle station owner Ian Sinnamon gave evidence that Bayerl had once lived on his one million hectare property for six months without assistance.

Weissensteiner told police he had a "special agreement" with Bayerl for work he did on the *Immanuel*, but would only say "*I know*" - as if it didn't matter what anybody else believed - and then shrug his shoulders when pressed for details. He was similarly vague about his movements since he arrived in Australia in June 1988, and refused to give details about "friends" whom he claimed had provided him with money and accommodation during his travels. Asked what made Bayerl such a good friend he replied: "He was clever (and) I liked him. I believe Hartwig. He doesn't believe, he *knows.*"

Wolfgang Link, a former inmate of Townsville's Stuart Creek jail, where Weissensteiner was held awaiting his trial, gave evidence the accused man told him Bayerl and Zack would never be found.

Link said Weissensteiner whispered "they can't find those two" in German so he couldn't be overheard, while they were standing together in a crowded prison yard.

Michael Sumner-Potts questioned why Link had only come forward a week before the trial when the alleged remark was made more than one year ago. Sumner-Potts suggested Link had only a poor understanding of the German language and he made the allegation with the sole purpose of ingratiating himself with the authorities.

Sumner-Potts: "Those German words weren't even said."

Link: "They were said. I know what he said and I remember it clearly."

In late 1993 during an interview at Lotus Glen Correctional Centre, Weissensteiner recounted yet another version of events - but once again stopped short of revealing the truth of Bayerl and

Zack's disappearance.

In this latest story, Weissensteiner said Bayerl and Zack were both on board the *Immanuel*, hidden below decks, when he sailed the vessel out of Cairns in January 1990.

The three sailed directly to Bougainville, where Bayerl and Zack rowed ashore in a dinghy. Weissensteiner was instructed to clear customs in Port Moresby and then make his way to Majuro and wait for Bayerl to contact him. On his way to Port Moresby he was intercepted by a Papua New Guinea patrol boat and turned back, so he headed for the Marshall Islands, admitting he sailed by "the seat of his pants" with the help of navigational equipment Zack had taught him to use. Later in the interview, however, he said he "didn't know" who navigated the vessel, but "it wasn't me". He said the cabin was constantly awash and the motor broke down, stalling the vessel in windless heat that turned the steel hull into an oven. Weissensteiner maintains he never saw Bayerl or Zack again.

Weissensteiner said the *Immanuel* was not running guns to Bougainville rebels, but he said with a smile the vessel was "well stoked", hinting that large amounts of marijuana were involved. And something crucial happened on that Bougainville leg of the voyage - something that Weissensteiner witnessed but was too afraid to reveal. He admits he was involved in *something*, but not murder.

"If I told what I knew in court about what really happened I would have been jailed for only six or seven years, but I would have incriminated myself, so I said nothing. I didn't think any court in the world would convict me of murder, but in Australia..." Weissensteiner shrugged and smiled bitterly at the word "Australia".

Weissensteiner hinted that he witnessed Bayerl assaulting the pregnant Zack on board the *Immanuel*, but was too afraid to intervene. He refused to elaborate on the incident, and remained silent when asked if Bayerl had murdered Zack. He said he invented the story of Bayerl and Zack hiding out in Western Australia to sidetrack police.

"I hoped a letter would arrive from Hartwig to help me, but I've laid on my bunk watching TV for years waiting for that letter," Weissensteiner said. "I've protected Hartwig all this time, but I'm not afraid of him anymore. Just because I didn't tell my story I'm in jail...so I've come to the limit...I have to get Hartwig. I covered for him, but what for?

"I am the key to what happened. When I tell the whole story it will prove I'm not guilty of these crimes. The world will know I'm not a murderer."

But Johann Manfred Weissensteiner has been in Queensland prisons for 14 years now and still hasn't told the truth of what happened on that fatal journey. Did a maddened Bayerl kill his pregnant girlfriend, dispose of her body, and disappear into the rebel-held mountains of Bougainville, or to an uninhabited island somewhere in the Pacific? Was the murder of Zack the "something" that Weissensteiner witnessed - and did he then, out of fear or self-defence, kill Bayerl and hope that the *Immanuel* would never be detected? Or did the quiet Austrian really murder them both and bury their bodies somewhere on a remote Cape York beach, or dispose of them at sea? If so, how did the inexperienced Weissensteiner manage to sail the heavily fortified and clumsy yacht single-handed on a marathon voyage from Cairns to the Marshall Islands. It was a journey through reefs, atolls and sand cays that qualified master mariners say would be highly dangerous except for experienced yachtsmen. One thing seems certain - and that is Susan Zack is dead. But is Bayerl, the self-trained survival expert and cunning prophet of doom, still alive? If he is, why doesn't Manfred Weissensteiner break his silence and reveal the truth?

Alleged "sightings" of Hartwig Bayerl have been reported over the years - strangely, but perhaps significantly, all from Austria. In February 1993, Stephanie Toeglhofer, a former schoolmate and neighbour of Bayerl's, claims she saw him and a blonde woman in a supermarket in his home town of Salzburg, but was "too embarrassed" to approach him. As she watched, she said the blonde woman called out to him: "Have a look over here, Hartwig." Toeglhofer reported the incident to police and claims to be "ninety-nine per cent sure" the man was Bayerl.

In March 1998 the Austrian newspaper *Kleine Zeitung* published a photograph of a man it believed to be Bayerl, sparking renewed interest in the case by Interpol and other police agencies around the world. The photograph was allegedly taken just before Christmas 1997 by Manfred Weissensteiner's long-time friend and supporter, Herbert Brabec, in a Salzburg cafe. Brabec has campaigned for Weissensteiner's release since his conviction and has visited Cairns several times protesting his friend's innocence. In an interview in 1993 Brabec said Weissensteiner was "my life" and he was looking forward to starting a new life in Canada with the convicted killer when he was released from prison.

Brabec claimed he followed Bayerl to his home and photographed him several times in the cafe, but at first police didn't believe him, and the fugitive escaped. Austrian newspapers followed up the story with reports of "Bayerl" and his girlfriend on the run across Europe in a dark BMW vehicle. And a German doctor, Silvia Fischer, said the man in the photograph had appeared freezing cold on her doorstep in Tyrol in the winter of 1995 asking for shelter. Another report stated Bayerl is living in a shed behind his parents' house.

Brabec's photograph, also published in Australia, shows a man smiling straight at the camera, bearing only a minimal likeness to the known pictures of Bayerl. It stretches the bounds of credibility that Bayerl, if he was alive and on the run, would allow himself to be photographed in his hometown of Salzburg - and smile broadly for the photographer as a bonus! Reason would suggest that the fugitive - if he was alive - would avoid Europe, especially Austria, and remain hidden in the more remote regions of the world.

In the meantime, Manfred Weissensteiner continues his life sentence. Under existing Queensland law he will be eligible for parole in 2004. He will be 38 years of age.

CHAPTER TWO

THE WHEELIE BIN MURDER

She came to enjoy the Great Barrier Reef, but instead she was brutally murdered and her body dumped in a garbage bin.

Michiko Okuyama had only been in Cairns for six days when she made a simple but fateful decision to walk into the city centre, just four blocks away from her shared apartment in Upward Street. It was 11.30am on Saturday 20 September 1997, and the 22-year-old Japanese tourist casually told her flatmates she was going to post some letters and stroll around the shops in the laid-back north Queensland city. The attractive, brown-eyed young woman from Yokohama was settling into the tropical out-door lifestyle, and, although she spoke little English, she was looking forward to starting a scuba diving instructor's course. Already a qualified diver, she had a 12-month working visa and was keen to upgrade her skills and eventually become a guide on the Great Barrier Reef.

Okuyama was wearing a blue singlet with a button-up front, black shorts and red and white thongs with the letter M on each heel. She was also wearing a black document bag - commonly called a "bumbag" - strapped around her waist, and carrying a camera. She was just one of many thousands of young Japanese backpackers who flock to Cairns each year searching for fun and adventure. They have long become an accepted part of the city's itinerant, multicultural population. On that sunny Saturday morning, Okuyama would have blended in perfectly with the Cairns streetscape.

But Michiko Okuyama didn't return home to her apartment that day.

Police later traced her movements to an inner-city post office where she posted two letters, and then shopped for groceries at Woolworths. But sometime after that, the young Japanese tourist became caught in a web of evil, her innocent city walk cut short by a dark force that took her life away in a random act of senseless horror.

The alarm was raised on Monday, two days later, by Okuyama's worried Japanese flatmates. She hadn't contacted them and all her belongings, including her passport and contact lenses, were still at the apartment.

Michiko Okuyama was missing.

Police scoured the city and appealed to locals and tourists to come forward if they had seen the young woman or had any information regarding her whereabouts. Detectives from the Brisbane Crime Operations Branch arrived in Cairns and a major incident room was set up at the Cairns district police headquarters.

Okuyama's sudden disappearance quickly became a murder investigation, code-named Operation Undergo.

Reports that the woman had caught a bus at 11.45am from an Upward Street location and alighted ten minutes later near McDonald's restaurant on the Esplanade were investigated by police. The bus driver remembered her handing him a handful of money, not understanding how much the fare was. Two passengers also identified her as the missing tourist.

But the bus stop was situated five blocks west from her apartment, 500m in the opposite direction to the city. If she had walked directly south along Grafton Street instead, she would have arrived in the city centre 10 minutes later.

Detective Senior Sergeant Gordon Thompson of the Brisbane Homicide Squad said the tourist may have caught the bus because she had lost her way.

"The bus driver is our only real clue at the moment, because he's sure he picked her up," Thompson said. "Our biggest problem is her description. She's got short black hair and there are thousands like that in Cairns at this time of the year."

Thompson said he understood Okuyama was a stable, conservative young woman who was meticulous in her planning and not the type to take chances or do things on a sudden impulse.

"She's disappeared in the middle of the day in Cairns when there are thousands of people about, so nobody could just grab her off the street. She's just vanished. This is a major incident and we're treating this very seriously. We'll be staying here until we find this girl."

Desperate for a breakthrough, police studied dozens of old crime files searching for clues that might link solved or unsolved attacks on female tourists to the disappearance of Okuyama.

A new lead that the missing woman had been seen at The Pier Marketplace shopping complex on the day she disappeared gave investigators new hope that this was the break they were looking for. A mannequin dressed in an outfit similar to that worn by Okuyama was placed on display in the complex and in other city locations in the hope the clothes would jog somebody's memory.

A contingent of about 30 Japanese journalists and television camermen had by this time descended on Cairns to report on a case that was creating daily headlines in Japan. Concerns that Cairns was being portrayed as a dangerous destination had city officials worried that visitor numbers would decline in an economy heavily dependent on tourism.

A week after Okuyama's disappearance, 15 detectives, plus intelligence and analyst specialists, were working on the case around the clock. The city and inner suburbs had been repeatedly grid-searched and police appealed for help from the public, but the puzzle was no closer to being solved. By this time, few believed that Okuyama was still alive.

On 29 September the missing tourist's parents, Mikio and Toshie Okuyama, held their first media conference. The distraught couple arrived in Cairns soon after their daughter disappeared. They were composed during a public plea for help they said came "from our heart, to help us find Michiko as soon as possible." Mikio Okuyama stood and read from a statement in Japanese with local interpreter Yumi Smith repeating his words in English.

"Michiko has been talking to us that her dream is becoming a diving guide to introduce the world to this wonderful Great Barrier Reef in Australia," he said. "We would love to fulfil this dream for Michiko."

THE WHEELIE BIN MURDER

Homicide detectives stepped up their efforts to trace Okuyama's last movements. Police foot patrols blitzed city streets, distributing her photo and questioning shopkeepers and pedestrians who may have seen her.

A Japanese-speaking police officer, who had lived and worked in Japan, arrived from Brisbane to take over the role of interviewing and taking statements directly from Japanese witnesses.

But Regional Crime Co-ordinator Detective Inspector John Harris made it plain that while police continued to vigorously pursue leads generated by Operation Undergo, the investigation had advanced little since Okuyama was reported missing.

On Saturday 4 October it finally happened. A naked and badly decomposed body of a young woman was found partly-covered with pandanus fronds in a swamp in the inner suburb of Manunda. The search for Michiko Okuyama was over.

A resident of Wilkinson Street made the grim discovery at 10am when he investigated a powerful stench coming from a dirt track leading into the scrub. Harry Howles told police he'd returned from a holiday with his family a few days earlier and immediately noticed the unusual smell, which he thought was a dead animal. Howles later told a Cairns court that he knew a Japanese girl was missing and as the smell intensified he decided to investigate and assure himself that it was nothing sinister. He said the buzzing of flies drew him to an area that had been freshly disturbed and he saw "a pair of human legs sticking out of the leaves". When he touched the legs with a stick "they moved, so I ran home to call the police."

No clothes were found at the scene but jewellery and dental records confirmed the body's identity. Okuyama died from severe facial fractures that had caused an inhalation of blood, meaning she had been savagely beaten and drowned in her own blood. Police said it was probable she had been murdered elsewhere, sometime between 20-25 September, and the body dumped after the event. It could not be determined if she had been sexually assaulted.

The entrance to the swamp quickly became a shrine as the dead woman's friends and the Cairns Japanese community flocked to the grim scene to lay flowers and leave behind sympathy cards, many staying quietly to pray.

The hunt for Okuyama's killer started with a doorknock of houses in the immediate area and a police appeal to the public for information that could assist them in what was now a high-profile homicide investigation.

The disappearance and murder of Michiko Okuyama had placed Cairns in the world spotlight, with the Japanese media reporting news on an hourly basis as events unfolded. It was attention Cairns didn't need and city leaders were nervous about the negative publicity. They wanted the killer caught.

The manhunt didn't take long. At 3pm on Tuesday 7 October, three days after Okuyama's body was found, police swooped on a disused warehouse in Grafton Street and arrested a 16-year-old youth. He was later charged with murder. The youth - who cannot be named because of his age at the time - was using the building as a "squat", along with a number of street kids who occasionally visited the premises. Police said after the arrest a wheelie bin found at the two-storey warehouse was most likely used to transport the woman's body to the swamp.

The warehouse, known locally as the Elphinstone building, is situated two blocks from the murdered tourist's apartment and just five minutes walk from the city centre.

The breakthrough for police came from a radio talk-back discussion on the murder that led to vital information. The broadcast sparked a flood of calls, including several reports of a man seen hauling a garbage wheelie bin through city streets. Building on what they called "an extraordinary amount of information" police followed a suddenly hot trail of clues to the warehouse and arrested the suspect.

After the youth's arrest, police revealed the shocking news that Okuyama had been brutally murdered in a security vault in the warehouse on the same day she disappeared. She was left there for the next 10 days before being hauled across the city in a wheelie bin taken from a next-door business premises. The walls and floor of the soundproof, walk-in Chubb vault were smeared with blood. Meat and vegetables believed to be part of Okuyama's shopping were found rotting on a kitchen bench.

Police revealed the youth had also been living in a city caravan park but owed back rent on his hired caravan and kept away during daylight hours. A park resident described him as a "quiet and conscientious youth who didn't take drugs".

"He was a good kid, the kind you'd take home to meet your parents," the resident said.

The day before Okuyama went missing, the teenager approached several television news studios seeking publicity over homeless youth issues and was interviewed on camera. The next day he appeared in a newspaper article, warning the public of used syringes being discarded on city streets.

The case took another bizarre twist when the Salvation Army announced it had been searching the streets of Cairns for the youth at the request of his mother, who lived on the Sunshine Coast and had lost contact with him.

The Salvation Army regional co-ordinator Captain Peter Sutcliffe said the youth's mother had phoned and requested help to locate her son for a reunion shortly before his arrest. He said his organisation had made inquiries and left messages at places around the city where the youth was likely to frequent, but without success.

On Friday 10 October Okuyama's ashes were taken by her family to the Great Barrier Reef, where she had dreamed of working as a dive instructor. At Vlassof Reef, about 35 kilometres off Cairns, her parents and brothers, Hideo and Takeshi, scattered some of her ashes and cast flowers onto the water during a private ceremony.

The next day a huge media scrum and a crowd of more than 200 wellwishers bearing flowers and gifts packed Cairns International Airport to bid an emotional farewell to the Okuyama family as they prepared to fly home to Japan. People from Mossman, Innisfail and the Atherton Tableland joined Cairns residents in a tearful public apology for the murder. Strangers wept openly and embraced Okuyama's mother, Toshie, while her father, Mikio, formally bowed to the gathering.

"Thank you all for helping Michiko and coming here today," Mikio Okuyama said through an interpreter. "Michiko's dream was not fulfilled this time, but if other young Japanese people would like to come to this country just like Michiko, we wish them well."

Japanese television reporter Ogata Shoichi said he had never before seen such a public outpouring of grief and sorrow, adding such emotional displays never occurred in Japan.

"Japanese people do not like to express our feelings in public, so I never expected to see such things," he said.

The shocking murder of Michiko Okuyama led to an unprecedented barrage of public opinion in north Queensland that called for tougher measures - including the death penalty - for convicted killers, and a change in legislation to allow the identification of children under 16 who commit serious crimes.

Talk-back radio shows, television surveys and letters to The Cairns Post newspaper were flooded with demands for swift and final retribution against murderers and harsher prison sentences for other violent young criminals. A petition urging the government to repeal the current law was signed by more than 4,000 people and presented to Parliament.

Cairns mayor Tom Pyne added his voice to the public outcry, saying he believed the naming of juvenile murderers was necessary to protect the public.

"The way existing legislation is now means the people of Cairns could be living next door to a young violent criminal and they wouldn't even know he was there," Pyne said.

On Tuesday 27 October 1998 the accused youth, then 17, appeared in the Cairns Children's Court to face a murder committal hearing.

The court heard police investigating the murder of Okuyama could not produce any witnesses or direct evidence that placed the deceased tourist at the alleged crime scene. Detective Sergeant Ian Thompson said although blood found in the vault could not be DNA identified, blood on boxes owned by the defendant, and containing the deceased woman's belongings, matched blood found on a bra believed to be hers.

Entertainer Warren Ellis gave evidence that he had legal access to the leased warehouse and had employed the accused - whom he had met through his son - to repair a truck he kept behind the building. Ellis said he picked the youth up from his caravan in the mornings and drove him home each night. He said he first took the accused to the warehouse on 20 September, the fateful day Okuyama left her Upward Street apartment to visit the city.

But Gordon Sleigh, who owned the business premises next door to the Elphinstone building, said the youth had been working on the truck for much longer - possibly for as long as two weeks - before Okuyama disappeared. Sleigh's wife Patricia told the court that on the Sunday after the Japanese woman went missing she complained to the accused about him using their wheelie bin and asked him to return it. She said that at about 10.30pm on the day Okuyama went missing she heard a scream coming from the area of the warehouse.

The court was told that 10 days later, on 30 September, police visited the warehouse to investigate reports of a bad smell in the area. Incredibly, the youth showed police the borrowed wheelie bin and removed rotting vegetation and other debris from the top for their inspection. But in a scenario that stretches the imagination, the police failed to empty the bin and Okuyama's body wasn't discovered.

The committal court heard the accused told police he first saw Okuyama about 12.30pm on 20 September as she walked along Grafton Street towards the warehouse, but he went inside when she was still a short distance away. He claimed he couldn't remember what happened after that but the next day he discovered her dead body inside the vault. At other times he claimed her death was an accident, that he hadn't had sex with her, and nobody else was involved.

The court heard that Michiko's injuries showed she had been repeatedly rammed head-first into a wall. Blood and hair were found on the inside walls of the security vault and bloodied clothing belonging to the dead woman were later found in the accused's caravan.

A 16-year-old youth told the court that a street acquaintance named "Martin" had boasted of murdering a Japanese woman, but this evidence was not taken further by the accused's defence counsel Kevin McCreanor, who argued police had not established his client was responsible for the woman's death and he should only be committed to stand trial on the charge of knowingly disposing of a body.

Throughout the two-day committal hearing, while his father sat quietly in the public gallery, the accused youth showed no signs of distress, instead appearing completely at ease and smiling to friends. His mother was not present.

Magistrate Trevor Pollock ruled that there was a prima facie case for the accused to answer and committed him to stand trial for murder.

On Monday 14 September 1998, almost a year after Michiko Okuyama set out on her last walk through Cairns, the youth accused of her murder pleaded not guilty in the Cairns Supreme Court. The crowded public gallery included the dead woman's parents and a throng of Japanese media representatives.

Crown prosecutor Jim Henry told the court the youth claimed he suffered from recurring blackouts that lasted as long as 30 minutes, and he couldn't remember if he killed the woman, but then, on another occasion, told police her death was an accident. According to police, he said he "might have" killer her, and appeared concerned that his parents and employer would find out about the incident.

Henry revealed that the youth first came to the attention of police on 27 September 1997 - one week after Michiko went missing - when he coolly approached a police officer and told him he had seen a Japanese woman dressed in clothes similar to those worn by a mannequin on display. He said he had seen the woman walking towards the Elphinstone building carrying groceries in white bags.

Henry told the court the youth "indulged in a game with police" by pretending to be a concerned citizen eager to assist them in their search for the missing tourist.

"He struck a thoughtful pose, put his hand on his chin, and said he was not sure if she was wearing shorts or a skirt," Henry said.

Detective Senior Constable Michael Dowie testified he was on duty at The Pier Marketplace where the mannequin was displayed when the youth approached.

"He said he'd seen her, so I asked him to make a statement," Dowie said. "He was very calm and laughing at me because I couldn't spell his name. I didn't suspect him at all."

Constable Peter Stevens testified he went to the Elphinstone

THE WHEELIE BIN MURDER

warehouse on 30 September to investigate reports of a foul smell, and directed the accused to open a garbage wheelie bin. He said he saw white plastic bags covered with a brown liquid on top of what he supposed was rubbish in the bin. The accused told him the smell was caused by rotting vegetables beneath the bags and he was going to dump them.

Stevens told the court he later became the butt of jokes and criticised for not emptying the bin but after experimenting with a colleague climbing inside a similar bin he was convinced a body could not be hidden inside.

"I don't believe there was a human body in the bin, but because the whole bin was not viewed, there is the remote possibility that there was someone in there," he said.

On the same day, at about 2pm, businessman neighbour Gordon Sleigh once again confronted the youth over the continued use of Sleigh's wheelie bin and suggested they empty it of its foul-smelling contents so he could have it back. The youth declined the offer and said he was going to dump "the rotting vegetables" himself.

Sleigh told the court the lid was tied down and black liquid was oozing from a crack in the bin as the youth hauled it across Florence Street away from the warehouse. The next morning the bin was returned empty by the youth, who told Sleigh he had used "two bottles of disinfenctant" to clean it, but it still had a "horrible" smell.

A week later police returned to the warehouse, this time finding rotting meat believed to have been purchased at Woolworth's by Okuyama on the same day she disappeared. Police also discovered bin wheel marks outside the vault and bloodstains on the walls and floor.

After media coverage following the youth's arrest, 12 witnesses came forward to declare they had seen the youth trundle the wheelie bin through city streets to the swamp where he dumped the body. The witnesses variously described the stench as comparable to a rotting animal, chicken mature or fish guts. At one point, in Gatton Street, the bin tipped over and the youth struggled to stand it upright - but not before decomposing blood leaked onto the roadway. After disposing of the body the youth borrowed a hose from groundsman Robert Allery at nearby Trinity Bay High School. Allery said the youth was sweaty and dirty and refused to open the bin and wash it out until he "left him to it" and moved away. When he returned Allery asked the youth what the smell was and was told it was "just junk".

The spectacle of a sweating and dishevelled youth dragging an obviously heavy, foul-smelling wheelie bin three kilometres across the city in broad daylight without being challenged is quite remarkable. It can only mean not a single witness to this unusual event was alarmed or curious enough to intervene. All this after 10 days of headline-grabbing international speculation into the whereabouts of a missing - presumed murdered - Japanese tourist. The fact that the youth thought he could get away with such a brazen act is astonishing enough. The fact that he did almost defies belief.

In a sensational incident on day three of the murder trial, Kuranda resident and environmental activist Graham Bell angrily shouted death threats at the accused youth before storming out of the court. The accused smiled during the outburst. Bell was barred from the courtroom for the rest of the trial.

On day four the court was shown a videotaped police interview between arresting officer Detective Sergeant Ian Thompson and the accused when he demonstrated how he dumped Okuyama's lifeless body head first into the wheelie bin. He told Thompson all he remembered was seeing the Japanese tourist walking towards the warehouse one day, and then the next day he saw her dead inside a cardboard box in the vault.

In a chilling description of the vault death scene the youth told Thompson: "She was in the boxes at the end of the room with her knees underneath her, crouched down with blood coming out of her mouth and nose. I picked her up and put her in the bin and blood ran into her hair. I just tipped the rubbish that was in the bin out on the floor and put her in head first. I just put some other rubbish on top of her, vegies, potatoes that were going off, so I dumped them in there."

The accused told Thompson he didn't tell anyone about the body because he was scared. "I thought I might have done something wrong (and they might) take me away and lock me up because that's what they do on television. I just remember her walking and then it goes black...I saw her in the vault the next day."

The youth's former girlfriend gave evidence that she had seen the accused faint twice during their two-year relationship.

"They only lasted for a couple of seconds. He seemed to fall and then just get back up again," she said.

Dr Susan McDonald told the court she had examined the accused in February 1997 after he complained of suffering blackouts at the rate of one a week for the past 18 months. She said after a blood test and cardiograph showed no abnormality she referred the youth to a specialist for a second opinion.

Cairns Base Hospital specialist Dr Mark Loewenthal gave evidence he could not make an accurate diagnosis of the youth's condition because of the absence of witnesses available who could describe the blackouts.

"I did think it was unusual that he had been having them every week for 18 months and that his girlfriend hadn't seen them," he said.

Prosecutor Jim Henry said it may be arguable whether the accused's claims of blackouts were genuine or a "teenage attention-seeking device" but they were brief fainting spells in any case and not long periods of amnesia as the youth claimed in interviews with police.

During a police video interview the youth said the woman's body was in the bin when police arrived and ordered him to open it up for inspection. He said he removed paper and plastic bags from the top of the bin and could "feel her in there" as he rummaged around with his hands. He said he told watching police there were only rotting vegetables in the bin and he would empty it that day.

The court also heard that on 1 October 1997 the accused ordered two teenage boys out of the warehouse vault when they attempted to clean up the interior.

Mitch Hardy, 14, and Benjamin Martin, 13, were cleaning rubbish out of the vault for Martin's father, who leased the warehouse, when the incident occurred. The boys said there was a large plastic bag in the vault that smelled "like a dead toad or a dead rat" and the accused smelled the same. They said the bag was too heavy to lift and they couldn't see what was inside because it was wrapped up. Two days later they noticed the bag was gone and the smell was not as bad.

Throughout the video evidence, Okuyama's parents watched and listened calmly as the grisly events surrounding their daughter's death unfolded. A search of the accused youth's caravan was shown, where police discovered the victim's bum bag, blood-soaked blue sleeveless shirt, shorts, panties and bra. The clothes - that had been cut from the woman's body - were found in plastic bags stored in a cardboard box sealed with masking tape, hidden under three teddy bears and a framed photo of the accused's mother.

In the interview the youth said he was "in a daze" as he hauled the wheelie bin across town to dump the body: "I wasn't going anywhere in particular, I just kept walking. I was so sweaty and thirsty, it was a very hot day. I stopped along the way and put the rubbish from the bin in other bins outside people's places."

When he arrived at the swamp the youth found a dirt track, apparently at random, and followed it into the scrub where he dumped the body.

"There was all this liquidy stuff in the bin so I tipped it up and she slid out," he said. "I covered her with pandanus leaves to keep the flies away."

The accused told Detective Sergeant Thompson he was too tired to take the bin back to the warehouse that day so he left it outside the nearby TAFE college and returned the next day to retrieve it. Once again, the wheelie bin was hauled a distance of three kilometres through city streets at the peak of a massive search for the missing tourist, apparently without raising a single eyebrow.

In his closing address to the jury, Crown prosecutor Jim Henry said "the big three" items of evidence were enough to prove a circumstantial case of murder against the accused. These were that the youth disposed of the body using a wheelie bin, that he was in the warehouse at the time of the killing, and the deceased woman's bloodstained clothing was found in his caravan.

Henry pointed out that the accused told police that he couldn't remember what had happened, but on another occasion said it had

THE WHEELIE BIN MURDER

been an accident with nobody else involved.

"He made a big blooper there and brought himself undone. He told police he couldn't remember the afternoon she disappeared but he had enough memory to know it was an accident."

Henry said the Crown did not have to provide a motive for the murder, or the exact circumstances of her death.

"Those things will probably remain forever unknown," he said. "There's no point applying normal thinking to some of the accused's behaviour."

But defence counsel Kevin McCreanor told jury members they should reject an automatic assumption of guilt as presented by the prosecutor and consider instead that the wrong person had been charged with Michiko Okuyama's murder. He portrayed his client as a young person who had found a body on his first day at work, "then panicking and acting stupidly."

McCreanor admitted the accused youth had disposed of the body in a wheelie bin and even had the opportunity to kill her, but suggested his client had been put "behind the eight-ball" by the media and the Crown, who had been against him before and during the trial.

"If the jury accepts Mr Henry's argument, not only does the real killer go free but a boy who was 16 at the time could be convicted," McCreanor said.

But the next day, on Wednesday 23 September 1998, the jury of seven men and five women disagreed and took just 50 minutes to reach a guilty verdict. The accused - who had not uttered one word during his eight-day trial - hung his head and shut his eyes as Justice Stanley Jones thanked the jury for the attention given to "disturbing evidence" while "under the spotlight and under media pressure."

The teenager's father showed no emotion in the packed public gallery as prosecutor Jim Henry asked for the maximum sentence of life in detention for the "particularly heinous nature" of the crime.

Jones adjourned the court until a later date, requesting a pre-sentence report on the youth.

At a media conference after the trial, Mikio Okuyama said through an interpreter his family considered the guilty verdict a "natural" conclusion to the trial. He said his daughter's killer had shown no remorse for the crime and should receive a life sentence.

"An innocent girl had all her belongings taken before she was brutally murdered and dumped in a swamp. The killer gave up his right to live as a human being," he said. "The people who raised this youth should apologise and compensate us but it is not for us to ask. The murderer has been well protected, but the victim's family has been ignored, and I don't think that's right."

Three days later Mikio and Toshie Okuyama attended an emotional unveiling of a landscaped garden dedicated to the memory of their lost daughter. The garden, funded by public donations, was built in the grounds of the Cairns Civic Theatre in Grafton Street - directly opposite the Elphinstone building where Michiko Okuyama was murdered.

A stone monument bears the inscription, in both English and Japanese: "In loving memory of Michiko Okuyama who tragically died September 20, 1997, aged 22 years, ending a lifetime dream to dive on the Great Barrier Reef. This Memorial Garden was erected with the hope this tragedy will never happen again."

The couple told a gathering of 100 mourners that the memorial was a lasting sign of friendship between Australia and Japan, and asked Cairns people to take care of the garden for their daughter.

"This memorial garden signifies our hope that such a terrible crime will never happen again in this peaceful city," Mikio Okuyama said.

On Monday 9 November Justice Stanley Jones sentenced the killer of Michiko Okuyama to life imprisonment with a non-parole period of 15 years. The sentence, for what Jones called a "violent and heinous" murder was the maximum penalty for a child under the Juvenile Justice Act.

The youth stared straight ahead without any sign of emotion as sentence was passed.

Jones, in his sentencing remarks, described the teenage killer as "highly dangerous and unpredictable," and his behaviour after his victim's death, "touches on the macabre and demonstrates a callousness which almost defies description."

He then described the probable sequence of events that led to

Okuyama's death after she had been lured into the Elphinstone warehouse.

"The injuries inflicted to bring about the death were most probably caused by her face being bashed into a concrete wall with considerable force. After her death, you stripped her naked and kept her clothes. You placed her body in a wheelie bin and allowed it to decompose, literally before your eyes. Your subsequent disposal of the body causes a sense of revulsion (and) your assistance to police to describe what Miss Okuyama was wearing at the time of her disappearance demonstrated cold bloodedness."

The court was told the youth had been sexually abused as a child by a family friend and had left home at 13 years of age, living on the streets before moving in with a girlfriend and her family for a period of time.

Jones said he accepted the youth had a caring side to his nature and had shown compassion for his former girlfriend, but there were concerns he had "a darker side" to his mentality.

"To some you are seen as a gentle, caring person, concerned for others. To others you are aloof, manipulative, controlled, controlling and cunning."

A psychiatric report submitted to the court revealed the youth had an above average intelligence, including an IQ of 110, and suffered no psychiatric disturbance.

The court heard despite the youth's claims of a history of mental blackouts, including no memory of Okuyama entering the Elphinstone warehouse, he had not suffered such an attack during more than a year in detention since his arrest.

Prosecutor Jim Henry said there was no evidence the youth had an accomplice in murdering his victim and his complete lack of remorse called for the maximum penalty.

"The manner of death where Michiko asphyxiated in her own blood underlined in a sickening way how appalling this death was," he said. "She was subject to a violent attack in a foreign country in a small windowless vault knowing no one would come to her aid."

But the convicted killer's defence counsel, Kevin McCreanor, said his client maintained his innocence and had told a pyschiatrist he did not murder Michiko Okuyama, but he knew the identity of the person who committed the crime.

In a surprise statement to a newspaper a few days after his son's sentencing, the convicted killer's father - who also cannot be named - said he believed his son was innocent and he would continue to stand by him. The Cairns businessman said such a crime was not in his son's makeup and the case against him had been largely circumstancial.

"If I knew for a fact that it was my son who actually killed the young woman I would feel obliged to apologise to her family (but) I cannot apologise for something I don't know to be factual," he said.

The man said his son came from a broken family and left home early to live on the streets with older youths, but had never shown any violent tendencies.

"I still cannot believe what has happened because my son never showed any signs of violence and, on the contrary, always tried to be of help to others," he said.

In January 1999 the convicted murderer lodged separate appeals against both the conviction and the sentence with the Queensland Court of Appeal in Brisbane. He claimed the sentence was "manifestly excessive", while the appeal against the conviction claimed there was insufficient evidence about the cause of death, the link between himself and the death, and his intent at the time.

He later abandoned his appeal against conviction but continued with his appeal against the sentence.

Brisbane barrister Tony Glynn, appearing for the youth, submitted to the Court of Appeal that the murder was "not particularly ruthless", but had "the ordinary brutality included in any murder".

Glynn said the sentencing judge had not been entitled to find the crime was "particularly heinous" - indicating it was highly criminal and odious - as there was no evidence of premeditation by the youth.

Under Queensland law a juvenile can be detained for life only if a judge finds the crime was "particularly heinous" otherwise the maximum sentence is 10 years.

Glynn said the manner in which the youth treated the dead woman's body should not have been held against him during sentencing, and a sentence of 14 to 15 years would be appropriate.

But Crown prosecutor David Bullock argued the murder was in the worst category of offences.

"She was lured into an abandoned building, then severely and brutally bashed inside the vault, enough to break bones in her face," he said.

In June the Court of Appeal unanimously upheld the sentence, describing Okuyama's death as being "inflicted by vicious and violent means (and) in our view, the judge was correct in categorising the offence as a particularly heinous one in all the circumstances."

Appeal Court justices Geoff Davies, James Thomas and Margaret Wilson found that the youth's actions were macabre and he had shown no remorse. They noted the evidence of a pyschiatrist who said that if the youth had committed the crime "he was presumably highly dangerous, unpredictable, and someone who will on the one hand deny doing it, while on the other hand drop hints that he has done it".

Labor Member for Cairns and clinical psychologist Desley Boyle said the murder of Michiko Okuyama was "outside the boundaries of known mental illness" with only a limited knowledge of such a crime available for research.

"We're looking way beyond psychology for answers to this - it's not any syndrome we can explain and it defies the human mind," she said.

Boyle said she had been heartened by the genuine concern shown by Cairns residents for the Okuyama family, in spite of the fact that "many ordinary people have been dreadfully unsettled" by the murder.

"Some people would suffer secondary anxiety because this could happen to them, and those who have had a relative murdered in the past would experience an awakening of that trauma.

"I'm proud of our community because we went to the heart of the matter in giving support to the parents, and there were certain people who stood by in the background without reward, who didn't even know Michiko, but were there when they were needed.

"Michiko was innocent, she was young and beautiful, and she

was a guest in our city. This makes her death more tragic in the public perception."

Father Kevin Lewis, rector of St John's Anglican Church, said he had never seen such an outpouring of grief in Cairns and he was reminded of the vulnerability of young people, including his own daughter, who was the same age as Michiko Okuyama.

"If she was to go off to Japan and this was to happen I'd be devastated beyond words. I'd have to go over there, just as Michiko's parents had to come here. This is an acceptance of the sad reality of life in our times and it hurts our city. Japanese people are a gentle people, courteous and trusting, as no doubt Michiko was."

Long-time Cairns resident and businesswoman Yumi Smith, who volunteered her time to interpret for the Okuyama family, said she refused to believe "one rotten apple" would spoil the bright image Cairns enjoyed in Japan and around the world.

"I'm sure nobody in Japan blames Cairns for Michiko's murder and my biggest concern is that the city doesn't suffer for this," she said.

Although the immediate horror of Michiko Okuyama's murder has passed, it was a crime that is etched irrevocably into the psyche of a city that can never forget the innocent young tourist whose dream of diving on the Great Barrier Reef was never fulfilled.

CHAPTER THREE

DEATH IN THE HINCHINBROOK CHANNEL

A story of drugs and death, a shark-mauled body, and a man convicted of murder because of his daughter's testimony.

When Brett Austin Scotton placed the barrel of a .357 Magnum in his mouth on a north Queensland marijuana plantation and pulled the trigger, he not only cut short his life, but became a key link in a bizarre sequence of events that would leave in its wake a convoluted trail of drugs, treachery and death, and ultimately the life imprisonment of his own father for murder.

Scotton should not have died on that sunny day in early June 1994. He was intelligent, strong, good-looking, and had recently turned 21 years of age. He loved the glamour and sparkle of the Gold Coast where he sometimes worked as a nightclub doorman. But it was that same lifestyle that led him into the dark world of designer drugs and his involvement as a crop minder in a massive $60 million marijuana-growing operation on the Burdekin River near Townsville.

And it was the effects of that lifestyle that finally commanded the demons of his unbalanced mind to pick up the gun and terminate his existence.

Scotton's body was unceremoniously dumped by his crop pals at a truck stop on the Bruce Highway, 35 kilometres south of Townsville. He was lying face-up on the gravel, the pistol, wiped clean of fingerprints, tucked beneath his body.

On the night of Sunday 5 June Brett's parents, Ken and Sophia Scotton, were sitting on the rear deck of their 24-metre cruiser

Peppermint, anchored in the tranquil waters of Magnetic Island off the coast of Townsville.

The couple had earlier celebrated their 23rd wedding anniversary at a restaurant and were reflecting on the ups and downs of their life together, and the two children their marriage had produced - Brett, their adored son, and daughter Natalie, then a month away from her 20th birthday.

Ken Scotton was worried about Brett, who had recently returned from the Gold Coast and openly confessed to his involvement in the designer drug scene, particularly with ecstasy, or "eckies" as he called them.

Brett told his father he was depressed from taking "bad shit" he had bought from a dealer he knew on the coast.

"I'm so sick from the drugs Dad, I'm having flashbacks and I feel awful," he said, adding he had work lined up in the bush and was looking forward to straightening himself out.

That was the last conversation Ken Scotton had with his son.

Before he and his wife dozed off to sleep, the phone rang. Scotton thought it would be Brett wishing them a happy anniversary. Instead, an anonymous caller informed him: "Ken, I have some really bad news for you. Brett has blown himself away."

Scotton went cold. Dimly, he heard the voice saying: "Ken, are you all right? Ken, I'll ring you back."

From that moment Ken Scotton's life became what he calls a "lousy nightmare". The phone rang again and he listened dully as the voice told him where his son's body could be found.

Brett's death sent Scotton into a spin of grief and hatred from which he would never recover - grief for his lost son and hatred for the dealer whom he believed dealt in bad drugs and death.

Kenneth Austin Scotton is the first to admit he is no stranger to trouble. He is in his sixties now and has done it tough, surviving a childhood of beatings from a violent father, then years of sadistic discipline in youth detention centres, finally graduating to safe cracking and armed robbery - which in turn led to lengthy stints in notorious jails such as Long Bay, Bathurst and the infamous Grafton Jail in the 1960s.

Along the way Scotton hung out with with legendary hard-head crims such as D'arcy Dugan and the notorious Lavender Hill Mob, ran around Sydney with Neddy Smith and Christopher "Mr Rent-a-Kill" Flannery, and knew John Andrew Stewart and James Finch.

In October 1971 Scotton - while on bail awaiting armed robbery charges after a gun dealer was shot in the neck during a holdup - decided he could not face the prospect of more jail time and absconded.

Astoundingly, in the next decade while the run, Scotton became a successful horse trainer in Victoria using the name Ken Kennedy and was photographed regularly without attracting police attention. Then, in May 1982, his run of luck came to an end when an unknown gunman almost killed him with a shotgun blast from the darkened doorway of his horse stables at Cranbourne. Scotton alias Kennedy had his photograph in the newspapers again, this time with his wife Sophia comforting him in hospital after part of his bowel was removed in a three-hour operation.

Scotton fled to Queensland but was arrested and extradited to Sydney three months later to stand trial for a crime committed 12 years previously.

During his trial Scotton was described by a judge as "one of those rare creatures - a truly reformed criminal", but he still copped an eight-year sentence. This time, though, the system was kinder, and Scotton walked free in less than a year. From that time on, Scotton says, he went straight and never put a foot wrong.

Scotton was under no illusion that his son's "work" in the bush was legitimate. He smelled a rat from the start and when Brett introduced Christopher James Honner, or "CJ" as he was known to his mates, as his fencing contractor boss, Scotton was not fooled. Later, Brett told him what he already suspected - that Honner was paying him $100 a day to help mind a marijuana crop. But that was a far better option, Scotton reasoned, than dicing with hard drugs on the Gold Coast.

"I should have talked him out of it, but I didn't," Scotton said later.

After Brett's death, Honner was unable to face Scotton and went into hiding. But a man later named in a Townsville court as the ringleader of the marijuana operation, Albert John Rhodes, visited

Scotton on board his boat, then moored at Dungeness, in the Hinchinbrook Channel near Ingham.

Codenamed Operation Broken Prop Two by police, the sophisticated drug operation involved five cannibas crops of up to 9,000 plants each growing on a 15 kilometre strip along the banks of the Burdekin River.

Rhodes told Scotton one of his workers had seen Brett's death after he had talked of suicide as the only way out of his depression, which he blamed on "bad shit". They thought he'd been talked out of the suicide plan after he said it would "kill my dad and I can't do that to him".

Sally Anne Innes, who was later sentenced to three years jail for her part in the dope growing operation, told Scotton she had been in the cooking area of the camp when Brett walked in. She asked him if he had sorted himself out and he had replied: "Yes, I've got the answer in my hand".

He picked up the gun off a table, walked outside and shot himself. When she heard the gunshot, Innes said she ran outside and saw Brett convulsing on the ground.

Scotton believed the story and did not go to the police. He saw no point in dobbing in a few marijuana growers after they had done the right thing and told him the truth about his son's death. Instead, he became obsessed with the drug ecstasy and the Gold Coast dealers who peddled it.

In December 1995 Albert Rhodes was arrested and charged with possession of one kilogram of amphetamines on the Gold Coast while awaiting committal proceedings on the Burdekin marijuana charges.

He was subsequently sentenced to 14 years in a maximum security prison for drug trafficking.

On 7 October 2002, Rhodes' son, 24-year-old Daniel Corey Rhodes, was shot dead by police on a Bundaberg street after he allegedly threatened two officers with a loaded automatic pistol. He had recently served a six month sentence for a number of charges, including robbery with violence. In 2001 he was found not guilty of the stabbing death of a Mackay man at a party, claiming he acted in self-defence.

In the grip of his own depression and blaming himself for his son's death, Scotton roamed the stretch of coastline between Ingham and Innisfail in the steel-hulled *Peppermint*, a former World War Two hospital ship, which had become a familiar sight to boat owners in the area.

In October, four months after Brett's death, Honner turned up and told Scotton he was finished with drug growing. The two men agreed to form a business partnership and convert the *Peppermint* into a supply ship that would service fishing fleets around Cape York Peninsula and the Gulf of Carpentaria. Honner gave Scotton $7,000 which he said was owed to Brett in "wages and bonus". Around this time Honner and Scotton's daughter, Natalie, began a relationship and moved on to the boat. Sophia Scotton was visiting her mother in Sydney.

Scotton's search for the dealer who had sold his son contaminated ecstasy continued. He put out feelers among his contacts on the Gold Coast but nobody admitted to knowing anything. Eventually he received a call from 44-year-old John Peter Saibura, an acquaintance from Beenleigh who had once chartered the *Peppermint* for a fishing trip on the Great Barrier Reef. Scotton asked him if he knew who had supplied Brett with the bad drugs. Saibura said he'd check it out, but asked if he could come up and talk to Scotton about something important.

"I agreed, thinking he had another one of his harebrained ideas to make money," Scotton said. "He also said he had some money for me. He didn't say why and I didn't ask."

Scotton didn't think much of Saibura, considering him a "big noter" who used Scotton's past links with the underworld to name-drop for his own advantage. He was the type, Scotton said, "who would talk in millions of dollars and then bite you for a hundred bucks - a bullshit artist with the chattering style of a bad used-car salesman". He also knew Saibura had a drug conviction in NSW and suspected him of dealing on the Gold Coast.

On Sunday 4 December Saibura arrived at the *Peppermint* and the wheels of fate clicked forward another gear. In less than half an hour Saibura would be dead and the nightmare of Scotton's life would darken even further.

From the start, Scotton sensed something was wrong.

"As soon as I picked Saibura up from the wharf in the tinnie I knew he was on speed because he didn't stop talking, and when we got on board and I made a cup of tea he started swallowing tablets at a furious rate. I said, 'What's that shit?' and he said, 'Medicine, only medicine'.

"Then out of the blue he asked me if anyone else was on board and I said no, even though Natalie was down below reading. I don't know what made me say it, I just had a bad feeling."

With good reason. According to Scotton, Saibura then produced a gun, holding it with his right hand resting on the table.

"I was stunned into silence when he pulled the gun. Then he said, 'We'd better get this thing about Brett straightened out, mate, it's been driving me up the wall. I know you've been poking around and that's why I'm here'."

Scotton claims Saibura pushed an envelope across to him and told him it contained $1,000 "for the drugs I sold Brett - that's yours, mate".

Saibura told Scotton that Brett had been sold a bad batch of ecstasy by accident and nobody knew it was bad until "kids started dropping dead and suiciding" and "the shit really hit the fan when the barrister's daughter died through the stuff". This was a reference to Deborah Lynette Hanger, who died in September 1994 after taking ecstasy tablets while celebrating her 18th birthday in a Brisbane nightclub. She was the daughter of barrister Ian Hanger and granddaughter of former Queensland Chief Justice, Sir Mostyn Hanger.

"Saibura told me he felt partly responsible for Brett's death and he was sorry, but it wasn't deliberate, and that was just the way things went sometimes in the drugs game," Scotton said.

Saibura said Brett had a falling out with one of his dealers, "a bloke called Mark", who threatened to "hot shot" Brett by giving him a fatal overdose, but "I pulled that up, mate".

Scotton said he sat "frozen in time", staring at the gun, which he noted was a small calibre Beretta, while he tried to make sense of what was happening. Scotton said he felt "threatened and intimidated" and "a thousand thoughts rushed through my mind".

Then a "red curtain of rage" clouded his mind and he suddenly lunged across the table at Saibura, grappling for the gun as both men lurched to their feet. According to Scotton he felt a blow to the side of his face as he "half-lifted and half-dragged" Saibura from behind the table and grabbed at his right arm. The gun went off as Saibura fell backwards, hitting his head on a washing machine before slumping to the floor.

Scotton said when he looked up and saw Natalie at the top of the stairs he told her: "It's all right he's just knocked out, go back downstairs." He then put a teatowel to a bleeding cut near his eyebrow and put the Beretta under a blanket in his bedroom. He noticed he'd left a trail of blood on the floor to the sink.

Scotton: "Saibura moaned and sat up and said: 'Shit Ken, I didn't do anything, the last thing I need is to be fighting you...I feel crook, mate, I took some stuff to help me face you. I thought you'd blow up, that's why I bought the gun to protect myself...no other reason, mate, honest...let me lay down for awhile and I'll get out of your hair when I feel better'."

Scotton pointed to the stairs and told Saibura there was a mattress in a rear bedroom below. He watched as Saibura "staggered like a drunk and slipped and fell down the stairs on his backside" before disappearing from view into the bedroom.

Scotton went out on deck and threw the Beretta as far out into the water as he could before retrieving his own Browning .32 pistol from its hiding place behind a television set. "I intended keeping it with me from then on. I didn't want him sneaking that one on me again."

But there was no need for the gun. John Saibura was dead.

When he went downstairs Scotton saw Saibura lying on the mattress on his back.

"He was unresponsive when I shook him and he smelled like he'd shit himself. I tried to resuscitate him but after about 10 minutes I checked his pulse and he had none.

"I don't know what Saibura died of, whether it was from a heart attack or hitting his head, or a drug overdose, but it wasn't from a bullet. I know for certain it wasn't the gun. He wasn't shot."

Scotton was in big trouble and he knew it. With his criminal past nobody was going to believe his story. An old mate of Neddy

Smith's pleading self-defence? No way. He was sure the cops would get him for Saibura's death one way or another.

According to Scotton he couldn't rely on Natalie as a witness because she had not witnessed the fight, and besides he wanted to keep his daughter out of it as much as possible. Over coffee he explained what had happened and the fact that Saibura had supplied her brother with the drugs that had bent his mind and in the end killed him. Scotton recalls Natalie stared at him with vacant eyes, as if numb with shock, or else she "didn't care".

Scotton began to operate purely on his knockabout instinct for survival, finely tuned by a lifetime of living on the edge. He had a dead man on his hands and things were not looking good.

"I was in a panic at the time and needed to talk to somebody, to have somebody tell me what to do."

Not thinking straight, Scotton drove Saibura's hire car to Cairns, taking Natalie with him. It wasn't until he was passing through Innisfail that he realised he was going the wrong way - Saibura had hired the car in Townsville. But Scotton kept going, and after parking the vehicle outside the rental company in Cairns with the keys in the ignition, the pair caught a late night bus back to Ingham, where they picked up Scotton's Kombi van and returned to the boat.

Scotton later claimed Saibura had asked him to return the car as a favour because a friend was going to pick him up from Dungeness.

The next morning Honner called from a public phone on the wharf, asking Scotton to come and get him in the dinghy. Honner wasn't feeling too good either. He'd had a couple of busy days on the booze and the night before he and a mate had ironed out a few differences brawling on the river bank. According to Honner he got the upper hand and "beat the crap" out of his mate.

Honner later told police Scotton admitted on the way out to the *Peppermint* that he'd shot Saibura "through the ticker" for selling Brett bad drugs and they had to get ready to dispose of the body on the high tide.

Scotton has a different story, however, claiming instead it was Honner who took charge and organised the dumping of the body.

"I was grateful at the time that CJ didn't hesitate to take control and do my thinking for me because I was a mess, knowing in a way

I must have caused John's death, even though I didn't shoot him."

According to Honner, both men shackled Saibura's body to to a galvanised garbage bin full of cement with an anchor attached and dumped it in a deep hole at the southern end of the Hinchinbrook Channel. He said they wore wet weather suits, placed cotton buds up their noses and covered their faces with handkerchiefs to avoid the stench as they prepared the body for disposal.

Scotton says he does not remember details about disposing of the body, except steering the boat "like a zombie" in the channel and at one stage hearing Honner say: "It's all right mate, let's get back, it's done."

Four days later, on Sunday 9 December, two Queensland Boating and Fisheries officers on a routine patrol of the channel stopped near Haycock Island to inspect what they at first thought were the remains of a dugong. But their gruesome find was in fact the shark-savaged remains of a human - the head and upper body of John Saibura.

While they waited for police to arrive, a five-metre tiger shark attacked the remains and, ignoring attempts by the officers to protect the macabre find, made off with an arm and shoulder.

Giving evidence later in court, Ingham-based fisheries officer Richard Kingdom said a white fertiliser bag and a one-metre long piece of "yellow-blue" rope were attached to the head. He said all the body parts had incision-like wounds and were in an advanced state of decomposition.

A grid-pattern search of the 25 metre-deep hole by police divers failed to find any more remains, nor did they find the concrete-filled bin, anchor, or any other evidence of the alleged disposal.

Saibura had earlier been reported missing by his wife, and police had enough of his body to identify him from fingerprints that matched his police file in New South Wales. On 19 December they boarded the *Peppermint* and arrested Scotton for murder.

At his committal hearing that started on Tuesday 28 March 1995, Scotton knew he was up against the odds. His daughter Natalie and her boyfriend Christopher Honner had agreed to give evidence for the Crown in return for an indemnity against prosecution. Both had been placed on the Criminal Justice

Commission's witness protection program.

Tight security provided extra tension to an already dramatic murder hearing as guards carefully checked every person entering the court.

Star witness Natalie Scotton, who was by then five months pregnant with Honner's child, gave evidence from an isolated room over a video monitor and microphone, telling the court in a shaky voice she saw her father standing with a gun in his hand on the day of John Saibura's death. She said she had heard a shot while she was below deck, and as she made her way up the stairs heard a man "groaning and making snoring sounds" before she heard somebody say: "I have not done anything." She told the court she couldn't see the man but her father told her to go back to her room because the man was "having a sleep". She testified that her brother Brett had kept diaries that contained entries about ecstasy, cocaine and "drug cocktails".

Ken Scotton, who represented himself, complained to magistrate Trevor Pollock about having to conduct a cross-examination over a microphone and television set.

"It would seem your worship that more consideration is being given to the witness than to the defendant," he said.

Natalie Scotton broke down when she heard the words: "Natalie, it's your father, love," forcing an adjournment. Later, she told the court she had overheard a telephone conversation between her father and a man named John who was coming to "buy some stuff". When asked by Crown prosecutor Jim Henry what she meant, Natalie Scotton replied: "Drugs and that."

Ken Scotton provided further drama to the courtroom proceedings by putting forward an application to determine if his daughter was under the influence of illegal drugs. This was refused by Pollock, who warned Scotton he was risking a contempt of court ruling if he persisted.

Pollock added his own criticism of the equipment used to allow Natalie Scotton to give evidence from another room, describing the electronic devices as "$20,000 worth of rubbish".

Honner testified that he had been with Scotton when the latter picked up a package containing a pistol from the Innisfail post office. Scotton later told the court he'd asked a friend in Sydney to send him a rifle to scare sharks away when he was fishing, but a pistol had turned up instead. He said it was a coincidence that the gun had arrived just prior to Saibura's visit.

"I could have (sent for it) in 1990, or 1995, or 1996," he said. "There was nothing sinister in it."

Honner described how he saw a body wrapped in a green floral sheet underneath a mattress in a downstairs bedroom on the *Peppermint* before he later accompanied Scotton and Natalie to Ingham where they purchased three bags of pre-mixed cement, two garbage bins and several galvanised shackles. Honner told the court he helped Scotton mix cement to dispose of the body while the boat was anchored in the Hinchinbrook Channel. After the cement dried, Scotton had said it was "time to get this bullshit out of the road" before the two of them pushed the bin and shackled body over the side.

In a dramatic start to the murder committal's second day, Scotton was rushed from a watchhouse cell to hospital after he was found on the floor complaining of chest pains. Doctors diagnosed his condition as an anxiety attack and Scotton was returned to court where he informed magistrate Pollock that he was not well enough to represent himself. In an angry outburst, Scotton claimed he had been poorly treated in the watchhouse and declared the hearing a "sham".

"You might as well send me back to Lotus Glen and then send me a telegram telling me I will be in there for life," he told the magistrate.

On day three of the committal hearing Scotton was ordered to stand trial for the murder of John Saibura.

At his 12-day trial, held in Cairns almost one year after Saibura's violent death, Ken Scotton stuck to his story. He had struggled with Saibura, the gun went off and Saibura went down, hitting his head on the washing machine. Scotton told police he believed Saibura may have choked on his own vomit, caused by the pills he had been taking.

The results of a scientific examination on Saibura's remains supported Scotton's story. State Government pathologist Dr Charles Naylor said Saibura's head and upper body, including the heart, showed no trace of either a bullet, bullet fragments or bullet track, but he did find flecks of a white substance in the stomach which could indicate the presence of tablets - but, he said, the substance could also have been "mashed potatoes". Naylor said the process of decomposition could mask the presence of speed or ecstasy. He could offer no opinion on the cause of Saibura's death.

Scotton was also charged with stealing $60,000 in cash from Saibura - money police alleged was for the purchase of marijuana from Scotton. Giving evidence at Scotton's trial, however, Deborah Saibura said she had no knowledge of any large amounts of money carried by her husband.

Scotton stoutly maintained there was no money except for the $1,000 Saibura gave him, and that the police based their claims on the fact that Scotton gave his daughter $10,000 for her and Honner to leave Queensland until the heat died down. That money, he said, came from his life savings of $18,000 that he kept hidden on board *Peppermint* for fuel, maintenance and emergencies. Scotton said he put $5,000 of what was left in a briefcase but forgot to put it away in his "snooker" (hiding place) behind the television, and the police later found it and took it away.

"The police have made a big deal of it (the money)," Scotton told the court during his committal hearing. "They have cast sinister shadows relating to a mythical 60 grand that was never, ever there. That is just bullshit."

Natalie Scotton and Honner fled to Alice Springs where Honner's father lived. They had the $10,000 Ken Scotton had given Natalie and they thought they'd lay low for awhile. By this time Natalie was pregnant.

Honner testified that while in Alice Springs Scotton had phoned him and said: "The thing that went down has popped up again and the shit has hit the fan."

It didn't take the police long to track the couple down and they were interviewed a number of times in a bizarre sequence of events that subsequently ended in amnesties against prosecution for both of them in exchange for their evidence against Scotton.

Natalie Scotton admitted in court she changed her police statement several times in the lead-up to her father's trial. In her earlier statements she insisted her father would not lie to her and strenuously denied he murdered Saibura. She told a senior detective: "It just seems that the police are always trying to cop something on my dad, that's all, and I'm sick of it." A couple of days later, however, she changed her mind, claiming this time she was "scared shitless" of her father and would tell the truth "because it is the right thing to do".

While in Alice Springs Natalie Scotton was booked into a motel by detectives after she was involved in a fight with Honner in a casino - where the same detectives just happened to be drinking.

Natalie Scotton later testified that Honner hit her about the head after she had verbally defended his brother Nelson, who had spoken to police about the murder case.

Later, a police constable named Richard Williams, apparently a personal friend of Natalie Scotton's, was flown from Sydney to be a "support person" for her. This was a surprisingly generous gesture by the police, but it was never revealed how Scotton had met Williams, nor what role he played in the Alice Springs interviews - except, in the words of a senior detective to Scotton later, "so that you felt more comfortable whilst you spoke with us". It was at this point, Scotton testified in court, that she decided to give evidence against her father.

Defence counsel Andrew Sinclair accused Natalie Scotton of fabricating her statement to police so she would be kept on the witness protection program. He said the story that her father had robbed Saibura of money intended to buy marijuana was concocted because that's what investigators wanted to hear.

"You are making this up because you want to preserve yourself," he said. "You were simply answering questions the police asked, hoping to be believed."

Scotton replied she was telling the truth and she did not care what the police thought.

Once Honner had accepted an amnesty, charges of accessory after the fact to murder against him were dropped and he joined Natalie Scotton on the witness protection program.

Honner proved to be a good find for the police. Not only did he save himself by turning on Ken Scotton, but he fingered his drug buddies involved in the Burdekin marijuana operation as well. Those who hadn't already been busted soon were, and the plantations were quickly raided and shut down. Operation Broken Prop Two resulted in the arrest of 25 people on a variety of drug charges.

During his committal hearing Ken Scotton told the court that Christopher Honner was "quick to take control (of disposing of Saibura's body) but quicker still to toss the ball back to me."

Scotton indicated the presence of the smartly dressed Honner and said: "I am used to seeing him in jungle greens, with a knife strapped to his leg, cocksure of himself and swaggering about with an answer to everything. But here he is presented to the court like a student straight from university - I take my hat off to whoever transformed him."

Scotton told the court that Honnor's evidence was a concocted story born out of "a basic human instinct for self-preservation".

"Chris's story comes across like a piece from a gangster movie - Al Capone and concrete boots - but I don't have any knowledge of that fairy tale. I wonder why he would exaggerate when simply the truth needed to be told. Ladies and gentlemen, the real fact is that what he has said is a blatant lie and it's not the only one he has told the police and this court."

Scotton insisted John Saibura was not murdered, but had met his death accidently during the fight, or from a heart attack, or the drugs he had been taking.

"John Saibura was not shot dead, or even wounded. A gun has got nothing whatever to do with his death.

"The real reason he came to see me was to ease his guilty conscience over my son's death. He gave me reason and motive to choke the daylights out of him, but I didn't. He gave me reason and motive to shoot him through the heart, but I didn't.

"I had the opportunity, but I am not guilty of murdering John Saibura. In truth I wish I did, I could live with that, I think."

At the murder trial, Crown prosecutor Jim Henry suggested Scotton was using his son's suicide as a ploy to gain sympathy from the jury.

"You're milking it for all it's worth," Henry said. "You're hiding everything behind the smokescreen of your son's death."

Henry accused Scotton of suspecting well before Saibura's arrival in north Queensland that he had supplied his son with bad ecstasy and Scotton had already made up his mind what action to take.

"If that was the case I'd have been chasing him down the Gold Coast and probably would have done what everyone says I've done and put a bullet through him," Scotton replied.

Scotton maintained his innocence throughout the trial, insisting Saibura had not been shot during the struggle for the gun on board the *Peppermint*.

"When the gun discharged it was pointing in such a direction that a bullet could not possibly have struck me or Saibura," he said. "The bullet could have gone anywhere, either into the roof, walls, the door, or out an open window.

"I am guilty, however, to losing my son to John Saibura's drugs. It appears also that along the way I might have lost my daughter to circumstances."

Scotton said his daughter's loyalty and ability to tell the truth had been lost through pressure applied to her during the police interviews that ultimately led to her accepting an amnesty against prosecution.

"I can't help feeling outraged at the manner that detectives have appeared to use my daughter without thought of the damage it may cause to her mental well-being when this is all over," he said.

Defence barrister Andrew Sinclair then accused Honner of agreeing to give evidence against Ken Scotton in exchange for police dropping drug charges against him.

"You gave evidence in my client's committal and at that time you had no indemnity - you were facing drug charges and digging a hole for yourself," Sinclair said. "You must have suspected that by co-operating with police things would be better for you."

On another occasion, Honner told the court that fear had prompted him to help Ken Scotten dump Saibura's body, but conceded the accused had never verbally or physically threatened him.

In his summing up to the jury, Henry said the remains of Saiburu's body "bobbing up again with sharks still at it would have been the accused's worst nightmare" and commonsense should be applied when looking at the evidence against Scotton.

"The accused did not believe his own flesh and blood could be so disgusted at what he had done, that she would tell the police," Henry said. "His daughter was shocked and upset and scared of her father. Is there any wonder Natalie Scotton took the time she did to come out with the truth and how difficult it was for her to say anything that was against her father."

Sinclair told the jury that if Scotton had killed Saibura it would have been the "worst planned murder ever", and the evidence showed his client had panicked and wasn't "thinking straight" when Saibura died after the pair struggled over the gun.

"Why would he dump the body in a popular fishing area where people could see it?" he said. "If he had planned to get rid of Saibura he could easily have come up with a much better place."

Sinclair said the medical report from the examination of Saibura's remains supported Scotton's version of events.

"There is no more evidence that Saibura died from a gunshot than he choked on his own vomit while unconscious," he said.

On 5 December 1995 Scotton was sentenced to life imprisonment after a jury took less than three hours to find him guilty of the murder of John Saibura. He was also sentenced to four years jail for stealing with aggrevation.

Before delivering their verdict, jury members asked to view post-mortem examination photographs of Saibura's shark-savaged remains. Scotton believes the granting of this request by trial judge Justice Kerry Cullinane sealed his fate.

"Those photos had no bearing on the case and served only to turn the jury against me," he said.

Before the trial Natalie Scotton signed an affidavit that she intended giving evidence against her father but she was "petrified" about incriminating him in the shooting of Saibura because she was still scared of "what he can still get his mates to do".

Yet in a letter she later wrote to her father in north Queensland's Lotus Glen Correctional Centre, she declared her love for him and how hard it was "lying to myself". The letter thanked him for "the wisdom, the experience and adventure you shared with me," and ends with: "Can you still love me and accept me as I am today?"

In July 1997 Scotton received a surprise phone call from his daughter, who was in a secret "safe house" somewhere in Queensland with her then two-year-old son under the witness protection program. Like all phone conversations in Queensland jails, the conversation between Scotton and his daughter was tape recorded. The tape was later confiscated by the Criminal Justice Commission - but not before a copy of the tape was smuggled out of the prison.

On the tape Natalie Scotton is heard tearfully explaining to her father that police in Alice Springs had intimidated and threatened her into changing her first statement while she was confused and under the influence of alcohol and drugs. She said she was told by detectives that if she didn't tell them the truth her baby would be taken away from her after it was born, and she would be sent to jail.

"CJ (Honner) had already told them what happened (but) they were playing games with me and screwed my mind around...accusing me...saying that you'd already put threats out against me," she said. "They took me out and got me drunk...I was on anti-depressants...they were going to put me in a psych ward and everything...you've got no idea what they were putting me through... I just wish I was wise to it then."

On the tape Natalie Scotton confesses to her father that when she was giving evidence at his committal hearing she would have tested positive to illegal drugs had his application for a test been granted by the court.

"I knew I had it in my system and I was hoping (the court would allow it) because I knew I'd fail a blood test," she said. "I didn't even know what I was there for...they just said they wanted to ask me a couple of questions...and they shoved me in this room."

Ken Scotton: "She said she was really whacked, as she put it, and the cops were shitting themselves because they knew she was smoking pot."

A request in 1996 by Scotton and his wife Sophia for an inquest into the death of their son Brett was refused by the Department of Justice as "unnecessary".

Although the Scottons believe Scott died by his own hand, they remain unhappy with the police investigation that followed the discovery of his body.

"The police treated my wife and I like suspects in our own son's death," Scotton said. "They called it murder at first and everyone who came near us was taken in for questioning. There were no inquiries by police into where, why or how he got the drugs that put him into that suicidal state."

Ken Scotton's appeal against his murder conviction was turned down, but he continues to maintain his innocence. He admits his role in the death of John Saibura, and in the disposal of his body, but not in his murder.

He believes he would be a free man today if not for his criminal past, Christopher Honner's decision to save himself, and the untruthful testimony of his daughter.

CHAPTER FOUR

WHERE IS PATANELA?

She was considered unsinkable, but just outside Sydney Harbour the steel lady of the sea suddenly disappeared - only to be seen sailing ghost-like off the north Queensland coast.

On Wednesday 2 March 1989, almost four months after the luxury steel schooner *Patanela* and her crew mysteriously disappeared off Sydney's Botany Bay, north Queensland caravan park owners Ted and Marie McCarthy were enjoying "happy hour" drinks with a group of park residents and friends in a beach hut at Tully Heads, a small seaside village 160 kilometres south of Cairns. It was a typical evening get-together as the friends relaxed and chatted in the balmy atmosphere of a spectacular tropical sunset. McCarthy, a 47-year-old former detective in the New South Wales Police Force, looked out at the breathtaking view of Rockingham Bay and noticed for the first time a handsome twin-masted sailing vessel, slowly cruising parallel to the beach. He took time to admire the sleek lines of the schooner. Although there was nothing unusual about sailing boats traversing the broad arc of Rockingham Bay, McCarthy noticed this one was moving forward "in a very strange way" - as if it had no purpose to its direction. Only the front and rear sails were aloft and they were flapping in a strong breeze. McCarthy, a keen sailor himself, felt something was odd about the vessel.

There was also something about the big blue-hulled boat that nagged at Marie McCarthy's memory. Suddenly she recalled reading a magazine story the night before about a missing Western Australian yacht with four people on board. She ran to the house for the magazine while Ted rounded up a pair of binoculars. The magazine article featured colour photographs of the 19-metre *Patanela*. McCarthy studied them and propped his burly frame against a coconut palm while he trained the binoculars on the schooner, about two kilometres out in the bay. The vessel appeared to be heading towards Dunk Island, which lay to the northeast.

McCarthy noted a dark blue hull, white decking and what appeared to be white canvas covering the midships area. There were square portholes at the bow port side, hatch covers and a large plaited section of rope on the bowsprit tie - all distinguishing features which appeared to match the magazine pictures of *Patanela*. McCarthy scanned the deck and saw three, possibly four, people dressed in shorts and T-shirts. One, a well-built male with dark hair, emerged from the wheelhouse. He was wearing a white and blue striped T-shirt, blue shorts and white shoes. McCarthy tried to zero in on the man to get a close-up view but couldn't see his face clearly.

McCarthy studied the vessel for a further 15 minutes. His police training was telling him this was unlikely to be the same yacht as the one in the magazine, but a sixth sense kept ringing alarms bells in his head, compelling him to try and identify the boat.

The Island Coast Van Park was one of the many listening posts for the Australian Coastguard Service, monitoring sea traffic twenty-four hours a day. McCarthy tuned his radio panel to Channel 88 and called the mystery yacht, giving his call sign: "This is VN4TU Tully Heads calling the schooner in Rockingham Bay heading for Dunk Island."

There was no reply. McCarthy tried again, this time receiving a message broken by static. The only words he could identify were "...yacht in Rockingham Bay..." He repeated his call a third time and again the transmission was poor, but he thought the schooner was attempting to relay a radio identification number.

McCarthy heard the caller switching the hand set on and off and judged whoever was using the radio was only making a half-hearted effort to respond. "It was as though they were making up what they were saying on the spur of the moment," he said. Finally, he asked outright if the schooner was *Patanela*. There was silence. McCarthy requested the skipper give an affirmative or negative answer. At that instant the line suddenly cleared and the response came back very clearly: "Negative...negative...negative."

McCarthy then said: "We are looking for the missing *Patanela* - what is your identification?" But there was no reply. All further attempts to communicate with the yacht failed. McCarthy returned to the beachfront and watched as the schooner slowly headed towards Dunk Island.

Oddly, McCarthy made no move to investigate the schooner at close hand. For an 18-year veteran of Sydney's CIB and the New South Wales Special Branch, it could be assumed McCarthy's suspicion would be aroused enough to motor out in a dinghy for a closer look at the mystery vessel. When asked during an interview why he did not venture out to the boat, McCarthy's wife interrupted and quickly pointed out that she feared her husband may have been shot and killed. But the former policeman scoffed at his wife's explanation. He explained he would have certainly investigated the vessel if he had been sure *Patanela's* disappearance had been caused by criminal activity. However, he understood from the magazine report that the vessel was "simply overdue" at Airlie Beach, its intended destination.

Tully Heads, though, is a good 400 kilometres north of Airlie Beach. If *Patanela* was still overdue on 2 March - 114 days after last contact was made with the vessel off Sydney, and sighted so far north of her destination, there would seem to be good cause for a closer inspection of the schooner the McCarthys and their friends had seen.

Later that night McCarthy reported the incident to Tully police and the next day he was interviewed over the sighting.

The mystery vessel was again sighted that night, and the next, by Shirley Walker, a resident of Hull Heads, a small township at the northern edge of Rockingham Bay. The schooner was seen at a spot locals considered too dangerous for sailing craft. Walker had first sighted the vessel anchored offshore and southeast of her beachfront home. She watched the yacht leave the next morning and return again the following afternoon - this time anchoring further out to sea. When she awoke at five o'clock the next morning, the vessel had gone. It was not seen again.

The Federal Sea Safety Centre in Canberra had issued coastal alerts on *Patanela* to Queensland Police, but were never notified of the north Queensland sightings.

On Sunday 19 March, Ted McCarthy watched the current affairs program *60 Minutes* on television, which included a story on the *Patanela* disappearance. He was now absolutely convinced the schooner he had seen 17 days earlier was the missing vessel. Finally, after reading a newspaper article about the mystery, McCarthy rang Alan Nicol, the vessel's owner in Perth, to report his sighting.

On Wednesday 6 April, Nicol and Perth-based private investigator Terry Hebb met in Cairns to investigate McCarthy's story. Hebb spoke to Frank Markert, owner of Jardine Shipping, a company that operates a fishing fleet around Cape York Peninsula and the Gulf of Carpentaria. Hebb made further inquiries at the Cairns Yacht Club and held a meeting with Sergeant Frank Clair, the region's Australian Federal Police officer in charge of the case.

On the morning of Friday 8 April, Nicol chartered a private aircraft and, together with Hebb and McCarthy, spent several hours searching the waters between Cardwell, Dunk Island and Cairns, where they believed a vessel the size of *Patanela* could be hidden. Although the search proved fruitless, pilot Colin Webb offered to continue the search during his regular mail runs to the tip of Cape York. Terry Hebb considered McCarthy's sighting to be the most credible of all he had investigated. But *Patanela* remained missing.

They said she was unsinkable, a tough princess of the high seas. In Tasmania, where she was built, she was known as the Ship of Dreams. Wherever she went on the oceans of the world, she was famous. She was *Patanela* - the big schooner made of steel. They said nothing could stop her. She had four watertight compartments that were designed to keep her afloat in the wildest seas imaginable. She had circumnavigated the world several times, survived storms in the North Atlantic, and sailed unscathed to inhospitable Macquarie Island, 1600 kilometres southeast of Tasmania. In late 1964, she was chartered for a scientific expedition to the bleak landscape of Heard Island in the South Indian Ocean, riding out freezing gales on the fringe of Antarctica.

On 1 July 1958, the steel lady proved once and for all how tough she was. On a cold winter night off the northwest coast of

Tasmania, with a full load of live crayfish in her tanks, *Patanela* slammed into an uncharted submerged rock and tore a 1.4 metre hole in her bow. Water rushed into the living quarters, but was held in check when a crewman closed the first watertight door. With her stern almost clear of the water and her bowsprit almost submerged, the sturdy vessel limped 80 nautical miles unaided to the port of Stanley. *Patanela* was considered by Tasmanian fishermen to be a miracle boat, blessed by the spirits of the sea, and virtually indestructable.

Yet in the early hours of 8 November 1988, within sight of the lights of Botany bay and Australia's largest city, *Patanela* vanished without a trace.

The rugged steel schooner, already a legend among seafarers, quite simply ceased to exist. The well-equipped yacht, with state-of-the-art safety and navigational equipment on board, went missing on a calm night in moderate seas in one of the world's busiest shipping lanes. No wreckage was found, no flares were sighted, no mayday call was transmitted, and the bodies of the four crew were never recovered.

Since that warm summer night in 1988, no answers have emerged as to her fate, but time has not eroded the intrigue, nor the bizarre events that led up to her disappearance. Instead, the passage of time has lifted the legend of *Patanela* into sharper public focus. People still want to know - where is *Patanela*?

Patanela sailed out of Fremantle on Sunday 16 October bound for Airlie Beach, north Queensland. On board were skipper Ken Jones, his wife Noreen, crewmen Michael Calvin, 21, and his best friend, 23-year-old John Blissett. Also on board were Alan Nicol, who had recently paid $200,000 for the schooner, marine electrical engineer Ray Mudie, and the Jones' daughter, Ronalee Dean. Mudie was along for part of the ride, to check the yacht's electrical systems and to have a short holiday. Dean was taking a break from a messy divorce and was also along for just part of the journey.

Patanela left her moorings to the cheers of a crowd gathered to watch her go. She looked sleek and graceful after a $40,000 refit to bring her up to luxury class. Her hull was painted a deep royal blue above the water line and red below, separated by a gold and white strip. On the stern was the word PATANELA and beneath it CYC FREMANTLE. On either side, facing the lettering, was a black and white penguin. Although she had outgrown her humble crayfishing beginnings, the steel lady still looked tough. The voyage to Airlie Beach, where she was to be chartered as a cruise vessel, should have been the easiest of journeys.

But 23 days later, in circumstances as strange as any in the annals of sea mysteries, *Patanela* vanished as though she had never existed.

Skipper Ken Jones' final, dramatic radio transmissions were picked up by Sydney Overseas Telecommunications Commission (OTC) Radio, beginning at 12.57am.

Jones: "Sydney this is *Patanela*...I believe we've run out of fuel approximately 10 miles east of Botany Bay...we've hoisted our sails and we're tacking out to the east, tracking about zero eight zero and our intention is to tack out for a couple of hours and then tack back in...we may need some assistance in the morning to get in the harbour...over."

Exactly one hour later, at 1.57am, Jones requested a wind forecast, stating the winds were "lightening off now and we don't want to get caught too far out with no wind". Curiously, Jones then asked how far south the coastal town of Moruya was from Sydney. Radio operator Keith McLennan replied that Moruya was "about five hours driving time" away.

At precisely 2.02am, McLennan received Jones' final message: "Three hundred kilometres is it...south?" The message ended in static. Nothing more was ever heard from Jones or the crew.

Only four people were on board at that stage. Ray Mudie had left the vessel at Esperance, in Western Australia. Alan Nicol and Ronalee Dean had both disembarked at Port Lincoln, South Australia, and flown back to Perth.

But *Patanela* was in competent hands. Jones was highly respected among mariners. He was an accomplished sailor, winning the West Australian Blue Water championship twice and taking out the 330-mile Perth to Albany ocean race on another two occasions. He held a commercial pilot's licence and was a qualified mechanic. Jones was known as a crack navigator and a fierce competitor who didn't like to come in second.

Michael Calvin and John Blissett were both knockabout adventurers with a keen taste for the sea. They sailed the Hobart to Sydney leg of Australia's Bicentennial Tall Ships race on board *Solway Lass*. They also crewed on the 33-metre brigantine *Golden Plover* that sailed as a tourist cruise vessel from Airlie Beach to the Whitsunday Islands.

Only three possibilities emerge from the events of 8 November. Either *Patanela* was run down in the dead of night with the loss of all hands, or she was hijacked by persons unknown - or she was stolen by the crew.

Even though a coronial inquest held in Sydney in February 1992 declared that *Patanela* had been the victim of a "catastrophic event" - most likely a collision with an unknown, larger vessel - there are still far more questions to a sinking theory than there are answers.

For a start, Ken Jones was an old hand at sea, a man used to aircraft, boats and machinery. His son, Peter, doesn't believe his father would ever run out of fuel. He says his father could sail into Sydney Harbour "backwards and blindfolded", with or without fuel. He also believes Ken Jones was under pressure when he transmitted for the last time off Botany bay.

"I don't believe any of Dad's last radio messages were his own words. It was his voice but there was too much indecision. Something or someone was forcing my father to say the uncharacteristic things he said. Someone, one way or the other, has managed to hijack the boat."

Even considering the unlikely possibility that Jones ran out of fuel, there is still the question of how an experienced, competent skipper on a safe boat would allow a larger vessel to run him down. It is inconceivable that all three men wouldn't be on deck at night, working the sails in a busy shipping lane. *Patanela's* lights would be ablaze, making the yacht visible for up to three nautical miles. The vessel had the latest satellite navigation equipment, colour radar, a radphone capable of calling anywhere in the world, a new VHF radio, a small CB radio and an RDF receiver. The aerials were fitted to the masts and a whiplash aerial was fitted to the stern in case the yacht was dismasted. On top of all that, *Patanela* was fitted with an Electronic Position Indicator Beacon (EPIRB), which, when activated, sends out continuous signals to passing aircraft for

48 hours - in this case, air traffic from nearby Kingsford Smith Airport would logically pick up a signal very quickly.

Alan Nicol was safety conscious and had equipped *Patanela* with flares, 28 lifejackets placed in several strategic locations, an eight-man liferaft containing two months' supply of food, a rubber motorised dinghy and two lifebuoys.

It would seem reasonable to expect Ken Jones to have at least one of the watertight compartments closed as added insurance against an emergency. One compartment closed, according to *Patanela's* builder, Bob Brinkman, would be enough to keep her afloat unless a "massive impact" cut her in half. Even then, the watertight section could be expected to float.

By any standards, *Patanela* was a safe yacht, with an experienced, competent crew. If she was run down by a larger ship, that ship would have to have been very large indeed, and travelling without lights to get close enough for Jones to fail to take evasive action. Jones' final radio transmission was received at 2.02am, which left only three hours or so to summer daybreak - yet there was no debris observed then or later, no evidence in the form of a lifejacket, a broken mast or a shred of sail. Such a sinking would need to be sudden, savage and fatal for none of the crew to escape. Clavin and Blissett were young, strong and known to be powerful swimmers. They could have stayed afloat for many hours, perhaps even made it to shore.

No debris, no bodies, no evidence. If *Patanela* went down that night within sight of Botany bay, it was the cleanest sinking in maritime history.

The "sudden sink" verdict, as it became known, was handed down by Deputy State Coroner Derrick Hand at the inquest more than three years later, and was based on a lengthy investigation by the Australian Federal Police which, in turn, relied heavily on a report prepared by Captain C.W. Filor, Inspector of Marine Accidents for the Department of Transport and Communications. Filor backed up his "sudden sink" theory with a series of complicated calculations which attempted to explain how, in his opinion, *Patanela* met her fate. However, in spite of detailed research into the number and movements of vessels known to have been in *Patanela's* reported area, the Filor Report - as it was called

- was unable to convincingly conclude just which "much larger" ship was responsible for ramming and sinking the steel schooner without trace - and without damage to the ship itself. In fact, only six vessels are known to have been in the general area of Sydney on the morning of 8 November. None of these vessels - or any other ship - entered Sydney Harbour or Botany Bay between the time of Jones' last message and 6am.

Although the Royal Australian Navy was conducting exercises somewhere off Botany Bay that night, no naval vessels were in *Patanela's* area at the critical time. Despite that clear-cut evidence, however, the Filor Report states: "The most likely explanation for the disappearance of the *Patanela* is that it was run down by a larger vessel, either commercial or naval."

But Commodore Tim Fox of the Royal Australian Navy was surprised at Filor's conclusion.

"We don't run down ships like that - it is most improbable," he said. "The largest vessel we have is a 20,000 tonne tanker. Most are 4,000 tonne destroyers, and if one of them ran into a boat the size of *Patanela*, everyone on board would know about it. I don't believe it likely even a large container ship would hit a steel schooner without feeling the impact."

Patanela's final known voyage across the underbelly of Australia and north along the coast towards Sydney was itself a journey of strange events. Her first two ports of call, Albany and Esperence, were uneventful, but at Port Lincoln the first of many inconsistencies appear in the story. For a start, owner Alan Nicol told Federal Police the yacht pulled into harbour on the night of 27 October. The Filor Report states, however, that the vessel arrived the following night.

Nicol and Ronalee Dean left the schooner at Port Licoln - Nicol unexpectedly, due to business commitments back in Perth. This was to be the last time he would see *Patanela*.

Nicol became convinced a plot to steal his yacht was hatched after he suddenly left the boat. He strongly suspected his old friend Ken Jones was behind the plan. "Either Ken or the boys could have masterminded the plot and persuaded the others to become part of it. After Port Lincoln and Portland there is a lot of ocean - and then South america. They had plenty of time to fake a radio message, supposedly off Sydney."

Nicol questions why all four of the remaining crew members had their passports with them - on what was supposed to be a holiday cruise in Australian waters.

As with its arrival, *Patanela's* departure date from Port Lincoln also remains confused. The Filor Report has assumed the vessel left in the "forenoon" of Saturday 29 October, but Wayne Murphy, Commodore of the local yacht club, said the steel schooner sailed out of the bay at 2pm on Sunday, 30 October.

Patanela's movements in and out of her last known port of call, Portland, Victoria, are even more confusing than those at Port Lincoln. On 1 November, Alan Nicol received a telephone call in Perth from Jones, who asked for $500 to purchase fuel in Portland. It was a strange request, as Jones had refused a fuel top-up in Port Lincoln as unnecessary. Although surprised, Nicol agreed to the request, just to keep his skipper happy. While on the phone, Nicol offered to send Jones two extra crewmen for the remainder of the voyage. Jones knocked back the offer, insisting that he, his wife and "the boys" could handle the yacht without any trouble. Although Nicol couldn't quite shake a feeling of unease, he decided not to push the issue.

On Thursday 3 November at 3.45pm, Ken Jones walked into the Portland branch of the Commonwealth Bank and identified himself to assistant accountant Maree Veronica Stanford, asking if the $500 had arrived from Perth. Incredibly, he told Stanford the money was from his daughter and was needed to buy stores for a yacht he was sailing out of Portland that night.

Patanela's visit to Portland is shrouded in conflicting evidence, confusion and mystery. Even though Nicol insists Jones phoned him on 1 November, Portland Port Authority slipway attendant, Ken Whistler, signed a police statement claiming *Patanela's* arrival date was actually 2 November.

Inquiries by police and private investigator Terry Hebb, working for *Patanela's* insurers, Club Marine, failed to find any evidence that Ken Jones purchased fuel in Portland.

Patanela's departure date from Portland is unknown. Not even the final police report would give a date with any confidence, declaring instead "a degree of confusion" existed over her departure.

The Filor Report, while admitting there was "an inconsistency over the date of departure", calculated that a radio call to Melbourne OTC coastal radio at 5.37pm on Friday 4, purporting to be from *Patanela*, "would indicate that the vessel sailed late in the evening of 3 November.

But Portland yachtsman Ted Meissner wasn't having a bar of that. Meissner is certain he saw *Patanela* pull away from the wharf at 11am on Saturday 5. Meissner phoned Australian Federal Police headquarters in Canberra just before the coroner's inquiry was due to start in February 1992, offering his testimony to the court. His offer was rejected.

While the police played down any sinister implications in *Patanela*'s confused arrival and departure times in Portland, Ken Jones' acceptance of $500 for fuel he never purchased, and his refusal to take on fresh crew, means there is no shortage of others who view those events with suspicion.

Terry Hebb is one. The private investigator is firm in his belief that somewhere between Portland and Wilsons Promontory, Jones decided - or was persuaded - to steal *Patanela* and alter course for an unknown destination. "It's too easy to say the boat sank off Sydney," Hebb said.

Peter Jones also believes that sinister events occurred either in Portland or just after *Patanela* departed - but his father was the victim of a crime rather than the perpetrator.

"My theory is that somebody got on board the boat, either before it left Portland, or just around the corner. It would only take two or three guys to blast up onto the boat with a Zodiac dinghy, climb up the back to the radio room with guns and just take control."

At 4.15pm on Saturday 5 November, the day Ted Meissner claimed he saw *Patanela* leave Portland, Peter Calvin picked up the phone in his Taree home and heard Michael say "G'day Dad" before the line went dead. That was the last time he heard his son's voice.

The next day, at 4.09pm, Jones contacted Sydney Radio, giving a position off Bega on the south coast of New South Wales and *Patanela*'s ETA (estimated time of arrival) in Sydney as midnight on Monday 7 November.

Apart from Jones' final dramatic message in the early morning of 8 November, *Patanela* would not be heard from again.

Around the waters of Victoria and Tasmania, the mention of *Patanela* is sure to bring the names Norm and Doug Hunt into the conversation. The famous schooner's history is inexorably linked to the brothers who sailed her for almost three decades - many of those years as a crayfishing boat in the wild seas off the southern and western coasts of Tasmania.

In 1963 she was chartered as a supply vessel for Warwick Deacock's scientific expedition to Heard Island and upon her return sailed to Perth where the Hunt brothers ran a ferry service to Rottnest Island. Norm Hunt spent 10 years refitting *Patanela* for a trip around the world which would take her to 46 countries in six years.

In 1987, Norm sold his half share in the vessel to Doug for $80,000 and a year later Doug sold *Patanela* to Alan Nicol for $200,000. Norm Hunt wasn't pleased. For a start, he still hadn't been paid his $80,000 and Doug had made an extra $40,000 on the sale to Nicol. Norm considered half that $40,000 profit should be his. Although he was eventually paid the $80,000, Norm claimed Doug had "dudded" him for $20,000, and a bitter rift formed between the two brothers.

But the enigmatic Norm Hunt seemed destined to forever be a part of *Patanela's* history and he became mysteriously linked to the proud schooner once again during her final voyage along the southern coast of Australia.

Hunt had purchased a badly run-down passenger ferry named Exy in Adelaide and when he finally received the $80,000 from his brother, completed a refit of the vessel and renamed it Explorer III. The Hunt brothers were well-known identies in the Gulf of Carpentaria and Norm intended to operate the ferry as a tourist vessel based in Karumba.

In early October 1988 the revamped ferry left Adelaide with Hunt and his girlfriend Linda Hornby on board, together with friends Trevor and Mary Blood. Hornby later told police the Bloods were Adelaide people who claimed they had sailing experience, but left the vessel at Robe, South Australia, because they were "too scared of the weather and the boat's handling in rough seas".

Although Hunt was later cleared of any involvement in a plot to steal or hijack the missing *Patanela*, his close proximity to the schooner during her last weeks in Australian waters has perplexed investigators.

Hunt claims he arrived in Portland on 6 October - roughly one month before *Patanela's* disputed arrival and departure times in the same port - and flew to Perth for his daughter's wedding. His movements from then on are confused - a hodge-podge of dates, times and events. Hunt's incredibly vague recollections and knockabout larrikinism heavily clouded any attempt to clarify his exact whereabouts as he sailed somewhere ahead of *Patanela* during the last half of her final voyage towards Sydney. During investigations into the schooner's disappearance, Hunt revelled in his reputation as a will-o'-the-wisp, likeable rogue who may, or may not, know the secret of *Patanela's* fate.

Hunt returned to Portland from his daughter's wedding on 10 October, but couldn't recall much of what he did there during the next few days, and couldn't remember when he left the coastal town. He did remember sailing on to Port fairy, a 45-kilometre hop across Portland Bay, where he spent three days socialising with friends. This visit was later confirmed by Terry Hebb's inquiries.

Apparently Hunt then worked his way around the rugged Victorian coastline, sheltering *Explorer III* at night and sailing by day. On Saturday 29 October - while *Patanela* rested at Port Lincoln after crossing the Great Australian Bight - Hunt tied up *Explorer III* in Sydney's Darling harbour. The fact that he was travelling the Australian coastline ahead of *Patanela*, albeit a considerable distance away, was in itself a bizarre coincidence treated by some with disbelief and suspicion.

Detective Superintendent David Lewington, the chief investigator when the Federal Police first became involved with the case in March 1989, believed Hunt had been only one day ahead of *Patanela*. Hunt denied this, claiming the police dates were inaccurate.

Lewington described Hunt as "an unknown kettle of fish" and further stated: "It was just too coincidental that the former owner of the vessel was in the same area. Hunt's movements were unexplained and as far as I know still haven't been properly explained."

Hunt was uncertain about the exact date when he left Darling Harbour but police believe he arrived at Nelson Bay, north of sydney, "about 7 November". However, records show *Explorer III* tied up at the marina on 4 November and spent three weeks in the harbour. That three-week period covers the night *Patanela* went missing just 240 kilometres to the south. Hunt's movements over most of that period are lost in confusion, conflicting reports, vague recollections and somewhere in the midst of it all, misleading information. Certainly, in the period from late 7 November to 18 November, Hunt can't remember where he was, except to say he was travelling with Linda Hornby in a Mini Moke, which he carried on board *Explorer III*, and they arrived back in Nelson Bay without it. He remembers only that he went somewhere "north" and came back by bus because of torrential rains that flooded the highway. Hornby told police she and Hunt drove to the Gold Coast where they stayed in a caravan park "for about one week" and the Mini Moke was left in a car park "by arrangement". She said the main purpose of the trip was to arrange a charter boat licence for *Explorer III* to operate in Karumba.

Norm Hunt later laughed at the fact that the time of his Mini Moke "disappearance" coincided with the 8 November disappearance of *Patanela*.

"Yeah, it was a bad time to go for a drive," he said. "But I'm a quiet sort of a bloke and I didn't bother to remember where I went. I don't need an alibi."

Although Federal Police investigators were satisfied with Hornby's version of the Mini Moke trip to the Gold Coast, Hunt's poor memory over the crucial time of *Patanela's* disappearance wasn't as easily dismissed by some close observers of the case, including Terry Hebb and his Sydney-based associate, private detective Nelson Chad. In a nine-page summary dated 8 May 1989, Chad reported to Hebb that there were "a number of disturbing features concerning the section of the inquiry that touches upon Norman Hunt and Linda Hornby (and) there is suspicion attached to this couple in relation to the disappearance of the *Patanela*."

Hebb and Chad weren't the only ones suspicious of Norm Hunt and his rumoured involvement with the missing schooner. Alan

Nicol strongly suspected the former owner of the vessel and said so to the police, and to the families of crew members Michael Calvin and John Blissett. But then, skipper Ken Jones was on Nicol's list, too.

One scenario widely mooted by some investigators and, later on, a small army of *Patanela* sleuths, is one that has persisted over the passage of time. This theory links Hunt and Jones, and possibly Calvin and Blissett, in a prearranged conspiracy to steal the yacht. The fact that Hunt's movements on the night of the disappearance are clouded in confusion serve to bolster the story. In this scenario, Hunt, enraged by his brother "dudding" him over the sale of *Patanela*, and, discovering that Ken Jones' Perth business was in financial trouble, set up a deal with the skipper and the crew to steal the schooner after making a bogus call to Sydney Radio. *Patanela* would then sail to a carefully selected destination, possibly southeast Asia or South America, where it would be heavily disguised and used in the drug trade or other illicit activities. Later, the vessel could be sold or scuttled in some isolated location.

Norm Hunt was amused by the speculation and appeared to enjoy the notoriety bequeathed on him by the disappearance of his old crayfishing boat, and had this to say: "Yeah, I'm the baddie in all this, a real scoundrel, but I didn't take the *Patanela*, which kind of spoils the whole picture, doesn't it?" He was even more amused by the tag "the mysterious Mr Hunt" given to him by by an intrigued media.

Hunt attracted further suspicion because he still owned one of *Patanela's* original dinghies, strapped to the top deck of *Explorer III*, which he said he kept for "sentimental reasons".

Despite the fact that Norm Hunt was a controversial key player in the history of the missing schooner and considered by many to be an integral link in the mystery of that vessel's dramatic disappearance, he was not called to give evidence at the coroner's inquest.

Explorer III left Nelson Bay on 28 November, 1988, and turned up several weeks later at Townsville's Ross River Marina. Soon after, Hunt and Hornby flew to Thailand for a month's holiday. On their return Hunt carried out repairs to the vessel before leaving on the final leg to Karumba around the tip of Cape York Peninsula, where they arrived on 27 March, 1989.

On the way north, Hunt anchored overnight on 9 March near Hinchinbrook Island, halfway between Townsville and Cairns - just seven days after Ted and Marie McCarthy claim to have sighted *Patanela* in nearby Rockingham Bay. Once again, coincidence had thrown the dice and the numbers came up suspiciously for Norm Hunt.

Hunt spent the next two years based in Karumba, taking tourists on wilderness trips along the mangrove and mudflat coastline of the Gulf. Included in his excursions were barramundi fishing sessions and crocodile spotting trips. He became somewhat of a celebrity in far north Queensland. To locals and tourists alike he became the man who once owned the famous *Patanela* - a crown he wore with good humour and showmanship. He was fond of baiting journalists with one-liners like: "*Patanela*? She's hidden up a creek where I left her", and: "*Patanela's* on a drug run at the moment so I can't show her to you!" It was all good for business and Hunt was seldom without an audience of customers to entertain with tall tales of *Patanela* and her mysterious meeting with fate.

A Brisbane newspaper article in September 1989 shows a picture of Hunt rowing his *Patanela* dinghy. Following the story, he was visited by two Federal Police officers - the first and only time he had been physically approached by the authorities over the yacht's disappearance. Once again, he was "hazy" about the time frame but remembered one was a male officer and the other was a "beautiful" female. Referring to the officers as "Dick and Dickless Tracy", Hunt said: "It took them all day to interview me because I bullshitted them about having the boat hidden up the river."

On a trip to Bamaga, a tiny settlement on the northernmost tip of Cape York Peninsula, *Explorer III* was boarded by a suspicious Queensland Boating and Fisheries officer who noticed *Patanela's* dinghy lashed to the deck. The officer - "a pompous redhead", according to Hunt - thought he had the *Patanela* mystery solved, but Hunt's wisecracking response to his questions robbed the occasion of any dramatic overtones. In the end, the officer gave up and enjoyed a beer with Hunt.

In November 1990, Hunt decided he needed a break from tourists and steered *Explorer III* out of Karumba on what was to be her last voyage. On 2 December, near the Aboriginal township of Lockhart River on the east coast of Cape York, the ferry sank in controversial circumstances. The crew of another yacht in the area, who had shared drinks with Hunt two nights before the sinking, claimed there was "a noticeable lack of equipment" on board *Explorer III*, and Hunt had admitted he had no personal effects on the vessel. They also claimed Hunt said he "hated the bloody thing and wished it would sink", and talked about "various boats he had owned that ended up sinking."

Six months later in Cairns, one of the yachtsmen boldly asked Hunt if he deliberately sank *Explorer III*, and alleges Hunt admitted to the sinking, saying the insurance company had paid out and he was looking around for a catamaran.

But Hunt laughed at the story and claimed the vessel sank because of rusted exhaust pipe fittings that allowed water to backflow into the boat while the engine was running overnight to recharge flat batteries.

"If this had been a put-up job I'd have put her down in very deep water. Every time a boat goes down someone says it was an insurance job. You've got to cop it if you're involved with boats. It doesn't worry me."

The *Explorer III* sinking was just one of several marine mishaps that had dogged the 58-year-old sailor during his 40 years at sea. In 1962 he lost a crayfishing boat, *Doris Bethune*, named after his mother, on rocks near a lighthouse off Cape Sorell, Tasmania. Ten years later, Doug Hunt was skipper on board another Hunt brothers' vessel, *Islander II*, a prawn trawler operating off Papua New Guinea, when she sank as a result of "an old-fashioned echo sounder working free from rotted boards". Norm Hunt wasn't on board at the time. The following year, a Hunt family-owned ferry, the Rottnest Hydroplane, caught fire in Perth and was destroyed while tied up at the wharf. The Hunts' believed sabotage was responsible for the blaze - the result of bitter rivalry between Perth-based ferry operators. And even *Patanela* was almost destroyed - gutted by fire in 1971 while undergoing a refit in the Swan River.

Too many coincidences, or just the odds attracted by a life at sea, where accidents and human error often result in disastrous consequences? But Norm Hunt claimed he was on board only one of the three vessels he and Doug had lost at sea - and that was *Explorer III*. He further claimed there was nothing extraordinary about the marine incidents that have plagued his career. Even though he admitted receiving paid-out insurance claims of "five or six hundred thousand dollars", he said he is innocent of any wrongdoing and has nothing to worry about from insurance companies.

"I've had bad luck with boats sinking and you can't help bad luck," he said.

Luck ran out completely for Norm Hunt in May 1998 when he died of a massive brain haemhorrage in Strahan, Tasmania, at the age of 64, taking his link with *Patanela* and any of her secrets with him.

Patanela had been missing an astonishing 11 days before the alarm was raised. During that time, Peter Jones had been trying to contact his father to sort out the family company's deteriorating financial affairs. At first he wasn't too concerned. He knew his father was trying to ignore the problems and didn't want to talk, but he kept trying. Business decisions had to be made and he needed help.

Finally he told Alan Nicol he was worried - *Patanela* had been out of contact far too long. With a growing feeling that something had gone terribly wrong, Peter Jones notified Perth police. But Nicol wasn't too worried. At that stage he was pretty sure Jones had decided to sail out wide and bypass Sydney, heading directly for north Queensland. After all, Jones was a master mariner and capable of making his own decisions.

But when *Patanela* didn't turn up by 18 November, when she was due at Airlie Beach, Nicol's confidence took a battering and he, too, became worried.

On 19 November, Canberra's Federal Sea Safety and Surveillance Centre - now known as the Maritime Rescue Co-ordination Centre - was advised by Perth police that Peter Jones was concerned for his father's safety and that *Patanela* was overdue at Airlie Beach.

The next day the families of Ken and Noreen Jones, and of crewmen Michael Calvin and John Blissett, were officially notified that *Patanela* and all on board had been declared missing at sea. Also advised were Federal Police, the Civil Aviation Authority, coastwatch agencies, and according to Maritime Rescue officials, "anyone else who could possibly give service."

But, in spite of mounting pressure from Nicol, Peter Jones and the Calvin and Blissett families, a full-scale search was never mounted for the missing schooner.

Bob McCulloch, director of the Maritime Rescue Co-ordination Centre, stood his ground as the *Patanela* disappearance became public knowledge and a national furore erupted over his organisation's failure to initiate a search. McCulloch defended the "no search" decision on the basis that he had not been notified of the schooner's disappearance until 11 days after the event. A rescue operation after such a space of time was considered "an impossible task that would require a minimum of 120 aircraft to search an estimated 200,000 square kilometres of coastland and ocean."

Federal Police investigators agreed, saying it was "impractical" given the time lapse and no "identifiable datum point" to begin with.

But the parents of Calvin and Blissett weren't impressed by the authorities' stubborn refusal to search for their missing sons.

"They will send out planes looking for foreign fishermen lost at sea, but not for my son," Dawn Calvin told reporters. "I think it is appalling that four Australians can go missing off Sydney Heads and no one will search for them. No one seems to want to help us at all."

On 9 May 1989, seven months after *Patanela* disappeared off Botany Bay, a barnacle-encrusted lifebuoy bearing the words PATANELA - FREMANTLE, was hauled on board a fishing boat off Terrigal, 50 kilometres north of Sydney. One of the fishermen, Brian Foster, noticed leatherneck barnacles growing on both sides of the buoy, estimating from the size of the barnacles that the lifebuoy had been in the water from six to eight weeks. Foster was local born and had spent 30 years of his life as a fisherman and he knew what he was talking about.

Professor D.T.Anderson, then head of the University of Sydney's School of Biological Sciences, considered by his peers to be one of Australia's leading marine biologists, later examined the lifebuoy for the Federal Police. He found that the lifebuoy had been in the water "for a relatively short time, certainly no longer than a matter of three to four weeks, possibly less."

Professor Anderson, however, was not called to give evidence at the inquest. Instead, evidence was given by Dr Patricia Hutchins, a marine ecologist at the Australian Museum in Sydney who said she believed marine growth found on the lifebuoy could have been "regrowth", which she claimed would make it possible for the buoy to have been in the water for seven months and yet be found with marine growth only weeks old attached to its surface.

The discovery of the lifebuoy, like the disappearance of the steel schooner itself, is a mystery. Official rhetoric, opinions and scientific conclusions have failed to establish how it came to be separated from the vessel and found seven months later.

In the first four years after she disappeared, 25 sightings of *Patanela*, plus a deluge of crank calls, were reported to the authorities and to Alan Nicol from as far away as southeast Asia and South America.

Federal Police gave little credence to the list of sightings, blaming many of them on media hysteria and the fact that some of them were reported to Alan Nicol before the witnesses could be interviewed.

Detective Superintendent Ed Tyrie gave evidence at the inquest that 22 sightings had been investigated "as best they could".

But as well as the McCarthy sighting at Tully Heads, another north Queensland report from Bowen gave Alan Nicol hope that his beloved *Patanela* was still sailing and hidden somewhere among the islands and bays of the Great Barrier Reef.

On 13 July 1989, Mackay travelling salesman John Benck was taking a breather from the heat on the Bowen foreshore when something out on the water caught his attention. A yacht tied up at the nearby marina seemed vaguely familiar. While staring at the vessel, Benck suddenly realised he was looking at *Patanela* - a sailing boat he hadn't seen since 1973 - "or if it wasn't *Patanela* it was a bloody good copy."

Benck had known the Hunt brothers in Perth during the years

Patanela was moored in the Swan River, undergoing the major refit before Norm Hunt's world voyage. Benck had owned a power boat which he berthed at a jetty "so close to *Patanela* you could spit on it", and had been on the schooner during a social cruise to Rottnest Island. Benck had also been on the river when *Patanela* was gutted by fire in 1971. Although Benck hadn't seen the schooner for many years, he was sure she was right in front of him now. But *Patanela* wasn't the regal lady he used to know.

"She was painted a ghastly cream or ivory colour for all the world like somebody had done it to neutralise her and make her look bland."

Benck walked down to the seawall to "have a gander" and look at the name on the stern - but she was facing bow to the shore and a locked marina gate prevented him making a closer inspection. Besides, Benck was a working man and had a full afternoon of calls to make. Strangely, he knew nothing of *Patanela's* mysterious disappearance nine months earlier.

Benck was halfway home to Mackay when the reality of seeing *Patanela* again hit him "like a thunderbolt".

"I was very tempted to turn around and go back and find out the name written on that boat, but I was pushed for time with appointments."

After speaking to his wife who had read about *Patanela's* disappearance, Benck phoned the Federal Police in Cairns and told his story. He said their reaction was "a bit blase". Nevertheless Federal Police did contact the Bowen harbourmaster who said he had no record of a vessel the size and description of *Patanela* having entered the port.

Two weeks before the coroner's inquest in Sydney was due to begin, Federal Police asked Benck how confident he was that the vessel he had seen was *Patanela*. Benck replied that he was "as sure as a bloke could be who took the trouble to ring the cops".

Strangely, the police did not take a statement from Benck in relation to the sighting, nor was he called to give evidence at the inquest.

In November 1989, one year after *Patanela's* disappearance, Cairns yachtsman John Shaw informed Federal Police that Michael

Calvin and John Blissett had plotted to steal the charter vessel *Golden Plover* at Airlie Beach in 1987.

Shaw, who was at that time skipper of the 30-metre brigantine, claimed the two boyhood friends from Taree had planned to sail the vessel to South America. He said they were frequent drug and alcohol users - often going below decks to "heat cannabis resin on knives and sniff the smoke." He also suspected they used LSD.

In June 1987, Calvin was hired as a rigger on the set of the movie *Dead Calm*, starring Nicole Kidman and Sam Neill, about a couple's ordeal at sea while trying to escape a deranged killer. For the movie, the *Golden Plover* was refitted to resemble a derelict ship during filming around Hamilton Island. Calvin is listed in the movie's credits. He allegedly told the movie crew of his hijack plan.

Shaw said he warned Calvin and Blissett that if they were involved in stealing the *Golden Plover*, they would never be able to return home to Australia without being found out.

"This prospect didn't seem to worry either of them and they stated on many occasions that they would love to spend their lives sailing around the world."

According to Shaw, another member of the *Golden Plover's* crew said he had contacts in South America where the vessel could be sold. Shaw said the plot - which included dropping crew and passengers on an island before sailing away - was abandoned when it was discovered the *Golden Plover* needed a major overhaul to make her seaworthy.

But the Federal Police were not impressed. Although the official investigation admitted Calvin and Blissett were "users of cannabis in the form of marijuana and resin" and a plot to steal the *Golden Plover* did take place, it was simply the result of "bravado uttered under the influence of drugs or alcohol by the boys and other members of the crew."

However, Shaw insisted the plot was "well-planned over a two-month period and wasn't just skylarking" and remains firmly convinced Calvin and Blissett were behind the disappearance of *Patanela*.

"There is no doubt in my mind what happened the night *Patanela* went missing - she headed east and then southeast. It's pure speculation from there. The *Golden Plover* wasn't a suitable vessel for what was planned - unfortunately, *Patanela* was."

The most intriguing of the many conspiracy theories that followed *Patanela*'s disappearance involves a shadowy American expatriate and alleged one-time bodyguard of Elvis Presley named Larry Horowitz.

The author first heard of Horowitz during the coroner's inquest in February 1992, when he was contacted by a man who claimed to have direct knowledge of *Patanela*'s fate. At a later meeting the man - ficticiously named "Max Branning" by the author - related a story that sounded like a Hollywood movie script, but was just bizarre enough to have some degree of truth.

Branning claimed to be a semi-retired US Drug Enforcement Agency (DEA) operative, then living in Sydney, but still in touch with the CIA and other covert US intelligence agencies, whom he trusted "absolutely" for information. According to Branning, Larry Horowitz was wanted by the FBI on fraud and drug charges and had been on the run since the early 1980s, sailing a yacht similar in size and appearance to *Patanela*. Although he said he was unable to prove any definite link between Horowitz and *Patanela*, Branning strongly suspected the fugitive was on board and in control of the missing vessel. He claimed a US military aircraft spotted a yacht on tidal mudflats in the Wessel Islands group, off the northwest tip of Arnhem Land, in late 1988, and although the vessel was not identified, it was believed to have been *Patanela*. Several months later, intelligence reports placed *Patanela* in the southern Philippines port of Zamboanga - a notorious area frequented by pirates and drug-runners. Branning said his sources reported that *Patanela* underwent major reconstruction, including a change of appearance to the bow and stern, and the fitting of powerful engines. He said the name *Patanela* was replaced with the cryptic legend *CX805* painted on the bow and stern.

Six months later, *CX805* was reportedly in the Arafura Sea, 100 nautical miles northeast of Darwin where a large drug shipment of buddha sticks changed hands. A 17,000 tonne cargo ship using the name *Carol Bell*, allegedly used as a drug mover, was the other vessel involved. Branning alleged a certain department of the Australian Government was aware of *CX805*'s movements and was secretly tracking it via satellite technology throughout the southeast Asian and Pacific regions. He said an Australian-based company with casino interests had financial links with the vessel's operations in and around the Solomon Islands and Fiji. Branning said Horowitz was the key to *Patanela's* whereabouts, but claimed his source of information was unable to pinpoint the vessel's location at any given time - nor does he know the fate of her crew. He said *Patanela* would be destroyed when it was no longer needed and Horowitz would run out of luck at the same time.

Several months later the author received a long-distance phone call from an anonymous male who gave some credibility to Branning's seemingly wild tale. The man said he had read Branning's account in a book about *Patanela's* disappearance - and so had Horowitz, who was then "somewhere in Venezuela, but he won't say exactly where", and that Horowitz - whom he described as "a big finance man" - was "pissed off" about the story. The caller said he had sailed for six years with Horowitz on a yacht named *Onza* that reputedly once belonged to Errol Flynn. He said he was on board the *Onza* with Horowitz in the Arafura Sea, as described by Branning, but Horowitz "had no involvement with *Patanela* whatsoever". The caller claimed he and Horowitz had been involved in "various deals" in Indonesia and elsewhere and their vessel had once been boarded and searched at Portland Roads, Cape York Peninsula, by Federal Police.

Larry Horowitz certainly didn't keep his head down in north Queensland. He was a well-known and flamboyant figure around Cairns in the early 1980s and remembered by many locals as "the Elvis Presley bodyguard" who lived on his sailing boat, anchored off False Cape, across the bay from the city. According to local reports, the vessel had a crane on board and carried a Mini Moke and a red Ferrari that Horowitz drove around town. Horowitz reportedly bought land in the isolated False Cape area and was suspected of growing marijuana there. One local remembers him as "tough looking and mean and you got the impression not to mess with him."

There are no shortage of conspiracy theories surrounding the strange circumstances of *Patanela*'s disappearance. Almost all of them involve drug-running and arms smuggling. *Patanela* under the control of Chinese triads or drug lords from southeast Asia. *Patanela* smuggling guns to Bougainville rebels. *Patanela* converted into an armoured gunship. *Patanela* used by pirates in the South China Sea.

But the conspiracy theories are no more incredible than the various sinking theories that claim the rugged steel schooner was somehow run down by an unknown supership, and sunk without trace in the early hours of that calm summer morning in November 1988.

Although the passage of years hasn't revealed the whereabouts of *Patanela* and her crew, seafarers have an old saying: "Missing ships have a habit of turning up." If that is so, then one day the steel lady may show her sails again.

CHAPTER FIVE

DARK JUSTICE

Kelvin Condren was drunk in a police cell when Patricia Rose Carlton was bashed to death, yet he was convicted of her murder. It took seven years to free him.

When Kelvin Ronald Condren walked out of Townsville's Stuart Creek jail in July 1990 he left almost seven years of his life behind those walls for a murder he didn't commit.

Condren was finally free because of only one reason - the judicial system couldn't hold him any longer and had no option but to release him.

As he walked through the gates into the winter sunshine and a barrage of waiting news cameras, Condren still felt he carried the brand of murderer, because although he had been set free, he hadn't been pardoned as an innocent man.

In March 1995 Condren received a $400,000 compensation cheque from the Queensland Government but still no pardon. Effectively, he had been paid off at little more than $55,000 a year for his time in jail, and left to get on with his ruined life. Except for his family and a loyal band of supporters who eventually forced his release, Condren soon became a forgotten man.

The mantle of freedom sits uneasily on Kelvin Condren's shoulders as he patiently waits for the pardon that would officially clear his name.

Condren can't remember how long it took to spend his compensation money, but he thinks it was about three years. It was, he says, his own fault, a "bit of bad management". But that doesn't matter too much. In the traditional way of the Aboriginal people, money, like everything else, is there to be shared, and he has no regrets. After all, he softly points out with a smile, he might need a helping hand one day.

He lives quietly in north Queensland now, existing on a government pension and showing no external signs that he holds a grudge against the white man's law that robbed him of his freedom and then turned its back on him.

But there's a sense of faraway sadness about Kelvin Condren. Perhaps the tragic events that led to his imprisonment are still too unfathomable for this simple man to comprehend. Perhaps he's given up trying to unravel the mysteries of a justice system that wrongly condemned, reluctantly rewarded, and then abandoned him for a crime that was not his.

Kelvin Condren was just a 22-year-old when Aboriginal woman Patricia Rose Carlton was brutally bashed with an iron bar in a vacant lot behind a Mt Isa hotel on 30 September 1983. Carlton was found in a coma at 5.40am the next day and died later that evening in hospital without regaining consciousness. An examination of her body revealed a stone had been inserted in her vagina.

Police spoke to a number of Aborigines that day, including Condren, who was drinking with a group of about a dozen friends in a dry creek bed. Condren was taken away to the police station and interviewed. Later, as a result of an alleged confession, he was charged with the attempted murder of Carlton, and when she subsequently died, with her murder.

Carlton and Condren associated with a band of homeless Aborigines who wandered the town drinking alcohol in a number of locations that included the creek bed behind West Street, a favourite spot because police had to get out of their cars and walk a considerable distance to reach the drinkers. Other areas were behind the Civic Centre and behind the Mt Isa Hotel, also used as a car park, where Carlton was found. A popular drink was a cheap flagon wine known as "Boydie's Special", bought from Boyd's Bottle Shop and often consumed until the drinkers passed out, or "choked down" as they called it.

Condren had been in Mt Isa for about a month after drifting across the state from Townsville where he'd been released from jail in May. He planned to meet his girlfriend and her family at the annual rodeo. Although his trip west was a breach of his parole conditions he was used to breaking the rules and thought he'd get away with it. Condren's frequent brushes with the law were over petty theft and heavy alcohol use. In July he attended an alcohol rehabilitation centre in Townsville but he still managed to get arrested for public drunkenness five times in August. Kelvin Condren's life was clearly on a downhill slide before he left Townsville.

In Mt Isa, police first arrested Condren for drunkenness on 20 September. Ten days later, on the same day Patricia Carlton was assaulted, police claim Condren was again picked up drunk at 5.50pm and held in the watchhouse until his release at 7.21am the next day.

Condren was back in the watchhouse at 12.40pm after police allege they received information that he was "keeping company" with Carlton prior to her death. Police claim he then volunteered to sign a written statement, confessing to the murder.

Later that day, five of Condren's drinking companions signed police statements implicating him in the murder. Susan Gilbert and de facto couple Louise Brown and Stephen McNamee said they saw Condren attack Carlton with an iron bar after an argument about her "playing up" with other men. Condren's former girlfriend Noreen Jumbo and Fabian Butcher, both cousins of Louise Brown, claimed Condren said he had "damaged" Carlton the previous night.

But within days most of the witnesses changed their minds and signed further statements saying the original police statements were false and made under duress by intimidation, harassment and threats. Stephen McNamee later claimed a police officer had punched him in the face at the Mt Isa police station and threatened him with a shovel, saying: "Every time you tell a lie you get this over your head." McNamee said he signed a false statement because he was "frightened, felt useless, and wanted to get out of the police station".

When the committal proceedings against Condren started at the Mt Isa Magistrate's Court in December 1983 only Fabian Butcher was prepared to give evidence supporting his statement. Claims were later made that Butcher was intimidated by Mt Isa police who watched his every move, relentlessly followed him around in a police car, and harassed him until he agreed to say Condren killed Patricia Carlton. Butcher, however, did not live to give evidence at Condren's trial. On 16 April 1984, four months before the trial, he was found hanging from a windmill tower at Bottle Tree Bore in Western Australia.

Following Condren's release from custody he formally complained to the Criminal Justice Commission with allegations of police misconduct. He was supported with written complaints from Brown, McNamee and Jumbo.

Condren was too drunk to remember the time he was arrested on 30 September, and he wasn't feeling too good when he was picked up by police the next day either. In fact he was drunk again - or "shaky from the grog" as he puts it. He'd resumed drinking early that morning after spending the night in a cell with a hangover and had trouble relating to events happening around him.

Condren was vulnerable. He was an alcoholic, a drifter with some prison form - and he was black. Although there were no witnesses to the assault on Carlton, and no physical evidence linking him to the crime, Condren had confessed, and, in police parlance of the time, he was "good for it".

"They came into the cell and said 'Kelvin, we're charging you with murder now, because she passed away in hospital'," he said. "I just went off completely, I didn't know what was happening, I didn't know where I was. I was in the horrors or something like that."

Condren claims he was verballed by police and given a bit of old-fashioned persuasion with a telephone book to help him make up his mind to sign the confession. He says he asked for a solicitor, but instead a Justice of the Peace "in a fireman's uniform" attended the interview sessions. Police claim they couldn't find a solicitor from the Aboriginal Legal Service and had to make do with a local JP. According to Condren the JP "started asking me questions too, just like the police," and directed him to pick up the steel bar and demonstrate how he used it to assault Patricia Carlton.

Throughout Condren's trial, two subsequent appeals and a Criminal Justice Commission inquiry, police who conducted the interview have denied intimidating or coercing him into signing the confession.

Condren still can't make any sense out of why he signed, except that detectives were "belting" him with the phone book, repeating the same questions over and over - and they promised to let him go if he signed. He said he was sick and confused and wanted desperately to get out of the police station.

"I kept telling them I didn't bash anyone and they would say 'of course you did' and they slapped me around the head and all that, and told me they'd still charge me even if I didn't sign a statement.

"They took me down to the carpark and asked me whereabouts I killed her and asked me to hold the bar and show them. They told me to look around and see if I could see anything. I saw a stain that could have been anything...oil...blood...so I said 'What's that there?' and they took a photo of me pointing at it. I didn't know they were trying to trap me."

Back at the police station the questioning continued. Finally, when he was told he could leave if he co-operated, Condren gave in and signed the confession.

"I didn't bother reading it (the statement)...there were too many pages and I didn't want to sit there all day... because it was pretty thick."

When the significance of what happened sank in, Condren went into shock, suffering from hallucinations, fear, and severe withdrawal effects from alcohol. He was placed in a padded cell and there he imagined he could see fire and smoke in the cell. He was found with his hands and feet wrapped in torn pieces of blanket to protect himself from the illusionary flames.

"I didn't know what was happening to me. Somebody came in, I think it was a doctor, and he gave me some pills while I was laying on the floor. My mind started coming back then."

Ernie Hoolihan, a Townsville Aboriginal and Islander Legal Service officer at the time, was alerted to Condren's plight by his mother Julia and prominent Aboriginal activist Gracelyn Smallwood. Hoolihan said he smelled a rat as soon as he read the official record of interview.

"Condren was blotto both times when he was arrested, yet he

was supposed to have pinpointed the time at exactly 4.15pm when he killed the woman. He'd been drinking for days, how would he know what time it was - or even what day it was? And Friday afternoon at 4.15 in the middle of town? A lot of people would be walking around that area at that time, but nobody saw it happen and nobody heard her scream. Why not?

"The police say Condren described what she was wearing right down to the last detail. He could not have remembered - drunk or sober - what any woman was wearing the day before. They just typed it up and made him sign it."

Hoolihan said police claim the motive was jealousy, that Condren believed Carlton was having sex with other men. "Patricia Carlton was never Condren's girlfriend, she'd just hang around in the drinking parties," he said.

Hoolihan went to Mt Isa and started asking questions. He says after talking to a number of people he came to the startling conclusion that Condren had been in police custody much earlier than 5.50pm on the day Carlton was assaulted.

"That day, 30 September, was a Friday and there was a Lions convention being held in Mt Isa," Hoolihan said. "Kelvin and his girlfriend's brother were jumping in the fountain to cool off at about three o'clock. Well, they didn't want drunken blackfellers mucking about with important visitors in town, so the council got them arrested and dragged off to jail. There were lots of kids coming out of school, so it was about three-thirty. The arrest sheet says 5.50pm but Kelvin was well and truly in custody when Patricia Carlton was bashed."

Hoolihan believes that not only was Condren too drunk to remember the time he was arrested, but he was too drunk to seriously injure anyone as well. "He was supposed to have killed her with a 15-foot (five metre) steel pole that weighed six and a half kilograms, but the state he was in I don't think he could have even lifted it.

"Stephen McNamee told the police he was too scared to try and stop Kelvin belting the woman, but the fact is McNamee is built like a wrestler and Kelvin wouldn't stand a chance against him."

Hoolihan said he was told by other Aborigines who were in the watchhouse that Condren had been assaulted by police, but the men "were in there under bodgie names and wouldn't put their hands up and admit they were there, so it never came out."

At Condren's trial, the issue of why an innocent man would confess to the crime of murder was raised. The court heard that many well-documented cases exist where apparently sane people have confessed to serious crimes which they could not have committed. Clinical psychologist Robert Walkely gave evidence that a phenomenon known as "gratuitous concurrence" occurred when vulnerable people, under certain circumstances, agreed with suggestions they had committed crimes when in fact they had not.

The Criminal Justice Commision report stated that it was clear that during evidence at the hearing some Aboriginal witnesses would agree to a certain proposition when it was put to them by one counsel and then, a short time later, agree with a contrary view put by an opposing counsel.

"Whether this malleability is caused by gratuitous concurrence or a general deference to authority, it may be a real problem for any tribunal before which an Aboriginal witness appears," the report said.

The Commission found that the inability to recall events at the hearing was not restricted to Aboriginal witnesses.

"Several of the police witnesses seemed to recall nothing at all outside the fairly basic details contained in their statements. Most of them could not recall with any certainty which witnesses they spoke to and had no memory of times or movements which were not recorded in their statements," the Commission noted.

Condren remembers being confused and frightened during his trial. He didn't expect to be found innocent, because by this time he realised he had no chance against the system.

"They'd rather take a white person's evidence because a murri is classed as low, like a low IQ and all that," he said later. "You get a barrister or a Crown prosecutor and you get a murri who hasn't been to court like that, they talk down at them. Murris don't know what to say. White people have been through school in towns or cities, and that's different. You've got a dark person and a white person...well, my witnesses didn't have a hope, the Crown just chewed 'em up."

Condren was found guilty of murder by an all-white jury on 15 August 1984 and sentenced to life imprisonment.

The case against Condren, always heavily dependent on his signed confession, became even shakier when, a few weeks after his arrest, and prior to his committal hearing, a white man being held by police in Darwin confessed to murdering Patricia Carlton because he "hated black bitches".

In November 1983, Andrew Christopher Albury told police he killed Carlton during a stopover in Mt Isa on his way home to the Northern Territory from Melbourne. He then caught a bus to Darwin.

Despite this remarkable information, it was January 1984 before a Mt Isa detective arrived in Darwin to investigate the claim. By this time Albury had changed his mind and refused to speak to the Mt Isa cop. He also declined to repeat his confession under oath at Condren's trial.

But Albury, who was jailed for life for murdering Aboriginal woman Gloria Pindan in Darwin shortly after Patricia Carlton's death, later repeated his claim to authorities. He told police: "It's not the first one. I killed a black gin in Mt Isa at the end of September. I don't feel sorry for them. I know I should be."

Albury stated he murdered Carlton about half an hour before catching a Greyhound bus to Darwin. A police investigation into Albury's confession later confirmed that he had stayed at a St Vincent De Paul hostel in Mt Isa the night before Carlton was bashed and had left town on a Greyhound bus at 8pm the next night - almost four hours after police claim Condren left the woman unconscious and dying behind the Mt Isa Hotel.

In November 1984, three months into his life sentence, Condren received a scribbled letter from Albury which read: "Kelvin, you tell your lawyers that if they care to call me for your appeal I will make full admission which would I believe get you off your murder charge. We both know you never did it."

Cairns solicitor Rowan Silva, who represented Condren through the Townsville Aboriginal and Islander Legal Service from early 1988, has no doubts that Albury killed Patricia Carlton.

"My view is that the murderer was actually Albury and the

information he originally gave the Northern Territory police was accurate," Silva said. "It seems to me that it's very consistent with a person having just committed a murder that they would then leave the scene immediately by - for example - taking a bus to another state. One of the High Court judges (at an appeal hearing) later noted that the original admissions made by Albury were startlingly consistent with the crime, and with Albury we're dealing with a person who had just murdered another Aboriginal woman in brutal circumstances. I've got every reason to believe that Albury was the person responsible."

In March 1987 Condren's appeal against his conviction was heard by a Brisbane court. During the four-day hearing, Condren's counsel, Tony Fitzgerald QC argued that Albury's confessions had been made independently to police, prison officers, lawyers and a prison chaplain. He told the court Albury suffered from personality disorders and admitted hating Aboriginal women.

In the Criminal Justice Commission's 1992 report on its investigation into the Condren case, the Commission found that there was an "inappropriate delay" between the time Mt Isa police learned of Albury's confession and the trip to Darwin by a senior detective to interview him two months later. The Commission softened the blow by suggesting the delay was not caused by the detective himself, but by his travel approval being held up by the Police Commissioner's office. "The delay in granting that approval is inexcusable," the report stated.

But a lawyer who studied the Condren case later said if Albury had made a formal statement, a full investigation would have followed, and if he was found to be guilty of the murder, serious questions about police handling of the case would be raised.

"An independent police officer should have investigated the confession by Albury, not an officer responsible for charging Condren," the lawyer said.

In any case, Albury was not called to give evidence at subsequent hearings - including the Criminal Justice Commission's inquiry. In its report, the Commission stated Albury was not called because available evidence suggested he would not be a credible witness and doubt was cast over his psychiatric condition, and "his alleged confessions to other killings, some of which confessions were considered to be false".

The stone found in Patricia Carlton's vagina was always a macabre and puzzling aspect of her violent death but remained a low-key subject during court hearings and national media coverage of the case. Rowan Silva, however, believes it provided additional evidence that Condren did not commit the crime.

"I've never come across anything like it in any of the cases where I've acted on behalf of Aboriginal people, and it indicates that the person who committed the offence was likely to be of unsound mind, to be suffering from a mental illness, and Kelvin never had any of those characteristics. In contrast, Albury was subsequently diagnosed as mentally ill, and did in fact volunteer details of the stone in his confession.

"It was always plain that this was an extremely violent crime with some very distasteful features to it, and Kelvin was really not the type of person who would do that, in my opinion. He struck me as a person who is simply not violent."

In the March 1987 Court of Criminal Appeal hearing, evidence was heard from two language experts who disputed the validity of Condren's confession.

Linguist anthropologist Dr Diana Eades, a specialist in the study of the way Aboriginal people use English in everyday life, testified she had concluded that the language attributed to Condren by police in his statement was different to that used by him at his trial and during an interview she had with him in jail. Dr Eades also appeared before the Criminal Justice Commission investigation where she gave evidence that Aboriginal people experience problems in communicating concepts of time and distance, were uneasy in formal interview situations, and experienced difficulties caused by their "deference to authority". She said being asked questions, in particular leading questions, as opposed to being allowed to give a narrative explanation, was not likely to result in accurate information.

The Court of Criminal Appeal also heard evidence from a world authority on languages from Scotland, the Reverend Andrew Morton, who said the record of interview was not in Condren's style of language and there was only a 500,000 to one probability that he was the author of the statements attributed to him.

But the court ruled that the language evidence was irrelevant and inadmissable to the only real issue before the court, which was Condren's personal characteristics.

In July 1989 Dr Eades told a journalist that in light of the recent Fitzgerald Report's finding of widespread verballing in the police force, her evidence in the Condren case should have been accepted. She said linguists had been accepted as expert witnesses in other cases, including the Russell Street bombing trial, and in 1959 the High Court set a legal precedent for linguistic evidence to be accepted in charges against Aborigines.

In late 1992, after the Criminal Justice Commission released it's report, Dr Eades criticised the Commission for failing to consider her findings of a detailed linguistic analysis of the Condren "confession". She said her 84-page report to the Court of Criminal Appeal should have been accepted by the Commission as vital evidence in its investigation. The report included the statement: "I do not believe that all of the utterances attributed to Condren, in reply to questions in the police record of interview (PRI) are verbatim reports of Condren's actual speech." Dr Eades said the Commission had the power to admit the evidence but had chosen not to.

"This is clearly relevant to Condren's allegation to the Commission that the PRI, which was used in evidence against him, was a false document," she said. "In my view, the question of the reliability of Condren's alleged 'confession' still remains unanswered."

The Criminal Justice Commission also investigated the allegations of "prompting" by police during their questioning of Condren after the assault on Patricia Carlton. The Justice of the Peace who witnessed the interview agreed with Condren's counsel at the hearing that police used a "multiple answer" technique to elicit answers from the suspect, and those answers were recorded in the official police record of interview. The JP - who was not named - agreed that when Condren did not immediately respond to the question: "How many times did you hit her?" he was then asked: "Well, was it ten, six, seven?" Condren allegedly then replied: "Oh, about seven times." Similarly, when he was asked what time the assault had taken place and Condren had not answered, the police officer suggested: "Well, was it three, four, quarter past four?" Condren allegedly answered: "Oh, about quarter past four."

The Commission's report said that only the initial question and answer were officially recorded - not the subsequent questions suggesting the answers. The JP testified that Condren was very quiet during the interview and that prompting was required in about 10 percent of the questions.

Both police officers who interviewed Condren denied any prompting had taken place but conceded the practice had occurred on other occasions.

The Commission found that evidence suggesting prompting had taken place during the interview with Condren, and at other times, was "a matter of great concern" and amounted to "bad police practice because it may encourage a suspect to make a statement that is not within his knowledge and may be untrue".

Condren's appeal heard evidence from two women who testified that they saw Patricia Carlton at the Mt Isa Hotel around 7.30pm on 30 September 1983 - the day she was allegedly bashed by Condren at 4.15pm.

Judy McConachie, a stenographer with the Mt Isa Aboriginal Legal Service, and former Mt Isa resident Lorraine Bauli, told the court they remembered seeing Carlton because she was wearing new thongs and they shared a joke about them. Both women denied making the story up to help Condren. McConachie said she had not realised the significance of the meeting and Bauli said she thought the incident was not important.

Solicitor Dennis James McCormick gave evidence that he worked for the Mt Isa Aboriginal Legal Service in 1983 and had been the instructing solicitor at Condren's trial. McCormick said he had been contacted by Condren's mother about a year after he had been sentenced to life imprisonment and she gave him the name of a woman who claimed she had seen Patricia Carlton in a hotel after 7.30pm. He said he was "astonished" to discover one of his staff, Judy McConachie, knew the woman, and told him she had been in the hotel too.

In May 1987 the Court of Criminal Appeal dismissed Condren's appeal for a retrial, ruling that the two new witnesses lacked credibility and their evidence contained significant inconsistencies. The court ruled that the new evidence was inconsistent with the large body of evidence given by witnesses at the trial.

In July 1988 Condren's lawyers petitioned the Queensland Governor Sir Walter Campbell for a pardon but the request was refused and the Attorney-General Paul Clauson declared he would not refer the case back to the Court of Criminal Appeal. In a complicated move that boggles the average mind, Condren's legal team then lodged an Application for Leave to appeal to the High Court against the dismissal of his appeal to the Court of Criminal Appeal.

Condren was getting used to the idea that he was destined to serve a life term in jail for a murder he didn't commit.

"It sounded real good going to the Appeals Court and all that," he said in an interview, "but when it gets to the end of it and it's dismissed, well, after all that building up hope, you know, it's all just gone. I gave up looking at calendars because every calendar you see in there is marked every day. The system was against you, so you got on with it the best way you can."

While he was giving evidence at the Criminal Justice Commision inquiry solicitor Dennis McCormick said police brutality in Mt Isa was commonplace in the early 1980s. He said police were feared in the western town and during his time working for the Aboriginal Legal Service he heard complaints of police misconduct frequently, "about a couple a week."

McCormick said reports of rough treatement by police were made by both white and Aboriginal people and a claim of being hit with a telephone book, such as the allegation by Kelvin Condren, was considered "a fairly mild sort of allegation for Mt Isa" at that time.

"Up there in those days general allegations of police giving someone a bit of a thump now and again were not uncommon," he said.

McCormick told the inquiry he had difficulties interviewing Aboriginal clients in police custody and there was a lengthy delay in gaining access to the brief on Kelvin Condren's case. He said tension between himself and police had boiled over on a number of occasions and at one stage beer stubbies started landing on his roof.

A Mt Isa senior police officer, whose name was suppressed at the inquiry, agreed that relations between himself and McCormick were poor but denied he avoided contacting the solicitor before interviewing Condren. He said he sent a car to McCormick's house after Condren's arrest but nobody was home.

Paul Gaffney, Condren's counsel: "You knew that if McCormick was called you knew that he would not allow his client to speak to police."

Police witness: "No sir."

Solicitor Rowan Silva, who later led a campaign for Condren's release, said although he never practiced in Mt Isa he understood that Aboriginal people living there were "disempowered" in their dealings with police.

"It's a western town with a bit of a frontier reputation, and Aboriginal people living on the fringes as they certainly do in the camps outside Mt Isa would generally have felt quite powerless in their dealings with police, and may very well have thought that there was little point in making official complaints," he said. "It was also a period when the Criminal Justice Commission itself didn't exist. "There was the old Police Complaints Tribunal, and in my experience as a lawyer I never had much faith in outcomes from that tribunal, and that was vindicated by the findings in the Fitzgerald Report that it had been extremely ineffective in dealing with police misconduct."

The breakthrough that finally led to Condren's freedom came after Ernie Hoolihan alerted investigative journalist Chris Masters to the case, and while Masters was filming a television documentary outside the Mt Isa Hotel he was approached by John Price, owner of the nearby Menzies Pharmacy.

Price dropped a bombshell that split the case wide open. He told an astonished Masters that he and assistant pharmacist, Barbara Milliken, had walked through the vacant lot behind his pharmacy and the Mt Isa Hotel sometime between 5.35pm and 5.45pm on the day Patricia Carlton had been assaulted, and they had seen no evidence of a body or an injured person. This was a regular route taken every working day by the pair, and they were both certain they would have seen a body on the ground.

Price and Milliken's evidence was startling and unshakeable. If, as the police claim, Condren had been arrested, drunk, at 5.50pm, then it would have been a mercurial task for him to have attacked the woman, flee the scene, and be picked up by police without blood on his clothes or any other evidence linking him to the crime. And if, as Hoolihan claims, Condren was picked up even earlier, around 3.30pm, then it was clearly impossible for him to have committed the assault.

In December 1989 new Attorney-General Dean Wells announced Condren's petition for a pardon would be referred for the second time to the Court of Criminal Appeal to review the fresh evidence.

On 26 June 1990 the Court of Criminal Appeal recommended Condren's conviction be set aside, and, by a two-to-one majority, recommended a retrial. But the dissenting judge, Justice Thomas, said there was no need for another trial and Condren's conviction should be quashed. He said in the unlikely event of a guilty verdict it would be followed by an appeal that would invariably lead to the conviction being set aside.

"It seems to me that to allow further proceedings would be futile and that the interests of justice would not be served," he said.

Thomas said the pharmacy witnesses had provided fresh evidence that "opened a crack (in the case) that ultimately permeated the whole windscreen".

"Condren's confession cannot now be looked at in the light of all the evidence and be safely regarded as effectively overpowering all the other countervailing considerations," he said.

Thomas said the evidence of Price and Milliken had cast grave doubts on the likelihood that Condren had assaulted Patricia Carlton because when they walked through the yard behind the pharmacy and the hotel, the woman was not there.

"Mr Price passed through the relevant area during that period and he was able to base his estimate of the time upon credible criteria," he said. "It is inescapable having regard to the route he took, that had the victim been lying in the vicinity, he would have seen her."

The Criminal Justice Commission report criticised a senior police investigator for his failure to interview Price and Milliken at the time of the murder. Although the officer gave evidence that he had interviewed one female witness at the pharmacy, he could not explain why he had not included other staff in his investigation.

"If they had been more thorough, the police would have spoken to these witnesses during the investigation and the witnesses would not have provided their first statements many years after the event," the report said.

The report states that the pharmacy witness interviewed by police provided "useful information" about seeing a woman lying in the carpark area at about 7.40pm on the night in question. The witness allegedly heard "moaning and gurgling sounds" at the rear of the pharmacy at that time but presumably did not alert her employer, John Price, or anyone else, to the situation.

Rowan Silva said it was quite clear on the basis of the woman's evidence that somebody was lying hurt in the carpark at that time, and had she acted on that knowledge, the events that subsequently unfolded may never have happened.

"The sad thing is she heard those noises, and it's quite sad that she did not do anything about it, to investigate whether the person she heard was injured and if so call an ambulance. If she had, perhaps there would never have been a murder charge at all."

In its report the Commission found that although "there were some unsatisfactory aspects to the (police) investigation", and regulations had been breached on several occasions, the evidence did not support allegations that a miscarriage of justice had occurred, and no disciplinary action should be taken.

Kelvin Condren did not seek bail while waiting for a decision on a retrial, instead deciding to stay in jail until he was declared a free man. He told his relatives, friends and legal representatives he did not want to look over his shoulder when the gates of the prison closed behind him, and he didn't want to experience fear every time he saw a policeman. Either he walked free, with no further legal threats hanging over his head, or he stayed where he was until it was all over.

He waited one more month. On 25 July the Director of Prosecutions, Royce Miller QC, advised Attorney-General Dean Wells that a nolle prosequi should be entered on the indictment against Condren and he should be released from custody. A nolle prosequi is a formal acknowledgement by the Crown that it does not intend to proceed further with a charge before a court. It is, in effect, a discontinuation of a charge, but is not equivalent to an acquittal. Or a pardon.

Two days later - after a murder trial, six years and nine months spent in jail, two appeals in the Criminal Court of Appeal, one Application for Special Leave to Appeal to the High Court, and two petitions for a pardon to the Governor of Queensland - Kelvin Ronald Condren was finally set free.

Rowan Silva remains critical of the Criminal Justice Commission inquiry, claiming it failed to conduct essential field investigations and also adopted legal procedures that led to the discrediting of evidence from Aboriginal witnesses.

"In my view the inquiry involved a lot of window dressing in terms of the evidence it received, and the recommendations it made about the position of Aboriginal people in the criminal justice system generally, but failed in its central task of unearthing the truth about how Condren and the other complainants had been treated by police."

Silva said Condren's placid personality and chronic alcoholism at the time did little to assist him as the police case gathered momentum following his arrest.

"He was the type of person who was always going to have great difficulty in adequately defending himself against any charge, whether it was murder or anything else," Silva said. "I gained the impression the campaign against him was launched on the basis of a rumour or statement that he was Patricia Carlton's boyfriend, but Kelvin always denied he was involved in a relationship with her, and that was confirmed to me by other Aboriginal witnesses who were in Mt Isa."

Prominent Brisbane lawyer and outspoken civil libertarian Terry O'Gorman, said the Condren case highlights the need for a miscarriage of justice unit, similar to the Criminal Cases Review Commission in England, which has the power to seize documents from police and government agencies in order to force deserving cases back to court.

"In Australia, the structure of the criminal justice system generally means that once you've been to trial and the appeal process is exhausted and fresh evidence comes to hand, you are then at the mercy of the Attorney-General of the day, and you somehow have to get through the eye of the needle of his office to get back to the Court of Criminal Appeal," O'Gorman said.

"The irony of this is that Condren got back to the Court of Criminal Appeal because the then Attorney-General, Dean Wells, was sympathetic to his case. But for that fact, he never would have got another hearing."

O'Gorman believes that miscarriages of justice similar to that suffered by Condren have happened before without being noticed - especially to people with little education and poor background - and will continue to happen under the present judicial system.

"The problems that cause a miscarriage of justice to exist are not only the problems relating to particular evidence not being known at the time of trial, but equally reflect structural problems in the criminal justice system which are as present now as they were then," he said.

"Statistically, I think there are many more Kelvin Condrens in jail, but nobody in the system collects those statistics, and there is a degree of cynicism among bureaucrats and others in the justice system that everyone in jail says they're innocent, so this bit of paper they see on the desk is just another person claiming he's innocent."

The Criminal Justice Commission, although not recommending disciplinary action against any police officer involved in the interview with Condren, made it quite clear in its 1992 report that Aboriginal people were extremely disadvantaged when confronted and dealt with by police.

"It is impossible to examine the case of Kelvin Condren without being struck by how badly Aborigines are likely to be served by the criminal justice system, even a well-intentioned system which makes allowances for and tries to protect disadvantaged people," the report stated. "Viewing the pattern of these lives, it seems somehow grotesque to expect people who have been living on the edge of society in every way to fit into the rigid structure of the criminal justice system."

The report also states: "Kelvin Condren was convicted of murder largely on the basis of his alleged confession to police. His case squarely raises the issue of how much reliance courts can or should place on confessional evidence."

Kelvin Condren was free, but in that peculiar Catch-22 of the criminal justice system, no legal pardon was granted to clear his name and officially inform the world that he did not murder Patricia Carlton. There was no apology from the government or the police - even though Police Minister Paul Braddy had publicly called Condren's case a "classic example of a miscarriage of justice".

Terry O'Gorman spearheaded Condren's $1 million compensation claim, first drafted by Rowan Silva, and presented it to the Queensland Government in September 1993. The claim included an ex gratia payment of $700,000 for the "incalculable loss" he had suffered from almost seven years of wrongful imprisonment, $100,000 compensation for his mother, Julia, for the "expense, trauma, inconvenience and public shame" she had experienced, and a further $210,131 for legal expenses to the Aboriginal and Islander Legal Commission.

The claim detailed compensation for loss of liberty and reputation, pain and suffering, physical assaults in prison and the loss of normal experiences.

O'Gorman told reporters at the time that Condren was finding it "very hard to reintegrate into his community".

"This is not an exercise in gold mining, it is a considered claim based on comparative material in Australia and overseas and it is a figure to which he is entitled," he said. "It would require a lot of ingenuity by the Government's lawyers to argue against it."

Nine months later O'Gorman complained of inaction by the Attorney-General Dean Wells in processing the compensation claim. "We were told it would be processed in a month," he said. "Now we can't even get replies to our letters."

Wells replied that because of the complexity and difficulty of the compensation claim and the fact that no precedent had been set for the Condren case, Cabinet was necessarily taking a considerable time to reach a decision on the application.

On 5 February 1995, O'Gorman told a civil rights rally in Townsville that Wells was "incompetent" and the then Premier Wayne Goss should take over the compensation claim. O'Gorman told a 200-strong crowd that if a "white man" had been in the same situation as Condren, he would have been compensated by now.

The next day Wells announced an ex gratia "fair, just and equitable" amount of $400,000 would be paid to Condren, even though there was no legal obligation for the government to do so. Wells said Cabinet had considered the case of Edward Splatt in South Australia during its deliberation. Splatt received $300,000 compensation in 1985 after spending a similar time in jail as Condren.

Five weeks later, Condren finally received his cheque, which was exactly half the amount he expected as compensation for his time in jail and his mother's traumatic experience.

O'Gorman, who waived his legal fees because he believed "this was a case that called for it", came out guns blazing, calling the payout a "laughable pittance" and an insult to the injustices suffered by Condren throughout his seven-year ordeal. He said Condren had been treated "appallingly" and the government had not explained how the compensation figure had been determined.

"This highlighted the mean-spirited, absolutely dastardly attitude of this government," he said.

O'Gorman said it was obvious the government considered "a black fella was worth only half a white fella" because Lindy Chamberlain had been awarded $900,000 compensation by the Northern Territory Government for serving less than half the time in jail.

But Wells said that was not a fair comparison because Lindy Chamberlain was found not guilty of murdering her child Azaria whereas there had been no specific finding of Kelvin Condren's innocence.

And that is the conundrum that Condren has lived with since his release from prison in 1990. He is not guilty of Patricia Carlton's murder but he is not legally innocent either.

But all that is a long way in the past for Condren now, far beyond the boundaries of this simple man's daily existence, and probably far beyond any real desire to pursue that final freedom that the system has denied him - a full pardon.

"I do think about it and it does bother me, but I'm out here and I'm not pardoned," Condren said with resigned logic. " It seems like I can't really do nothing."

CHAPTER SIX

"TRIAL BY TELEVISION FRAMED ME FOR MURDER"

Miranda Downes died mysteriously on a North Queensland beach, but was she murdered?

Ernest Arthur Knibb has served 16 years of a life sentence for the murder of scriptwriter Miranda Downes in 1985, but he continues to protest his innocence, claiming he has been denied any chance of parole by a justice system intent on keeping him behind bars.

According to Knibb he is permanently out of favour with the system because he won't admit to a crime he didn't commit. He says he has no intention of backing away from his accusation that he was railroaded by a combination of circumstantial evidence, police harassment, and a bizarre campaign against him by Channel Nine's *60 Minutes*, which led to what he calls a "trial by television that framed me for murder".

Although prison authorities say 90 per cent of all inmates claim they're innocent, the crucial role played by *60 Minutes* in Knibb's arrest and conviction in 1987 left many observers of the case wondering if the jury had indeed been sidetracked and the wrong man sent to jail.

Miranda Beverly Downes was 35 years of age when she died. She was an attractive, talented writer with films such as *Undercover* and *The Last Resort* to her credit. At the time of her death she was working on a television script called *Cane*, later to become the successful mini-series *Fields of Fire*.

Although Downes had made a late start in her writing career, she was at last on the road to top. Before that, though, she had led a gypsy lifestyle. After graduating from the University of New South Wales she taught English to adult immigrants before setting off in the early 1970s to southeast Asia on what was then a common pilgrimage for adventurous young Australians.

In 1976, Downes married Shawn Smallwood, an old university friend, and for a time they lived in London, where the couple formed a close friendship with Roger and Elizabeth Lewis. But the marriage was not a happy one and they were divorced in 1981. One year later Smallwood fell to his death from a treehouse in a game reserve in India.

Depressed and lonely, Downes made up her mind to break into the Australian film industry as a writer and in the space of two years created a niche for herself in Sydney where she was suddenly in demand for her script ideas and writing skills.

Ernest Arthur Knibb was 44 years of age and had recently been awarded $85,000 compensation for injuries received in a 1981 motorcycle accident in Sydney that had left him with a permanent limp. Knibb had a history of petty crime in his youth, but for the past 20 years had not offended. He was a drifter, preferring the open spaces of the country to the crowded congestion of city life. His passion was exploring outback mining fields, fossicking for opals and gold.

They were from vastly different backgrounds, but on the night of 3 August 1985, fate locked Downes and Knibb together in a bizarre sequence of events that resulted in one of the strangest murder cases in Australia's criminal history.

Buchan Point juts into the sea 26 kilometres north of Cairns. It's a chunk of natural bushland that looks out over the Great Barrier Reef and a string of pristine beaches that stretch north to Port Douglas. The headland was a multi-million dollar developer's dream that had somehow survived the bulldozers of progress. The beach lies at its feet, a one-kilometre stretch of sand protected from the highway by a buffer zone of native trees and scrub. A third of the way from the southern end of the beach, a large boulder protrudes from the sand like a lonely sentinel. The rock marks a section of beach that has long been Cairns' traditional nudist spot, a popular haven for nature-loving locals and tourists. The rest of the beach, on the northern side of the rock, attracts large numbers of conventional bathers due to its bush car park and easy access to the highway.

In the late afternoon on that winter Saturday in 1985, Buchan Point residents Roy Turner and his girlfriend Anna Heyer greeted Heyer's sister Elizabeth and brother-in-law Roger Lewis and their two children from London at Cairns airport. A short time later, Miranda Downes arrived from Sydney to meet her English friends and spend a two-week holiday with them first at Turner's house and later at Cape Tribulation. Heyer had known Downes for 10 years, but this was the first time Turner and Downes had met.

The party arrived home at about 5.30pm and sat on the verandah, high above the beach, drinking wine and admiring the view. Downes, a keen fitness enthusiast, had one glass of wine, and, according to Turner, left the house at 6pm to jog on the beach. She was wearing grey-blue track suit pants, a pink T-shirt, and a pink "sloppy joe" sweater tied loosely around her shoulders. Turner watched her go, losing sight of her in the bush until she reappeared on the beach, jogging northwards with an "easy gait" in the fading tropical light.

That was the last time any of the group saw her alive.

At 1.50am, Sergeant First Class Roger Walsh from nearby Smithfield police station, who headed the search for Miranda Downes, found her body at the high tide mark of the northern end of the beach. She was face down in the sand, her long hair streaming seawards. She was naked, except for a necklace with a small key pendant around her neck, a wristwatch, ear-rings, and a ring on each hand.

Walsh later recalled in his official police statement the drama of his tragic discovery: "Shortly after the police team left the car park I also left the car park and commenced to walk along the beach in a northerly direction. The moon was quite bright, however at times a cloud would darken the sky for short periods of time. As I walked along the beach I noted that the tide was running out and that a wind of about 15 knots was still blowing from the South East. I had walked along the beach near to the bank of grass and when about half way from the car park to the rocks at the northern end I saw at the water edge what I at first thought to be a palm branch. As the cloud was blocking out the moon light I waited until the cloud had passed and the area became considerably better lighted and I saw that what I had originally thought to be a palm branch was in fact the body of a human."

Miranda Downes' innocent run on the beach had ended in her lifeless body gleaming in the moonlight of a tropical north Queensland night.

Several tyre tracks and footprints were noted by police at the scene, but many more had been obliterated by the tide.

Although Downes' body was marked by abrasions and bruising to the neck and shoulder the official cause of death was drowning. Later, police declared she had been struck from behind by a vehicle, strangled, sexually assaulted and thrown into the sea still alive.

The discovery of Downes' body marked the beginning of a murder investigation that became buried in a confusion of circumstantial evidence and vague witness recollections, lacked a true suspect and motive for the alleged crime, but led to the eventual pursuit of the only target the police could find - Ernest Arthur Knibb.

Indeed, it was Knibb who presented himself to the police as a suspect, thus setting in motion a sequence of events that would ultimately result in him being convicted as a cold-blooded killer and sentenced to life imprisonment.

Less than two days after the discovery of Downes' body at Buchan Point, Knibb was in his Cairns motel room watching a television news report requesting information about a four-wheel-drive vehicle that had been seen on a beach north of the city where a woman had drowned.

Realising he had been on the same beach with his own vehicle that day, Knibb telephoned the police and volunteered his movements, offering to help in any way he could before he left Cairns. Had he not picked up the phone, it's extremely unlikely that Knibb would ever have become involved in what was to follow.

After a lengthy wait at the police station Knibb said he gave a statement concerning his movements on the beach, and even volunteered details of his petty criminal past in Sydney. It didn't take Knibb long to realise the police were showing more than a passing interest in him, especially when they asked for pubic hair and blood samples. He agreed, even though he said the samples were taken in front of other people and he was extremely embarrassed. He was even more upset when his vehicle was confiscated by Detective Sergeant Bruce Gray for forensic testing.

The next day when Knibb went back to pick up his vehicle he had a solicitor with him. According to Knibb there was fingerprinting "dust" all over the paintwork and the burglar alarm was broken. An argument broke out over who should clean the vehicle and eventually the police "got a steam cleaner and gave it a bit of clean".

Knibb claims his solicitor repeatedly told him to leave Cairns as soon as the police had finished with him. When he protested, pointing out such a move would make him look guilty, the solicitor firmly replied: "Take my advice and leave."

But Knibb was not arrested. He denied any knowledge of the woman's death and the police had no proof of guilt. The case against Ernie Knibb was shakily constructed on a framework of probabilities that would never have gone to court without the involvement of *60 Minutes* a year and a half later.

Knibb arrived in Cairns two weeks before Miranda Downes' death, driving a new Ford Bronco he had bought with the insurance payout from his motorcycle accident. The Bronco was his pride and joy - a yellow and white four-wheel-drive fitted with a fibreglass canopy and an impressive pair of spotlights attached to an aluminium bullbar. He left behind a caravan in a park at Gosford, north of Sydney, intending to travel to Cooktown where he hoped to set up camp and prospect for gold.

Instead, he says he "came to sunny Queensland for a holiday and was framed by *60 Minutes* for murder".

In the late afternoon of 3 August, Knibb left a youth hostel in Kuranda, where he had been staying for two days, and drove down the mountain range overlooking Cairns to the coast.

Knibb intended to find a beach to test his vehicle in sandy

conditions before the long haul to Cooktown.

The first beach he came to was Buchan Point. As he crested a rise overlooking the beach he saw two vehicles bogged in the sand and decided this was the perfect opportunity to try out the Bronco. Around this time, Miranda Downes was either descending the hillside track or she was already jogging on the beach.

Knibb is very clear about what happened next. He drove into a carpark clearing, got out to engage the four-wheel drive hubs on the Bronco's front wheels, and then drove onto the beach. He noted two vehicles in the carpark, and remembered one of them was a red, late model Mercedes with an elderly couple sitting inside. On the beach, Knibb took a right hand turn near the water's edge and swung up towards the two cars he had seen bogged in the sand. By now several youths had pushed one of them free, and Knibb had troubles of his own in the loose sand, until one of the youths told him to let some air out of his tyres for better traction. Knibb then attempted to free the other car by pushing with his bull bar and then using an old tow rope which broke. Finally he drove over to the couple in the Mercedes, borrowed another tow rope and easily pulled the bogged vehicle clear.

After returning the tow rope to the couple - Roland and Marjory Murphy from Victoria - and chatting with the youths in the carpark, Knibb drove back onto the beach and turned left heading north along the top side of the beach. As he did so he passed a blonde woman walking briskly in a southerly direction. He went as far as he could go, to a natural rock barrier at the northern end of the beach. It was now dark and Knibb turned both his headlights and spotlights on to scan the rocks area to see if there was a track off the beach onto the highway. There was no exit and he turned to drive south, this time along the water's edge. As he drove down the beach he saw in his headlights a figure jogging past the blonde woman. Knibb told police he didn't notice if the person was male or female, but remembered the running figure was wearing a dark coloured, possibly blue track suit and was taller than the blonde woman.

Knibb continued south, passing the blonde woman, then turned near the base of the large boulder protruding from the sand and stopped, facing back towards the carpark entrance. Knibb said the blonde woman stopped in his headlights, and, worried that he had frightened her, he drove slowly forward, wound his window down and called: "Don't worry love, I'm just trying out my new vehicle." He then waved to her and she waved back, saying something he couldn't hear. Knibb drove off the beach, sounding his horn at the entrance before entering the carpark.

The blonde woman was American teacher Janice Cunningham who, at the time of Downes' death, was sharing a house on the hill overlooking the beach. Cunningham gave police a different story to that of Knibb. She told them Knibb drove *past* the rock to the southern end of the beach before turning around. She said he slowed down and spoke to her about testing his vehicle, to which she replied: "Righto, go for it." According to Cunningham, Knibb then drove past and continued north without leaving the beach. Giving evidence in court, however, Cunningham stated she couldn't tell how far north he had gone because "I didn't turn to watch it (the vehicle) go, other than just to (briefly) look."

During her walk along the beach, Cunningham had passed the jogging figure Knibb had seen and later positively identified her as Miranda Downes. The two had exchanged smiles and said "hello" as they passed each other.

Cunningham said in her statement she arrived home from the beach "at about 6.35pm", but giving evidence in court four months later she said she arrived home at "approximately 6.20pm". Police originally took a statement from Cunningham on the day after Downes' death, but waited almost two years to re-interview this crucial witness, by then living in New South wales.

The beach at Buchan Point was a very busy place late on the afternoon of 3 August, 1985.

Michael Holland - who shared the house with Cunningham, together with a pilot named David Rickward and Rickward's girlfriend Gail Richmond - was on the beach at 3pm, waiting for Cunningham to join him for a walk around the rocky point to Ellis Beach. At about 3.45pm they walked north, passing a number of swimmers, sunbathers and two men who hired out jet skis on the beach. They also passed a woman with fair hair hanging freely to "mid-back length", jogging along the beach.

At Ellis Beach, Cunningham said she decided to have a beer with friends in the restaurant while Holland headed back home. Holland, though, clearly states he waited for Cunningham for 10 minutes while she used a "nearby toilet" before he started for home "just as the sun started to go down". On the way back, Holland passed a group of eight adults and children playing cricket on Buchan Point beach and "a few people just sitting on the beach". He also passed "two or three" beach strollers. Half way down the beach he met Gail Richmond jogging northwards.

Holland watched as two cars raced up and down the beach, doing "some fairly tight turns" until one became bogged. Even though he thought the youths in the cars were "stupid and I didn't want to have much to do with them", he helped them push the car free. During this time, Holland noticed a man, about 40, sitting alone on the beach watching him. Holland then walked home and Richmond turned up 10 minutes later.

Janice Cunningham said she stayed at the Ellis Beach restaurant for half an hour before leaving for home. Along the way she passed a group of "male and female adults and children playing in the water", presumedly the same group Holland had seen. Cunningham, however, remembered a man wearing a "long black clergyman's coat" and a wide-brimmed black hat standing in the middle of the group. Police later identified the man in the black hat as a mock "preacher" mourning the "loss of youth" of a friend at a beachside 40th birthday party.

Still walking down the beach, Cunningham passed a "middle-aged" couple and then the female jogger she greeted with a "hello".

Gail Richmond left the house at precisely 5.27pm. Richmond was a dedicated runner who wore a watch to time her distances whenever she trained. She ran north, passing the youths and their bogged vehicle, "a couple in their thirties holding hands" and Michael Holland on his way home.

Richmond said she reached the northern end of the beach at 5.34pm and sat on the rocks for eight minutes, getting her breath back. While she was there she saw a male "in his thirties with short black hair and a moustache" climb over the rocks onto the highway, where he met three other men and a young boy in a golden-coloured Holden Kingswood, which then drove off heading south. At

"TRIAL BY TELEVISION FRAMED ME FOR MURDER"

5.42pm, Richmond ran south "in half-light" along the water's edge, arriving home at 6pm.

David Rickward was the only member of the household not on the beach that evening. Instead he sat on the balcony smoking a cigarette and watching Richmond jog along the beach. He watched as the youths "did a couple of doughnuts" and bog one of their cars, then he went inside to read a book. After "10 or 15 minutes" he heard a loud scream which "sounded like a female voice" come from the direction of the beach and, concerned for Richmond's safety, went back to the balcony to investigate. Relieved, he saw her about to leave the beach and come up the path.

There appears to have been little effort by police to investigate the source of what Rickward insisted was a scream on the beach as darkness fell.

The subsequent police case against Knibb relied heavily on the suspect driving north a second time and murdering Downes before leaving the beach. Knibb, however, insists he drove off the beach immediately after speaking to Cunningham, and stopped in the carpark where he unlocked his wheel hubs and checked his deflated tyres. After considering whether to pump the tyres up to their correct pressure manually he decided against it and drove slowly south along the highway to a service station at Clifton Beach, where two witnesses swear they saw and spoke to him at 6.45pm. Knibb pumped his tyres up, chatted to a motorist, and asked the attendant if any food was available. He was told the kitchen had closed because the service station was due to shut down at 7pm.

Then, incredibly for a man who had supposedly just committed a brutal murder, Knibb drove north again to the crime scene and was seen by witnesses on the highway opposite the beach adjusting his spotlights. Knibb said he stopped to carefully adjust the lights for maximum vision because he was heading to Port Douglas and was unfamiliar with the winding, coastal road.

If Knibb was a killer, he showed remarkable stupidity in stopping at that spot, the scene of a crime that, if he was caught, carried the maximum penalty of life imprisonment.

Just as incredible was the fact that Knibb pulled up again at Hartley's Creek, a few kilometres north of Buchan Point, to help at the scene of a car accident. Witnesses placed him at the scene betwen 7.30pm and 8.15pm and confirmed he offered to call police, emergency services, and a tow truck on his two-way radio.

Knibb then drove on to Port Douglas, where he had a meal and drinks at the Court House Hotel in the town's main street. The barmaid later told police that Knibb was "a pain in the neck and was demanding my attention all the time". Knibb explained that he asked for coins for the cigarette machine and was short-changed 20 cents, complaining to the barmaid that he was telling the truth, and wasn't desperate enough to try and cheat her out of 20 cents.

After leaving a clear-cut trail of his movements for police to follow since allegedly murdering Downes, Knibb decided against going on to Cooktown, and, not liking the "attitude of the woman in the pub", drove back to Cairns - once again passing Buchan Point. If Knibb had indeed killed Downes, it looked like he was intentionally trying to get caught. But her body had not yet been found and there were no police swarming over the beach.

Knibb booked into the Northern Heritage Motel in Sheridan Street, signing the registration book at precisely 9.45pm. After depositing a package of opals and a sum of money in the motel safe, Knibb showed the manager how to switch off the alarm on the Bronco in case it was activated in the night, explaining his injured leg made him slow to respond to emergencies.

The next day Knibb drove to Kuranda and enquired at the hostel where he had previously stayed if anyone was interested in going to Cooktown with him. He then spent several hours at the local craft markets and bought some opals off a dealer, intending to have one made into a brooch for his mother. On Monday, Knibb arranged for a jeweller to make the brooch and that evening, almost two days after he had booked into the motel, he notified police he had been at Buchan Point on the evening Miranda Downes died.

It was extraordinary behaviour for a man who police allege had murdered a stranger in bizarre circumstances.

Even though Roy Turner was sure Downes had left his house at 6pm, Roger Lewis is equally certain it was 6.15pm, because at 6.30pm he accompanied his wife and children down the track to the beach for a short walk. The children ran towards a lone woman

"TRIAL BY TELEVISION FRAMED ME FOR MURDER"

walking towards them, thinking it was Downes, but most likely it was Cunningham. The Lewis family then turned back and returned to the house, arriving at 7.05pm.

It was now dark and Downes was still not home, but nobody in the Turner household was alarmed. At 7.30pm the group watched a television documentary at a neighbour's house before returning for dinner nearly an hour later. Turner later said Downes' whereabouts were discussed during the meal, but it was 9pm, three hours since she left the house, before Turner and Lewis went looking for the missing woman. They drove three kilometres north to the restaurant at Ellis Beach, hoping to find her there, before returning to pick up Turner's girlfriend, Anna Heyer, and driving to the northern end of Buchan's beach, where they searched the rocks and waterline. It was moonlight and Turner had a torch, noting "six or seven" footprints in the sand and a pair of tyre tracks partly obliterated by the incoming tide. By then it was just after 10pm. Clearly, Miranda Downes' body was not on the beach then. At 10.30pm the police were called.

One hour later police officers and a tracker dog found Downes' Adidas running shoes and socks at the bottom of the track leading up to Turner's house. The team then searched the beach, north and south. Still no body.

It was almost eight hours since Miranda Downes had left the house before Sergeant Roger Walsh found her lifeless body. She was less than 700 metres from where she had left her running shoes at the base of the hill, yet three searches had failed to find her.

The mysterious death of Miranda Downes created national headlines and sparked a press frenzy that ran hot with lurid accounts of how she'd been run down on the beach, strangled, raped and then drowned by an unknown assailant. But disturbing gaps in that scenario appeared and continued to surface with alarming frequency.

The discovery of her clothing was one such gap. At 7.15am, Detective Sergeant Terry Brooks of the Cairns CIB found a pair of "pink, mauvey coloured" panties near a rubbish bin in the carpark.

Two years to the day after her daughter's body was found, the panties were finally examined by Downes' mother at police headquarters in Brisbane. Although she failed to positively identify the underwear, now described as "light beige coloured", Diana Combe declared they were "similar" to items that her daughter purchased after "a large quantity" of her underwear had been stolen prior to her trip to Cairns.

"I made an inspection of this garment and they are of the same size that my daughter wore, size 14," Combe said in her statement. "The briefs are also of the same style and colour that my daughter always wore. I am not able to positively identify the briefs as being the property of my daughter, Miranda Downes, however they are the same in all aspects to those she would have had."

Three days after Downes' death, a resident of a nearby beach suburb found a "sloppy joe" style sweater in the water at the southern end of the beach, close to where Downes' running shoes had been located. He also found a T-shirt, which "appeared to be ripped" down the front. For some reason he left the T-shirt in the water and waited an hour with his wife before leaving the beach with the sweater and notifying police. Later that day the man led Brooks back to the beach where the T-shirt was recovered.

But he wasn't finished yet. On the following Saturday, a week after Miranda Downes died, he was back on the beach, this time finding a pair of tracksuit pants in the same spot. The pants had zip style pockets "so full of sand that I didn't think that you would be able to get another grain of sand in them". Right on cue, two plainclothes police officers appeared on the beach and took possession of the garment.

These items of clothing were later identified as belonging to Downes. They had lain at the water's edge for several days at the opposite end of the beach to where her body was found, remarkably undetected by police and resisting all efforts by the tides to carry them out to sea.

Scientific examination showed Downes' body contained a small number of non-intact spermatozoa with no seminal fluid activity detected, indicating sexual intercourse could have taken place up to five days before the night of her death. Downes' Sydney film maker boyfriend Jim Gerrand later told police that he and Downes had sexual intercourse just three days before her arrival in Cairns and that she had no other lovers.

"TRIAL BY TELEVISION FRAMED ME FOR MURDER"

No blood or seminal fluid were found on any of Downes' clothes. Head and pubic hairs found on her track suit pants did not belong to her, nor did they belong to Knibb.

Despite an intensive police examination of Knibb's clothing and his vehicle, nothing was found to link him to the alleged murder of Downes. A medical examination revealed not a single cut, scratch mark or bruise on his body. Further, there was no evidence that Downes' was raped or sexually assaulted in any way.

The evidence also clearly shows Knibb was only one of many using the beach that late afternoon and evening. Others were camped in the bush along the highway. Buchan Point has always been a popular recreational beach and Saturday, 3 August 1985, was no exception.

Phillip Gilbert, a 25-year-old mechanic from Southport, saw a "four-wheel-drive with big sand tyres fitted" on the northern end of the beach around 7pm, just after two witnesses spoke to Knibb while he pumped his tyres up at a service station 20 minutes drive to the south. Gilbert said the vehicle, which he thought was an "International Scout, fawn in colour", was being driven very slowly by a man "sitting tall" in the driver's seat. He said after he waved to the man, the vehicle increased its speed.

Almost 40 witnesses gave differing versions of vehicle movements in and around the beach area, conflicting descriptions of vehicles and occupants, and a hodge-podge of time frames that point clearly to the fact that, if Miranda Downes had indeed been murdered, then others, besides Knibb, had the opportunity to kill her.

A key police witness, Roland Murphy, the elderly Victorian tourist who loaned Knibb the towrope, claimed Knibb drove back onto the beach after he returned the rope and returned "twenty to thirty minutes" later, stopping in the carpark to examine his vehicle before driving onto the highway.

Murphy and his wife had both been on the beach earlier, walking north towards the rocks, and had seen a woman with long hair "blowing in the breeze" walking ahead of them. According to Murphy, the woman was "carrying something in her left arm", which he thought were her shoes, because he had noticed her bare footprints in the sand. Murphy said he then saw the woman "standing still" in the fading light near the rocks.

The police made much of Murphy's evidence that Knibb "examined" his vehicle in the carpark. It was alleged Knibb had struck Downes with the side mirror of his vehicle before murdering her, and was inspecting the mirror for damage. Knibb, however, explained he was merely turning his four-wheel-drive hubs back into the normal drive position and checking his deflated tyres. He pointed out to police that his side mirrors were designed to swing harmlessly inwards at the slightest impact, making bush driving easier and less hazardous.

And why would he stop in the carpark for any reason if he had killed the girl?

The case against Knibb was weak, and the police knew it. Before voluntarily presenting himself, the police had nothing - no suspect, no description of a vehicle, and no real proof that Downes had even been murdered. And certainly no grounds for arrest.

Knibb was a free man, but for the next 18 months he was tracked from town to town by Queensland police in what he claims was a campaign of intimidation and harassment, including a verbal threat by one officer who allegedly told him: "If we don't get you on this one we'll get you on something else."

True to their word, police kept tabs on Knibb's movements as he travelled down the Queensland coast. At Maryborough, his vehicle was confiscated, loaded onto a semi-trailer and taken to Brisbane, where extensive tests were carried out on the Ford Bronco's side mirrors. Knibb claims the vehicle was returned to him damaged with an extra 900 kilometres on the clock. The tests on the mirrors proved negative. Twice the police had comprehensively examined the Bronco and twice failed to find a single piece of evidence that connected Ernie Knibb to the death of Miranda Downes.

A few weeks later, two male and two female undercover police officers befriended Knibb in a Maryborough caravan park. Posing as bikies on the run, the male officers claimed they regularly raped women on the Gold Coast just for the fun of it, and tried to trap him into confessing he murdered Miranda Downes. Over a period of several days Knibb was kept under surveillance as the "bikies" shouted him drinks in a hotel and in his caravan. According to

"TRIAL BY TELEVISION FRAMED ME FOR MURDER"

Knibb, attempts were made to spike his drinks, but he knew all along the so-called bikies were really police trying to trap him. The two female officers later admitted they were "used as bait" to lower Knibb's guard.

But Terry Brooks said although the operation failed to trap Knibb, the suspect wasn't aware he was being set up.

"He might say now he knew they were police officers, but that's not how he acted then," Brooks said. "He actually fell in love with one of the female officers and wanted to marry her."

During this period newspaper articles appeared quoting police as saying they knew Downes' killer and were closing in on him. Several reports carried physical descriptions that clearly fitted Knibb.

But Knibb didn't take the police attention laying down and hit back with a media campaign of his own. In a Maryborough newspaper article he accused police of the harassment and persecution of an innocent man who merely wanted to get on with his life. "I have committed no crime," he said.

But Knibb was forced to move on in an attempt to escape police attention. In Bauple, a small town between Maryborough and Gympie, he was raided by five plainclothes officers and subsequently asked to leave by local residents. At Gympie he sold his vehicle and caravan and bought a light truck to go outback opal mining. Later at Blackall, in central Queensland, he was questioned by police about outstanding warrants for traffic offences. Knibb, by this time broke and living on an invalid pension, agreed to pay the fines on pension day. He claims the police told him they always knew where he was and could arrest him at any time.

Knibb said he was eventually forced to flee to a remote cattle station called Highlands where he hoped he could dig for opals and live peacefully.

He was wrong. Events were soon to unfold that would thrust him back into the limelight and ultimately lead to his downfall.

Enter *60 Minutes*. In January 1987, then executive producer of *60 Minutes* Gerald Stone was looking for a good story to kick off the ratings season when he remembered reading about the murder of a scriptwriter in Cairns. Stone put researcher Stephen Taylor onto the story to see what he could dig up. Taylor at first approached Downes' mother and her boyfriend, Jim Gerrand, who both declined offers to be part of the program. But Stone was reluctant to let a good story idea slip through his fingers and sent Taylor looking for the man they knew to be the prime suspect, Ernie Knibb. Eventually, Taylor's long distance calls to the owners of Highlands station paid off and a message finally reached Knibb, asking him to phone Taylor back, reverse charges.

Knibb fell for it. He contacted Taylor and agreed to tell his story. Taylor flew to Longreach, hired a vehicle, and drove to Knibb's bush campsite. Knibb said he was offered $400, plus expenses, to return to Cairns and undergo a lie detector test to prove his innocence. Unwittingly, he was sowing the seeds of his own life sentence for murder.

In February, with Knibb booked into a Cairns hotel, *60 Minutes* producer John Penlington and reporter Ian Leslie held a meeting with local police. Knibb claims a deal was then made between Leslie and the police to "stitch him up". Although police and Leslie denied this, Detective Sergeant Bruce Gray, one of the officers who arrested Knibb, admitted in court to defence barrister Bob Pack that *60 Minutes* "were privy to some of the information in statements", and this was later confirmed by Leslie himself.

February 3 was a busy day for Knibb and the *60 Minutes* team. First Knibb was interviewed at the hotel, then taken to Buchan Point in a hired Bronco for a re-enactment of his movements on the beach the night Miranda Downes died. But this was the middle of the north's wet season and heavy rain washed out the day's shooting before it was completed.

That night, a willing Ernie Knibb submitted himself to a lie detector test. Despite the fact that that such tests are inadmissable in court, *60 Minutes* had scoured Australia to find a polygraph machine, finally locating one owned by Bill Glare, a Sydney private investigator. Glare and his machine were flown to Cairns to conduct the test on Knibb. After the test, Glare wrote and signed a report, witnessed by Leslie and Penlington, that Knibb's responses in relation to "relevant questions" showed "significant emotional disturbances indicative of deception" but went on to conclude: "However it must be clearly understood that the results of any polygraph test in itself is not sufficient evidence to find a person guilty or innocent. In my opinion this polygraph test alone or of itself does not mean John (sic) Knibb is guilty or innocent of the murder of Miranda Downes."

Two days later Knibb volunteered for a hypnosis session with Brisbane psychologist Dr Gordon Milne. With cameras rolling and Leslie and detectives Bruce Gray and Terry Brooks watching a monitor out in the corridor, the stage was set for high television drama. The net was closing.

The *60 Minutes* tape that was shown in court and eventually broadcast in Queensland shows Knibb in an agitated state, eyes closed, describing events in the beach carpark, including the presence of an unidentified vehicle with its lights on full beam and a sinister, shadowy figure with a knife in the driver's seat.

Knibb claims the tape was heavily edited in an effort to suggest he was not under hypnosis at all.

Milne later stated that Knibb could have been faking, or drifting in and out of hypnosis, but the question "cannot be answered with any certainty" and that his report "should not be accepted as evidence unless it is confirmed by other evidence as a result of independent investigation."

Giving evidence in court Milne said he conducted a "practice" session with Knibb before the camera was turned on "because I didn't know it was going to be a court case - as far as I knew it was a television show." Milne was convinced Knibb was hypnotised at that stage, but Knibb quickly became agitated when Penlington walked into the room. Milne agreed during his testimony that he had no specialised knowledge in "detecting the difference between simulators and genuinely hypnotised people" and that the process of hypnosis was unreliable for legal and forensic purposes.

Clinical psychologist Peter Stoker, who interviewed and assessed Knibb in prison over a six month period in 1991, wrote in a five-page report that after Miranda Downes' death and subsequent harassment by police, Knibb agreed to go on *60 Minutes* "only after he was close to suicide from this harassment". Stoker also suggested that the two-year time lag between Knibb's first interview with police and the lie detector test, plus the stress of "possible incarceration" would increase Knibb's sense of vulnerability.

"Because of these factors he would have been highly conditioned to the name Miranda Downes and any mention of her name would create a physiological response (ie increase in heart rate etc that could be measured) and interpreted as evidence of guilt," Stoker wrote. "It was little wonder that he agreed to do the lie detector test and also little wonder he failed. Psychologically Ernest Arthur Knibb does not have the personality to commit a murder like the one alleged."

On the same day as the hypnosis session, *60 Minutes* had Knibb back on the beach at Buchan Point for another shot at the re-enactment. The tape shows Knibb driving the hired Bronco along the beach for the camera while answering Leslie's persistent questions. Knibb stuck to his story, insisting on the night of Downes' murder, he had driven up and down the beach once and then back to the carpark. This was the same story he had given police for the past 18 months.

But Leslie was ready to spring the trap. When he asked Knibb how long he had been on the beach that night the reply was: "I'll be quite honest, I would not know."

Leslie: "Any idea?"

Knibb: "Not the foggiest, but it wouldn't have been more than half an hour, top price. It wouldn't have been more than half an hour by the time I went up there, then down around there and out. That's on this beach, on this actual drive, I'm talking about."

Leslie (a few minutes later): "You said to me earlier that you were on the beach for no more than about two or three minutes."

"Okay, so I was on the beach no more than two or three minutes then," Knibb replied, clearly irritated by Leslie's questioning.

Leslie: "Well, what do you think it was, two or three minutes or half an hour?"

At this point Knibb's abrasive personality clearly shows itself in his reply.

"I wouldn't fucking know mate, I am not a computer and I don't look at my watch when I'm driving down the beach, so I don't know, it's as simple as that. You want a direct answer, that's your answer - I don't know how long I was on the beach."

Knibb had a valid point - that on a beach people are naturally more relaxed and tend not to be as conscious of time as in other places and circumstances. Police witness Roland Murphy stated Knibb had been on the beach after returning the tow rope for 20-30 minutes. By this time it was dark and Murphy and his wife had just moved their car and were preparing for bed. They had no reason to be conscious of Knibb's movements. It could well have been 15 minutes, or even less.

Knibb doesn't recall telling Leslie he had been on the beach "no more than two or three minutes", but he didn't try to hide the fact that he was unsure of the time frame. Nevertheless, that uncertainty was enough to send him to jail for life.

At 5.30 that afternoon Leslie and the *60 Minutes* crew took Knibb back to his Cairns hotel. Detectives Bruce Gray and Terry Brooks were waiting in the foyer. Producer John Penlington had conveniently been tipped off and the cameras were in place and ready to roll. Gray placed his hand on Knibb's shoulder and recited in TV-cop tones: "Ernest Arthur Knibb, I am placing you under arrest for the murder of Miranda Downes on the third of August 1985." It was compelling television.

Gray later said in court that police had only made up their mind to arrest Knibb that day and there was no deal with *60 Minutes* to film the scene.

Ian Leslie was the key witness for the prosecution and the *60 Minutes* tape was clearly a linchpin in the case against Ernie Knibb. The tape was widely discussed and shown several times throughout the four-week trial in September 1987. At its conclusion, the jury of seven men and five women decided that, although there was obviously no direct evidence that Knibb had killed Downes, the opportunity for him to have done so existed. The jury took six hours to find him guilty.

Subsequent appeals based on the grounds that the film footage, including the hypnosis sessions and a "cross-examination" of the accused by Leslie should not have been admitted as evidence, was refused.

Leslie backed up Gray in denying he had done a deal with police to give them the leverage they needed to arrest Knibb in exchange for live film footage. But under cross-examination by defence barrister Bob Pack, Leslie admitted that he was "prepared for the possibility" that police might make the arrest at the hotel after the beach re-enactment because that was "a very professional thing (for a reporter) to do."

But on 6 February 1987, just one day after Knibb's dramatic arrest, *60 Minutes* producer Gerald Stone was quoted in a newspaper as saying: "Acting on our information, police were waiting nearby yesterday and moved in for the arrest."

In March the following year - before Knibb's appeal against his conviction was heard - a magazine article quoted Leslie as saying: "Because of that story, the police got their man. We worked hand-in-hand with the police (and) I also believe that, knowing we were doing a story on Knibb, they felt they would be embarrassed publicly if they hadn't acted then."

In another article, *60 Minutes* supervising producer, Cliff Neville, had this to say: "We simply set out to do a story and it turned out the way it did. We didn't set out to prove he was a murderer, but as the story progressed he fell into a trap he set himself."

But Detective Sergeant Terry Brooks, in charge of the Cairns CIB at the time of Miranda Downes' death, later said the police "had no case" without the assistance of *60 Minutes*, and went on to say: "*60 Minutes* gave us additional information and we helped each other."

Brooks admitted there was little chance of Knibb ever being arrested if he hadn't come forward voluntarily after the police appealed for information. "We didn't even have a description of the vehicle before he came in."

In a bizarre twist to the case, solicitor Mal Cleland took up the legal aid case for Knibb after he was recommended as a defence lawyer by Gerald Stone. "I don't know how *60 Minutes* recommended me - somehow it just happened."

Both Cleland and Bob Pack strenuously objected to the use of the *60 Minutes* tape, but because Knibb had volunteered to the interview on camera it was deemed admissible in court. Cleland said that without the tape, Knibb would have walked away a free man, because there was insufficient evidence for a murder verdict and the minor inconsistencies in Knibb's police statements were "not enough to put him away for life".

The court also allowed statements made by Knibb during the hypnosis sessions to be presented as evidence - even though such material would not normally be admissible in Australian trials - because the Crown successfully argued that Knibb was faking his hypnotic trance.

Cleland later commented: "The jury obviously didn't take a shine to him and two appeal processes agreed with them".

Knibb elected not to give evidence after advice from his legal team that such a move could work against him in what Pack called a "tense" courthouse, pointing out that Knibb's abrasive personality could cause a hostile reaction among the jury.

Cleland: "We felt why take the risk? The fact that he didn't take the stand should have worked in our favour by causing the jury to have doubts about the evidence."

Knibb's long-standing claims of jury bias are supported by anecdotal evidence that alleges a "stand-up argument" took place among jurors before all the evidence was heard, and that one dominant juror berated others who were leaning towards an acquittal. As well, a juror allegedly boasted to friends at a party that Knibb was guilty and the jury would convict him "at any cost".

After the verdict, Knibb wrote to a friend from jail: "I knew it was going to be a kangaroo court and I knew it was no good defending myself because they had me branded - they had me marked."

Bob Pack says the *60 Minutes* tape was damaging enough, but the trial judge's summing up to the jury finally convicted his client. "After the summing up Knibb called us over and said, 'I'm gone aren't I?' and I said, 'Yes.' I have no doubt the judge put him down."

Pack said his cross-examination of Ian Leslie revealed a man with "a steel gaze without expression".

"Ian Leslie has the coldest eyes I've ever seen," Pack said.

Knibb was always up against the odds. He's a loner who doesn't make friends easily. He wears a steel plate in his head, courtesy of a bashing in jail. He clashes with prison officers. Ernie Knibb doesn't like jail and jail doesn't like him.

Knibb once told a prison officer he was guilty only of being in the wrong place at the wrong time. Certainly he has never made any admissions and never admitted any guilt, and the only evidence against him was circumstantial.

Knibb had no motive for the alleged murder. The evidence that he had the time and opportunity to kill Downes is at best shaky and can be shared by others, known and unknown, who were on the beach at Buchan Point that night. In spite of diligent efforts by police, no forensic evidence was found to connect him to Downes. Knibb was not reported as wet or sandy when he left the beach. Why not, if he had just minutes before run her down, strangled her, stripped her naked and thrown her body far enough into the water for the tide to take her out and then wash her onto the northern end of the beach? Or did he kill her where her body was found. If so, how did her clothes get to the southern end of the beach? How did he have the time to do all this, and why didn't someone see him in the act? And surely, after such murderous actions, he would not have stopped in the carpark and risk being seen and later identified. And, of course, there is no clear-cut evidence that Miranda Downes was murdered at all. She had bruises and abrasions on her body which most likely were caused by rocks or sand, and the official cause of death was drowning.

There is no doubt *60 Minutes* played a major role in Knibb's arrest and conviction. Indeed, on the eve of the program's 20-year anniversary special in November 1998, executive producer John Westacott publicly declared: "It's not every day you catch a murderer - it is one of the stories of which we are most proud."

60 Minutes had earlier approached Knibb to appear on the two-hour special after being granted permission by the Department of Corrective Services to interview him at Rockhampton Correctional Centre, where he was then a medium-security prisoner.

Knibb's tongue-in-cheek reply contained a demand for two lawyers and a journalist to be present - plus a fee of $2 million.

He also demanded the show be broadcast live without editorial interference.

Westacott called the conditions "way over the top" and the special went to air showing only part of the original program with presenter Ian Leslie.

In a letter to *60 Minutes* Knibb accused Leslie and the program's producers of luring him on to the show in 1987 with the promise of helping him clear his name.

"Well, you helped me all right," he wrote. "Helped me be framed for life for a crime I had not committed.

Knibb said he had no intention of co-operating with *60 Minutes*, either then or in the future.

"Why would I? I'm an innocent man and I'd be free today if *60 Minutes* hadn't worked with the police and prosecution to wrongfully put me in prison."

In December 2001, Knibb - then an inmate at the Borallon Correctional Centre at Ipswich - wrote to the Queensland Director of Public Prosecutions, Leanne Clare, demanding a DNA sample recently taken from him be compared with evidence found at the scene of Miranda Downes' death. He said advances in forensic technology, if applied to Downes' clothing and body samples, would prove he did not murder her.

"DNA testing is now used to clear up crime and hunt down those who have escaped justice, so I'm asking that the same principle be used to prove I was wrongly convicted," he wrote.

In February 2002, Knibb received Clare's reply.

"I am unable to assist you as this office does not retain scientific exhibits after criminal proceedings have been finalised," Clare wrote. "I have made unsuccessful enquiries of both the Police Service and the John Tonge Centre who would normally have custody of those things. It is 15 years since your conviction and it seems that the scientific evidence was disposed of some time ago."

In desperation, Knibb has presented his case to the Griffith University Innocence Project, a program that brings together lawyers, academics and law students from the university's Gold Coast campus to investigate claims of wrongful conviction. The project - the first of its kind in Australia - is based on an American scheme that has used DNA technology to secure the release of more than 30 innocent prisoners, including people on death row.

At the time of writing, the Innocence Project team was considering a review of Knibb's case.

CHAPTER SEVEN

THE KILLING OF JASON TYLER

Jason Tyler was young and strong but he found himself in the wrong place at the wrong time and it cost him his life.

In the early hours of Sunday 20 August 1995, Jason Matthew Tyler was winding down his shift as doorman at The Nest nightclub in Cairns. Tyler liked his job. His girlfriend Allison worked there, the pay and conditions were good, and the security work allowed him to mix with his mates and meet new people. Tyler was a tough, fit 24-year-old who knew his way around. He was also an easy-going type, a bit of a larrikin who enjoyed a good time and didn't take life too seriously.

Tyler knew quite a few patrons in the club that night, including three bikies who were quietly playing pool and enjoying a few beers. They were Michael Anthony Rousetty and Troy Charles Mitchell, members of the Cairns chapter of the Bandidos Motorcycle Club. Rousetty was the chapter's sergeant-at-arms, a powerful position in the club's hierarchy. With them was Robert Michael Sainsbury, a Bandido "prospect" serving his apprenticeship with the club, whose job that night was to drive the other two around and do whatever else he was told to do.

Tyler was not a Bandido club member, but he got on well with them, as he did with members of the Renegades Motorcycle Club, and other local bikies. After all, he was a bit of a rebel himself - at 180 centimetres tall and solid build, he sported a distinctive mohawk haircut and goatee beard combination that mirrored the image of the outlaw Harley Davidson riders.

After the club closed at 3am, the group hung around and had a few more drinks. Some time later Rousetty spoke to Tyler and invited him for another drink at the Bandido's clubhouse, located in a secluded rainforest setting at suburban Edge Hill.

Tyler went home to his shared unit in Mulligan Street, Manoora, and after changing his clothes, knocked on the bedroom door of his brother Scott and Scott's girlfriend, Melissa Sarkinnen. He told them he was going to the Bandido's clubhouse. Scott Tyler advised Jason not to go, because it was late, but Jason said: "I'm right. Wait here, I won't be long." Tyler's girlfriend Allison Shinnick-Spoor was also home. She gave him the key to her blue Toyota Corona and Tyler drove off around 4.45am.

Later that day, at about 3.30pm the Toyota was spotted abandoned on the side of the road, five kilometres north of Ellis Beach, by taxi driver Shane Walsh - who, coincidentally, happened to be the husband of Tyler's mother, Pamela Walsh.

Shane Walsh was driving his taxi to Port Douglas when he recognised Shinnick-Spoor's Corona by the letters "VB" on the registration plate. Police later found the radio damaged and the ignition tampered with, as if the car had been "hot wired".

A search of bushland and beaches in the area failed to provide police with any clues to Tyler's whereabouts.

A Mossman sugar mill employee later came forward and told police he had seen the car heading south from Mossman just after 12pm on the day Tyler went missing.

The search for Jason Tyler involved a large-scale police investigation that included a dozen local detectives, a Brisbane Homicide Squad detective and a Bureau of Criminal Intelligence officer. It was no secret police were interested in the Bandidos, but the bikie organisation was sticking to the well-known outlaw code of silence and all efforts to interview members hit a blank wall.

"They're showing some reluctance to assist us with our inquiries to date," Regional Crime Co-ordinator Detective Inspector John Harris announced with typical police understatement.

A few days later however, a large contingent of police headed by Special Emergency Response Team (SERT) members stormed the Bandidos clubhouse and confiscated "a number of items" as part of the investigation.

One week after his disappearance Jason Tyler was officially declared a missing person and, although stopping short of calling it a murder investigation, police were now treating the case as a major incident.

But as the weeks passed - and despite Pamela Walsh admitting her son occasionally "took off" unannounced for short periods of time - it became clear that Tyler had met with foul play and was unlikely to still be alive. Police followed up a number of leads, including an anonymous tip-off that a bloodied rock located in rugged Barron Gorge bushland could mean Tyler's body was hidden in the area. Police and State Emergency Services volunteers made their way to the rock about three kilometres downstream from the Barron Gorge power station, but a thorough search revealed no sign of Tyler.

In September another anonymous phone call led police to the discovery of a body in thick hillside scrub about 800 metres off the Captain Cook Highway, just south of Ellis Beach. The body was wearing jeans and Johnny Reb motorcycle boots similar to those worn by Tyler, but forensic tests later revealed the man, who had been dead for about six weeks, was not the missing bouncer. Police said the body had been found beneath a noose fashioned from a shirt that was still hanging in a tree. The dead man was later identified as Darwin resident Scott Anthony Koum, who was declared a missing person on the same day his body was discovered.

In a bizarre twist, the man who originally found the body was arrested for growing cannibas plants in the area. Daryl Bruce Emery, an unemployed 24-year-old, was later jailed for six months in the Cairns Magistrate's Court for producing and possessing a dangerous drug. The court heard Emery stumbled across the body near his cannibas crop and told friends who subsequently informed police of the discovery.

The unsolved mystery of Jason Tyler's disappearance continued to haunt his anguished family. In August 1997, Pamela Walsh said she had endured two years of "absolute hell" as she agonised over the fate of her son. She said every conscious moment of her life was a personal struggle between the realisation her son might be dead and the possibility he was still alive.

"If he's out there I want to know. If he's run away for some reason or he's been murdered, and if it means that whoever killed him has to go free, so be it, I just want to know," she said. "I've been told so many things - that he was dealing in drugs, that he's been fed to the sharks, that he's gone into hiding - I don't know what to believe anymore."

Then, two years to the day after Tyler drove away in his girlfriend's car, a man who identified himself only as "David" phoned Walsh and told her Jason had been murdered by a bikie gang and buried under tonnes of concrete on the site of the Cairns Reef Casino complex. The man, who called again several times, told Walsh he feared for his life and would only identify himself if police investigated his claims.

Walsh publicly appealed to the man to come forward and co-operate with police, saying the calls were only adding to her grief.

"He's called half a dozen times but he thinks my phone is tapped and won't stay on the line for very long," she said. " But he sounds genuine in what he is saying."

Walsh said "David" told her he was a former criminal who "now believes in God and has grown a heart" and wanted to help her. She eventually set up a meeting with the mystery caller in the food hall of a Cairns shopping plaza but he failed to appear.

"I didn't tell the police about this because I didn't want to frighten him off but he didn't show up anyway," Walsh said. " I was very nervous because I didn't know if he was watching me all that time or not. I don't want to believe this has happened to Jason but I can't ignore it and I can't get rid of the feeling that this person really does know something. But if he doesn't offer some proof, they're not going to dig up the casino, are they?"

Andrew Pearce, who was design manager for Concrete Constructions, the company responsible for laying the casino's floor and surrounding approaches, said most of the concrete - except for the driveway and minor works around the site - had already been laid before Tyler's disappearance.

Pearce said from Sydney that workers had been on the casino site 14 hours a day during construction and security guards had patrolled the site after hours.

"The chances of what is purported to have happened are so remote as to be farcical (and) to the best of our knowledge it didn't happen," Pearce said. He added that to be 100 per cent certain that a body wasn't under the casino was a "fine line to draw", but said company records of concrete pouring times existed and were readily available for police inspection.

Detective Sergeant Ed Kinbacher of the Cairns Casino Crime Squad said he believed the calls to Pamela Walsh were the work of a hoaxer, and although police had interviewed Pearce it hadn't been necessary to inspect the company's files.

"We don't believe there's any substance to this caller's claims, but we require him to come forward with any evidence that he may have, and if he does that we'll investigate the matter."

Kinbacher said he couldn't say "absolutely" that Tyler wasn't buried under the casino but it was such a highly unlikely scenario that police didn't consider it a serious option during the investigation.

"The reality is impossible to establish one way or another, but our view is Jason went to meet a particular group of people that night and there's only a very slim hope that he's still alive."

Just over one year later, in September 1998, the Jason Tyler case took another dramatic turn when police launched a search for his body in the murky, crocodile-inhabited waters of Mackey Creek, near Edmonton, on the southern outskirts of Cairns. The search was sparked by new information police said strongly indicated Tyler had been murdered and dumped in the secluded creek not far from the Cairns Crocodile Farm. A special taskforce had been established to investigate the promising leads, which, according to police, had been uncovered during a routine examination of the Tyler file in March.

But specialist police divers from Brisbane combed the creek bed for three days without success. The divers were protected from estuarine crocodiles by nets and the regular firing of explosive devices to keep the animals at a distance.

Police conceded the presence of crocodiles in the creek, plus regular wet-season flooding, made the task of finding a body after three years very difficult, but it was necessary to carry out the search.

Detective Inspector John Harris: "The search was something we had to do. We have done that and now can move on."

Harris said taskforce detectives would pursue inquiries in Sydney and Cairns over the next month as part of the renewed investigation and police were cautiously hopeful of an arrest by the end of the year.

Harris, of course, knew more than he was saying. The operation, codenamed "Hudad", was by now a big-time investigation involving local detectives, the Brisbane Homicide Squad, the Bureau of Criminal Intelligence, and - because an outlaw bikie gang was involved - the National Crime Authority. The trail was now hot and the police were moving in fast.

Jason Tyler's remains were found in a shallow mountainside grave on 11 November 1998, following information given to police by a Bandido informant. Forensic tests on Tyler's bones later revealed he had been shot in both knees and then bashed to death. Further injuries included a broken jaw and cheekbones and a fractured skull. Personal items including boots, a set of car keys, a belt and remnants of a vest were found near the remains.

The macabre discovery followed a two-day search of dense rainforest on the Rex Range Highway, a winding mountain road that links the Atherton Tableland with the coast near Mossman.

Nine days later on Friday 20 November, police arrested four bikies in simultaneous dawn raids on the Bandido's clubhouse and several homes in the Cairns area. Included in the bust were Michael Rousetty and Robert Sainsbury, the two Bandidos who invited Tyler back to their clubhouse on the night he disappeared. The others arrested were Peter James White and David Barry Houghton. All four were charged with Tyler's murder and remanded in custody to await committal proceedings. Houghton was also charged with possession of cannibas and incorrectly storing a 9mm semi-automatic pistol. Rousetty was also charged with possession of cannibas and methyl amphetamines.

The next day Bandido member Grant William Clear, was arrested in Sydney. Two days later fellow Bandido member Troy Charles Mitchell - who was also with Tyler on the night he disappeared - was arrested on a fishing boat in Townsville. Both men were charged with Tyler's murder and flown to Cairns.

Mitchell was later granted bail with strict reporting and residential conditions.

Pamela Walsh spoke publicly of her feelings after the men had been arrested for Tyler's murder. She said police had taken her to the place where his remains were found and the family intended to plant a rose bush there in his memory.

Walsh praised the efforts of police in tracking down the men accused of her son's brutal killing and said she was grateful to the informant who had come forward to help them.

"That person is not a nark or a lagger, he is a person who knows the wrong thing has been done, and he has given me the opportunity to bury my son."

Walsh said she was shocked and horrified at the way her son was killed.

"I can't believe any human being could kill someone in that manner," she said. "It is totally cowardly and inhumane. There are codes in life but if my son had done something so bad, why not just put a gun to his head and shoot him. There is no reason and no excuse to kill someone in this way."

At a Cairns Magistrate's Court hearing in January 1999 Troy Mitchell was the only accused to appear in person. The other five defendants were represented in court by their lawyers. Their absence was excused earlier by the court because of the costs and inconvenience of transporting the prisoners to Cairns from various jails across the state. Bail applications by Grant Clear and Peter White were refused. Troy Mitchell remained free on bail while Robert Sainsbury was released and placed in a police protection program. On 26 February, Sainsbury was granted an indemnity against prosecution after agreeing to give evidence against his fellow Bandido members.

Police said they dropped the murder charges against Sainsbury because they had no evidence against him.

In early March the five remaining accused appeared in court to face committal proceedings for the murder of Tyler. Special Emergency Response Team police officers guarded the handcuffed men and metal detectors were used to screen members of the public before they took their seats in a packed gallery. It was a tense courtroom scene and requests from lawyers to have the prisoners' handcuffs removed were refused. All five accused pleaded not guilty.

Peter Otto Klarfeld, who was the Cairns chapter president of the Bandidos at the time of Tyler's murder, testified he had been told of the killing by Michael Rousetty on the weekend it happened. Klarfeld - known as "PK" in outlaw motorcycle circles - said he was told Grant Clear shot Tyler during a fight and David Houghton forced a sock down his throat "until he croaked". Klarfeld gave evidence that Houghton told him Tyler was shot in the legs to "slow him down" because Tyler was getting the best of the fight, and then his attackers "kicked the crap out of him".

"Rousetty said Tyler deserved it and they couldn't get on top of him," Klarfeld said. "I told him he'd gone overboard."

Klarfeld told the court he considered Rousetty a psychopath and a "loose cannon who was not fit to use a gun", and had stripped him of his sergeant-at-arms position because he was unstable and unpredictable.

Klarfeld told the court he chose not to inform the police about the murder because of his loyalty to the Bandidos.

"I was trying to save the club. It was general knowledge in this town that I was a prime suspect for Jason Tyler's murder, though, and I wasn't going to cop that crap for the club."

But Klarfeld admitted he had been offered an indemnity against prosecution if he co-operated with police and provided them with information about the murder. It was later revealed Klarfeld had turned against his former associates during National Crime Authority investigations. The police now had two indemnified witnesses who were crucial to their case against the accused Bandidos.

Detective Sergeant Ed Kinbacher told the court that although members of the Bandidos were always the murder suspects in the case, police were unable to pinpoint who the actual killers were. He said phone taps were used on White and Clear and electronic listening devices planted in the Bandidos clubhouse. Kinbacher said police seized club colours and other items in a series of raids on the clubhouse and members' residences.

Kinbacher testified that Peter Klarfeld had led police to where Tyler's remains were eventually found.

"He had been removed from the Bandidos, so I thought it was the perfect opportunity to talk to him," he said. "He showed us a clearing on the side of the road and said Rousetty and Houghton had told him that was where they had parked the vehicle and removed Mr Tyler's body."

Rousetty's former de facto, Robyn Kay, gave evidence that Rousetty had talked about the killing in his sleep, but he denied having ever met Tyler when the murdered man's face appeared on television. She said Rousetty had picked Grant Clear up at the airport on the afternoon before Tyler was murdered.

A distressed and emotional Pamela Walsh was shown a studded leather belt and asked if it belonged to her son. She said it was similar to one he had worn.

"It looks like Jason's belt," she said. " I wish I could say it didn't."

She was also shown a black leather boot and agreed that it appeared to be her son's.

When she had completed her evidence, Walsh was directed to leave the court after Tony Glynn, defence counsel for Houghton, Mitchell and White, claimed her presence could taint other witnesses who may appear in a future trial against his clients.

All five accused were committed to stand trial for Jason Tyler's murder.

On 12 March 1999, Pamela Walsh farewelled her son at a moving funeral service attended by a large gathering of relatives and friends. Several detectives who worked on the case were scattered among the mourners.

A video of Tyler, smiling and joking for the camera was shown to the congregation as No Mercy's song "When I Die" played in the background.

"He never had a chance to say goodbye to us, so we can only see him as he was then," his mother said. "We don't want to talk about how Jason died, but about how he lived. This will be Jason's homecoming, but I wish he wasn't coming home this way."

After the service Jason Tyler was cremated, but only after considerable thought by his mother.

"I don't believe in cremation, but I wouldn't bury him again after where they put him," she said. "His ashes will go in the grave with me. It's in my will."

Six weeks later, at 10.30pm on Sunday 25 April, Grant William Clear was found hanging from a bed linen noose attached to a louvre in his cell at Townsville's Stuart Creek jail. Clear was alone in his cell and was last seen alive at 8.30pm. Prison authorities said there were no suspicious circumstances and it appeared Clear had taken his own life.

There were now four Bandidos left to face trial for the murder of Jason Tyler.

On Monday 19 April an advertisement appeared in The Cairns Post's classified "Personal" column. Underneath a photo of Peter Klarfeld the advertisement read:

LOST BROTHER
Peter Otoa Klarfeild (sic) P.K.
Reward 4 information to locate him

A disconnected mobile phone number was listed below the advertisement. It was the second time the advertisement had appeared in the newspaper.

Warren James Taber, 32, a former Bandido club bar manager, was later charged with attempting to pervert the course of justice by placing the bogus advertisements for the purpose of threatening Klarfeld, the Crown's star witness in the upcoming murder trial.

Police arrested Taber after handwriting and fingerprint experts identified him as the person who placed the advertisements.

It was December before Taber faced a committal hearing over the incident.

Giving evidence at the committal, Klarfeld said he was not afraid of local Bandido members, whom he described as "a bit of a joke", but he felt intimidated by the advertisements because he did not know Taber or what he was capable of doing. Klarfeld said Cairns Bandidos were weak as individuals "but they hunt in packs and in packs they can be dangerous."

At Taber's trial in the Cairns District Court in May 2000, Klarfeld again said he felt the advertisements were a threat to intimidate him before he gave evidence at the Bandido murder trial. He said he had taken extra security measures to safeguard his family at his Atherton Tableland home after the advertisements appeared.

"I've got a wife and three children and they're a major concern here," he said. "I know how they (Bandido members) operate. If they're too wimpy to come after me they go after other people. They've bashed friends of mine, 18-year-old kids."

Crown prosecutor Barry Murray told the court Taber was known as a "hang around" with the Cairns chapter of the Bandidos and was expected to impress the members before being accepted into the club. He said the term "brother" was commonly used only by members when referring to each other.

Two employees of The Cairns Post gave evidence that when Taber placed the adverisements he told them he was Klarfeld's brother whom he had not seen for a number of years but wanted to find again.

Taber was acquitted of the charge.

In August 1999 a jury of five men and eight women was empanelled to decide if the four accused Bandidos were guilty of murdering Jason Tyler.

Once again Peter Otto Klarfeld was the star attraction for the Crown, doing the job he was required to do in return for his amnesty - point the finger at his former clubmates. For that decision, the Bandidos had expelled him from the club, so Klarfeld was on his own. Early in the trial the court heard Klarfeld had been assaulted by Bandido club members and his motorcycles confiscated.

Klarfeld told the court he only broke the outlaw club's code of silence after he and his wife were subpoenaed to appear before a National Crime Authority inquiry into Tyler's disappearance.

"I was not prepared to commit perjury at an NCA inquiry," he said.

The second star of the prosecution show was Michael Sainsbury, who had called police from his jail cell to organise his own indemnity deal. Unlike Klarfeld, though, Sainsbury appeared in court under the state witness protection program.

Sainsbury testified he was acting as the Bandido club's "chauffeur" on the weekend Tyler was murdered and had driven Grant Clear to Klarfeld's home the day before the killing. He said he had taken Michael Rousetty and Troy Mitchell to the Nest Nightclub where Tyler was working and later back to the clubhouse. Sainsbury said he knew Clear had flown up from Sydney to "talk to some bouncer who was more than likely going to cop a slapping" but he didn't know when that was due to happen. He said after arriving back at the clubhouse Clear told him to go home, saying: "We'll call you if we need you". When he returned a few hours later several club members were "cleaning up."

Jason Tyler's former girlfriend Jasmine Cheadle said she started a relationship with Tyler in Sydney when she was living with her aunt, who was Grant Clear's de facto. She moved to Cairns with Tyler in March 1995, but returned south in early August after Tyler started seeing fellow Nest Nightclub employee Allison Shinnick-Spoor. She told the court she believed she was pregnant with Tyler's child at the time, but she later discovered this was not the case.

Cheadle's evidence established for the first time publicly the link between Clear's arrival in Cairns and the plot to lure Tyler into an ambush to "cop a slapping". It appeared Cheadle was unknowingly the catalyst for the horrific events that followed.

Crown prosecutor Craig Chowdhury admitted the Crown's case hinged on the evidence of Klarfeld and Sainsbury and compared the case to the FBI using informants to chase down and convict mafia mobsters.

"The FBI would have no convictions against organised crime without the evidence of insiders," he told the jury.

As he had at the accused Bandido's committal hearing, Klarfeld implicated Houghton, Rousetty and Clear in the savage attack that killed Tyler. He said he had been told by both Houghton and Rousetty, and also by Troy Mitchell, that Clear shot the bouncer in the legs with a gun left at the club for that purpose by Peter White. Rousetty then allegedly handed Houghton a sock tied in a knot and said: "Let him eat this". According to Klarfeld's evidence, he was told Houghton stuffed the sock down Tyler's throat and the three men then proceeded to kick him to death.

But defence barristers for the four accused called on the jury to reject Klarfeld's two days of evidence, challenging his credibility as an indemnified witness.

"You would be more likely to believe the tooth fairy than to believe Mr Klarfeld," barrister Tony Glynn said at the conclusion of the two-week trial. "Mr Klarfeld is a compulsive liar."

Glynn told the jury everyone agreed Grant Clear instigated the attack that killed Jason Tyler, but Klarfeld had lied about the extent of his contact with Clear and the fact he led police to Tyler's body could mean Klarfeld killed Tyler himself.

Greg Lynham, representing Peter White, told the jury there were a number of weapons at the Bandidos clubhouse where Tyler was killed, including - according to Robert Sainsbury - a pistol hidden in a vacuum cleaner.

"No one saw White hand over the weapon (and) there is no evidence one of the other weapons seized by police wasn't used," Lynham said.

Lynham told the court Klarfeld's evidence couldn't be relied upon because of contradictory statements he had given to police, the National Crime Authority, and his appearance at the trial.

After deliberating for more than 10 hours the jury returned at 10pm on Wednesday 13 August 1999 with its verdict. Rousetty and Houghton were found guilty of Jason Tyler's murder and sentenced to life imprisonment. Mitchell and White were judged not guilty and released from the dock by Justice Stanley Jones.

In his sentencing remarks Jones said the verdict was a warning to young men who were considering joining violent organisations.

"You chose to become involved in an organisation which in the long term only offered you trouble and ultimate misery," he said, addressing a stony-faced Houghton.

Five days after Rousetty and Houghton were sentenced, Peter Klarfeld's car was found at the bottom of the Barron River. The Ford station wagon had been stolen and dumped in the muddy river near a popular boat ramp. Police agreed the incident could be related to Klarfeld's evidence against his former associates in the murder trial. It was alleged Klarfeld gave the vehicle to a young male friend who was involved in a minor collision with another driver three days earlier. Police said a third person - Bandido club member Mark William Genrich - intervened and a scuffle broke out between Genrich and the young driver, who fled on foot with his female companion.

Genrich was charged with a number of firearm offences and with fighting in a manner to cause public alarm.

Six months after her murdered son's funeral Pamela Walsh was informed by the government that she was ineligible for a $6,000 compensation grant because Tyler died several months before the Criminal Offence Victims Act was passed in December 1995. The notice came as a shock for Walsh, who filled in an application for funeral assistance two weeks after her son's remains were found in November 1998. She said she had been led to believe by the Justice Department the costs of the funeral service and cremation ceremony would be paid for by the government.

A spokesperson for Attorney-General Matt Foley said there had been some initial difficulty pinpointing the time of Jason Tyler's death, but following advice from the police, the director of public prosecutions and the coroner, that 20 August 1995 had been established as the correct date, no retrospective payments could be made.

"We are not trying to opt out or duck for cover over this but we are compelled to follow by law this legislation and unfortunately Mr Tyler's death precedes the legislation," the spokesperson said.

Pamela Walsh: "How can the government be so petty over a time limit when a human being has been murdered? Well, it was my son who was murdered, so the government can send the bill to the Bandidos."

In November 1999 Peter Klarfeld was again in the spotlight when he walked free from the Cairns Supreme Court after pleading guilty to serious drug charges. Klarfeld was found in possession of cannibas and a traffickable amount of lysergic acid diethylamide (LSD) during a police raid in Rockhampton in July 1998. Although he copped a three year sentence on paper, Justice Stanley Jones halved it to 18 months for co-operating with police in the Jason Tyler murder investigation. Jones then suspended the sentence entirely for five years, explaining to the court Klarfeld would be placed at risk in prison for giving evidence against his former Bandido clubmates. Jones said Klarfeld's course of action had provided "solace" to Tyler's family.

The court heard Klarfeld had drug convictions dating back 20 years but was not a user of LSD and had freely admitted the drugs found in his possession were intended for commercial use.

On 16 December police busted a number of Bandido haunts around Cairns in a series of dawn raids involving about 90 armed officers. Five Bandido members and four club associates were among 20 people arrested on a total of 108 drugs and weapons charges. Bandido president Maxwell Patrick Geary was picked up in the operation - codenamed Celeste - along with Peter White, who was acquitted of Jason Tyler's murder and Mark Genrich, who was earlier charged over the street fracas involving Klarfeld's car. Warren James Taber, who had been acquitted of attempting to pervert the course of justice in the "bogus adveriesments" affair, was also caught in the net and arrested on drug charges.

In a subsequent Cairns Magistrate's Court hearing following the mass arrests, police said 11 witnesses to alleged Bandido criminal offences were in fear of their lives and were under police protection in secret locations. The court heard one witness had been told he would "end up like Tyler" if he tried to back out of dealing and distributing drugs. Another former Bandido insider detailed a drug trafficking ring involving a network of club associates in the Mission Beach and Tully area.

Police claimed Bandido members used standover tactics to distribute drugs through tattoo shops and stripper agencies.

One informant told police Bandido club members had kidnapped and tortured him because of an outstanding $5,000 drug debt. The court heard the man was tied up in the Bandido clubhouse and tortured for four hours with cable, plastic tubing and an electric "stun gun". The man said he was later taken to Innisfail where he escaped and made his way to Brisbane and contacted police.

Defence solicitor Gelma Meoli told the court it was wrong to judge the alleged offenders simply because they were affiliated with the Bandidos.

Maxwell Geary was later jailed for 12 years for trafficking and producing drugs but in March 2002 had his sentence reduced to 10 years on appeal. However, an appeal against his conviction for trafficking was dismissed.

In August 2000, one year after they were sentenced to life imprisonment for the murder of Jason Tyler, David Houghton and Michael Rousetty had their convictions set aside and were granted new trials by the Court of Appeal in Brisbane.

In its unanimous decision the Court of Appeal considered defence submissions that a miscarriage of justice had occurred because the jury had not heard evidence from Tracey Hancock, the former de facto of indemnified witness Robert Sainsbury. Hancock allegedly claimed Peter Klarfeld was present at the Bandido clubhouse at the time of the murder and threatened Sainsbury with "the same treatment" if he spoke of the killing.

In its judgement, the court found there was a "significant possibility" that the jury would conclude Houghton was not at the murder scene if it had heard Hancock's evidence. It said the case against both Houghton and Rousetty hinged on the confessions they allegedly gave to Klarfeld - an "unsavoury witness" with a strong interest in seeing others convicted of the murder. The judgement said that while the fresh evidence was not convincing enough to conclude a guilty verdict could not be returned by a jury, it did cast a doubt on the key testimony "based solely on confessional statements said to have been made by Houghton to Klarfeld."

But although Tracey Hancock's "fresh" evidence had a significant influence on the Court of Appeal's decision to order a new trial, she wasn't around to back her claims up on the witness stand. Hancock, it appeared, was living somewhere in America, and wasn't interested in coming home to give evidence.

On Monday 12 November 2001 - three years and one day after Jason Tyler's remains were found - David Houghton and Michael Rousetty stood together in the Cairns Supreme Court dock, and, for the second time, pleaded not guilty to the bouncer's murder.

Both men admitted to being accessories after the fact of the murder and pleaded guilty to that lesser charge.

Tight security added tension to the trial with media and members of the public searched before being allowed entry to the courtroom.

Counsel for Houghton, Tony Glynn, objected to the security measures, complaining to trial judge Justice Stanley Jones that he was concerned about the detrimental effects heavy security and the strong police presence might have in the minds of the jury. He asked that police be disallowed from sitting in the well of the court.

"This (could raise) suggestions about my client, and they (police) should sit in the back of the court where the jury can't see them," he said.

Before the trial began the jury was reduced to 11 members after one juror revealed she was a former neighbour of a witness listed to give evidence.

Justice Stanley Jones advised the jury that there were in fact two separate trials in progress at the same time and jurors must endeavour to "keep the evidence in separate boxes".

Crown prosecutor Terry Winn told the jury in his opening address that Jason Tyler was murdered in brutal circumstances and the evidence they were about to hear would not be pleasant.

Winn later said the evidence of Peter Klarfeld and Robert Sainsbury might suggest to jury members that the two men were also involved in the murder.

"If so you'd be dead right, but the evidence of Klarfeld is crucial to this case, and little fish must be used to catch big fish."

Winn told the jury that Houghton and Rousetty were not alone when they murdered Tyler.

"Another man, Grant William Clear, was involved," Winn said. "Clear is dead. Were he not, he'd be sitting here today. A higher jurisdiction will deal with him."

Peter Klarfeld, by this time a seasoned veteran in the witness box, again gave evidence against his former bikie associates. In his third court appearance as the prosecution's star witness, Klarfeld was earning his indemnified status the hard way.

Klarfeld told the court he was "not well liked" when he was the

Bandidos club president, but he closely abided by the national chapter's rules "or I would be removed". He said he had the power to order local chapter members "to do anything, including criminal activity" and a strict criteria existed for attending club meetings.

"You turned up for the meetings unless you were in hospital or in jail," he said.

Klarfeld gave evidence that he didn't attend a club function on the Friday night before Jason Tyler was killed because he had food poisoning and he didn't fully recover until the following Monday.

"Other members couldn't question my excuse. If I say I'm sick, I'm sick," he said.

Klarfeld repeated evidence that Robert Sainsbury and Grant Clear visited him at his home on the Saturday and they discussed club business. On Sunday he received a phone call from "Mick" Rousetty, who said he'd run out of petrol on the highway near Mt Molloy and asked Klarfeld to help him out.

Klarfeld said when he arrived with a can of petrol, Rousetty and Clear were standing next to Rousetty's utility. Clear allegedly said the two were "just taking care of some business", but didn't elaborate and Klarfeld returned home.

When he visited the Bandido clubhouse that afternoon, Klarfeld said "a lot of cleaning" was going on and "things were burnt" in 44-gallon drums. He said Rousetty, Houghton, Sainsbury and Peter White were present, but Clear was not.

"I asked Mick Rousetty what the fuck was going on and Mick said the big prick deserved it so I whacked him."

Klarfeld testified that after Rousetty described the killing, he angrily replied: "How the fuck did it get to this? This is your shit, you've gone overboard again." He then gave Rousetty instructions "to clean the place up and then clean it again, and keep your mouths shut".

"There was a murder on my hands and I had to do something about it. How he died I didn't care."

Klarfeld gave evidence that Rousetty later repeated his version of the killing, adding that Tyler was stripped and "dumped" in the bush on the Rex Range. Rousetty said Tyler's clothing was burnt, together with "some of our own".

Klarfeld said Rousetty told him Clear had shot Tyler in the legs with a .32 pistol belonging to White. According to Klarfeld, Houghton had confessed to shoving the sock down Tyler's throat because "Mick told me to".

Klarfeld said he drove Rousetty and Houghton back to the Rex Range "about six or eight weeks" later and dropped them off so they could "clean up properly" and rebury Tyler's body. He said he drove to the bottom of the range and waited for half an hour before returning to pick up the two men. Rousetty had remarked: "Gee that stunk, it made me sick."

Under cross-examination by James Sheridan, counsel for Rousetty, Klarfeld said he had left a rival motorcycle club, the Renegades, in 1993 "under somewhat difficult circumstances" and established the Bandidos Cairns chapter a short time later.

Klarfeld denied he was an "experienced liar" but admitted he lied to police about the Tyler case because "I didn't want to talk about the subject". He also agreed he had several aliases and possessed a fake birth certificate and driver's licence.

When asked by Sheridan why he hadn't mentioned to police earlier that he had an alibi, that he was at home with food poisoning when Tyler was killed, Klarfeld said: "I said as little as possible to police, that's always the best remedy. We didn't waste words in those days."

Sheridan: "I would suggest you have a powerful reason for concealing the murder, that's because you and Clear killed him."

Klarfeld: "No, that's a figment of your imagination."

Sheridan: "You lied about everything to get an indemnity from prosecution, didn't you?"

Klarfeld: "No. I was facing drug charges, thanks to the club. I left the club because of the drug charges. I couldn't get out of it."

Klarfeld said he hadn't deliberately lied to National Crime Authority investigators but he had sometimes made mistakes about dates and times because he was under stress and had "mixed days up" on several occasions.

Tony Glynn suggested a senior detective had put Klarfeld "under enormous pressure to blame others (for the murder) or they'd blame you".

Klarfeld: "That's rubbish. I remember him saying if the shit goes down the club may blame you."

Margaret Klarfeld gave evidence that she had been in a relationship with Peter Klarfeld for 27 years and had been married for 18 years. She told the court her husband was sick and never left their home until Sunday afternoon on the weekend Tyler was murdered. She denied a suggestion from Tony Glynn that she had provided an alibi for her husband.

"I wouldn't cover for my husband if he committed murder," she said. "I take my vows seriously but it doesn't extend to murder. If my husband was involved in this he'd be sitting where the boys are sitting today."

Detective Sergeant Michael James Moatt of the Covert Surveillance Squad said on 17 October 1995 police followed a blue Ford Falcon station wagon driven by Peter Klarfeld from Smithfield to the Rex Range. He said Houghton and Rousetty were in the vehicle but later when it was observed parked at the bottom of the range only Klarfeld was inside.

A police surveillance video tape played in court showed Klarfeld, Rousetty and Houghton arriving at the Bandido clubhouse later that day. Houghton was shown cleaning a shovel with a hose.

Houghton defended his actions by claiming he helped rebury Tyler's body to improve his standing in the club.

In a sensational and abrupt conclusion to the week-long trial, Justice Stanley Jones ordered a mistrial against Rousetty after evidence judged to be prejudicial was heard from indemnified witness Robert Sainsbury. Jones ordered Sainsbury's evidence be suppressed from publication. Rousetty was remanded to reappear in court to stand trial for a third time at a date to be set.

The next day Jones directed the jury to find David Houghton not guilty of murder because the evidence against him failed to show any intent to kill Tyler. He said the only evidence put up to incriminate Houghton was a very short statement by Peter Klarfeld that Rousetty and Sainsbury told him that Jason Tyler had fought back and "we couldn't get on top of him".

Jones said the Crown tried to show there was a common intention to assault Tyler, but the words "we couldn't get on top of him" could mean that Houghton was merely trying to restrain Tyler during the fight and was not involved in his death.

"It is my view that passage does not show a common intention and I am required to direct you to find a verdict of not guilty," he told the jury.

Jones also said there was no evidence to prove Houghton had "complied with the request" to shove a sock down Tyler's throat.

Houghton was sentenced to eight years imprisonment with no recommendation for early parole on the accessory after the fact of murder charge.

A shattered Pamela Walsh reacted to the trial with disbelief. She said although she felt no anger towards the judge it appeared that justice was structured for the perpetrators of a crime and not the victims.

"What can I say, except the law is to blame for this, and the law needs to be changed," she said. "I don't want them to cry for my son like I do, but I cannot accept this as justice. Where do I go from here, do I have to go through another court case? It's like having to go through his murder all over again.

"Give me Jason back and they can go free, but I can't have him back so they should stay in jail. They get another chance but I don't get one."

But the drawn-out aftermath of her son's brutal killing continued to deny Walsh a final conclusion to his death.

In May 2002, six months after his conviction for helping to dispose of Jason Tyler's body, David Houghton had his eight-year sentence reduced by one year on appeal.

In a majority 2-1 judgement the Court of Appeal ruled the original sentence was excessive and seven year's imprisonment would more adequately balance the mitigating factors in Houghton's favour.

In August 2002 Michael Rousetty again pleaded not guilty to murder at his third trial in the Cairns Supreme Court. The six-day trial was mostly a replay of evidence heard in court on several previous occasions and there were no surprise witnesses called by either the prosecution or defence.

Forensic pathologist Dr Anthony Ansford gave evidence that an examination of Jason Tyler's remains revealed he had been shot twice in the left leg and possibly another three times, but in his opinion the victim died of massive head injuries caused by a blunt instrument, such as heavy footwear.

Once again the star prosecution witness was Peter Klarfeld, who toughed out yet another two days in the witness box denying he was a liar, but admitting he had made unintentional errors of fact when interviewed by police and National Crime Authority investigators.

Crown prosecutor Peter Kelly said in his closing submission that while Klarfeld was "not perfect" the jury should believe him because there was enough evidence to substantiate his story, and, despite intensive cross-examination by the defence, he had firmly maintained his account of the events that followed Jason Tyler's murder.

But barrister James Sheridan, representing Rousetty, said Klarfeld was an unreliable witness who had evaded certain questions about his dealings with the police and National Crime Authority.

Sheridan reminded the jury of Klarfeld's various aliases over the years and asked why an honest man would need assumed names.

"From the beginning of his life he has been living a lie," Sheridan said.

On 20 August 2002, seven years to the day after Jason Tyler was bashed to death, Michael Anthony Rousetty was found guilty of his murder and sentenced to life in prison. The jury took just over four hours to reach its verdict. When handing down his sentence, trial judge Justice John Byrne described Tyler's killing as "treacherous (and) callous".

Rousetty was also sentenced to seven years jail for his role in burying Tyler's body.

Pamela Walsh said she was relieved that justice had finally been delivered to Jason and his family but the memory of how he died could never be erased or forgotten.

"He's with me every day in my heart and mind and I can still hear him say 'love you Mum' before he'd hang up the phone," she said in a tearful interview. "A man is going to jail for the rest of his life for killing my son, and now his life will be wasted like he wasted Jason's life. That person can't hurt anybody else now."

But the trauma that Pamela Walsh called her "recurring nightmare" was not over. A month after his trial - the third, following previous appeals - Rousetty again appealed against his conviction on the grounds the jury's verdict was "unsafe and unsatisfactory" because of reliance on evidence given by Peter Klarfeld and Robert Sainsbury.

In appeal documents filed with the Court of Appeal, Rousetty's lawyers said the evidence of Klarfeld and Sainsbury should not have been considered by the jury as reliable because of the "many inconsistencies" in their testimony, and the fact that the two former Bandidos were indemnified witnesses.

But on 31 January 2003 the Court of Appeal rejected Rousetty's submission to have his conviction overturned and the long-running series of court appearances finally came to an end.

In a bizarre episode that added to Pamela Walsh's grief over the loss of her son, she received a notice from the State Government threatening to suspend Jason Tyler's driver's licence unless he paid an outstanding debt of $838 for failing to wear a bicycle helmet in 1993.

The notice was sent by the State Penalties Enforcement Registry (SPER), an agency of the Justice Department, demanding her deceased son pay the original fine of $126, plus accrued costs, or lose his licence.

Walsh was outraged. She said she was trying to resume her life after the trials and appeals but the letter had reopened emotional wounds caused by her son's violent death.

"Jason's been dead all those years and he's still copping it," she said. "What's next - will they come knocking on the door to arrest him?"

The State Penalties Enforcement Registry was formed in February 2000 to take over a debt recovery system previously administered by the police, but although SPER claimed it was highly successful, it admitted no data cross-matching program was yet in place to ensure fines were not sent to the dead.

Walsh said a high-ranking SPER official phoned her to personally apologise for the mistake.

"That's all very well, but why isn't there a mechanism in place to detect when a person is deceased, especially after seven years? It's just unbelievable that they can't get their act together."

The tragic irony of Jason Tyler's brutal murder lies with the fact that he almost certainly died as a direct consequence of his own strength and courage. He was lured into a trap where he was to be taught a lesson by his assailants, but he refused to submit and fought back with courage and gritty determination. That decision led to the savage frenzy that ended his young life.

Pamela Walsh said the entire community of north Queensland seemed to have supported her over the years and helped her deal with the brutal circumstances of how her son died.

"Family and friends and even strangers in the street have shared my grief and for that I'm truly thankful," she said. "I know it would have been a much tougher battle without them.

Walsh said the years of court cases have left her disappointed with the legal system but she has no choice but to move ahead with her life.

"I've tried to put it all in perspective and walk away from the hurt, but sitting through those trials without being able to say anything has changed me," she said.

"I try to remember how Jason was in life, not what happened to him. I don't let that evil drag me down."

CHAPTER EIGHT

MISSING ON MT SORROW

Daniel Nute walked to the top of Mt Sorrow and disappeared - and he wasn't missed for 23 days. Did he die on the mountain, or is he still alive?

On the morning of Tuesday 29 July 1997, British backpacker Daniel Fraser Nute set off on a hike to the top of Mt Sorrow, near Cape Tribulation in far north Queensland. The 19-year-old traveller from the Devon township of Totness had arrived at the famous tourist destination - known around the world as "Cape Trib" - just the day before, intent on enjoying the tropical surroundings of an area renowned for its pristine, rainforest-clad mountains and picture-postcard beaches. The young Briton had pitched his tent in the grounds of PK's Jungle Village resort, a popular camping and meeting spot for thousands of backpackers who flocked to the area each year on their shoe-string budgets.

Cape Tribulation on that Tuesday was bathed in brilliant sunshine. Although it had rained the week before, it was the traditional mid-winter "dry season" in Australia's north, and fine days for bush-walking and swimming could usually be counted on for a relaxing holiday.

Early that morning Daniel Nute packed his wallet, personal papers, mobile phone and a camera in a light backpack, zipped up his tent, and walked to a Queensland National Parks and Wildlife Service ranger station two kilometres up the road from PK's.

Nute, who had arrived in Australia six months earlier, was a dedicated conservationist and had worked briefly for the Australian Trust for Conservation Volunteers charity group in Canberra and the Snowy Mountains. He had also worked with the group in the

McDonnell Range near Alice Springs, and in Darwin.

Before heading north to Cape Tribulation, Nute spent a few days camping and relaxing on Magnetic Island, off Townsville.

There's little doubt the backpacker would have been excited about the idea of experiencing a trek through the Daintree National Park's spectacular rainforest environment.

The tall, athletic traveller was an experienced bushwalker and had hiked extensively in Europe, Indonesia and Canada before deciding on a trip to Australia. He was due to start university back home in Bath in September.

The climb up the rugged slopes of the 797-metre peak should have been a straightforward and easy trek for Nute. Although described as "moderately difficult" by rangers, the walk from the coast to the top of Mt Sorrow and back is not considered too arduous for fit hikers. The three-kilometre track was well defined with marking tape and a lookout at the top clearly indicated the end of the journey.

It was just after 8 o'clock when Nute filled out a standard bushwalker safety form at the ranger station and listened as ranger Jan Grace explained to a group of Italian tourists how to follow safety procedures during the three-hour climb to the top of the mountain. Half way through Grace's talk, ranger Hans Nieuwenhuizen arrived to take over and she left to take up her normal duties for the day. Before he finished his talk, Nieuwenhuizen noticed Nute had slipped away, leaving his completed form on the desk. Nute had filled in the date and the starting time of his Mt Sorrow walk as 8am, also indicating he would be back at 5pm.

Nieuwenhuizen noted the fit young backpacker had all the right gear for a day-long hike, including hat, walking boots, and a water bottle. He looked capable and prepared, a welcome change for frustrated rangers who say many visitors have no idea what they should take when they enter the mountain environment.

Although the ranger station was manned only between 8am and 10am because of the many other tasks the rangers were required to carry out, a notice requested hikers who intended to climb the mountain to leave a note recording the time they left and confirmation that they had arrived back safely.

There was nothing that morning to alert the rangers that this was going to be anything other than what north Queenslanders proudly call "just another day in paradise".

But Daniel Nute didn't come back that fine day, and for his family and friends in England, paradise became synonymous with hell and the ominously-named Mt Sorrow became a monument to their grief.

Nute wasn't reported missing until Thursday 21 August - an astonishing 23 days of mystery and silence. For an incredible three weeks the young Englishman was missing from the busy backpacker resort without anybody noticing his absence. Finally, resort staff raised the alarm after realising his accommodation bill hadn't been paid and his tent left unattended. It was a scenario that was almost impossible to believe. It was almost as if Daniel Nute had never been there at all.

Police at first believed there were a number of options to explain Nute's absence. High on the list was the possibility he could have gone off sightseeing somewhere else in north Queensland. After all, he had his phone, camera and wallet with him, so he could have made a spur of the moment decision to alter his plans and return later to his camp at Cape Tribulation But for 23 days? Police conceded it was a long shot, but one that had to be considered.

Sergeant Graham Coleman of Mossman Police pointed out the Mt Sorrow track had been used by many walkers since 29 July and nobody had seen any sign of Nute. The Italian tourists who had been on the track the same day as the Englishman left a note on the door of the ranger's office, advising of their return. But there was no such message from Nute.

Over the next few days, Mt Sorrow and the surrounding wilderness were subject to a massive land and aerial search involving police, park rangers, and volunteer emergency rescue teams. Obscure tracks and thick forest on each side of the main walking trail were scoured metre by metre for any clue that could provide a lead to the backpacker's disappearance. Queensland Rescue helicopters scrutinised the terrain below in carefully-plotted search patterns, but there was no trace of Nute and no visible sign that he had been on the mountain. Authorities were left no choice but to cling to the slim hope that he had gone somewhere unannounced and would return to collect his belongings.

Four days after Daniel Nute was reported missing, his father, Fraser, and 16-year-old brother Ben arrived in Cairns to help in the search.

Fraser Nute told a media conference that he had been worried for some time because his son's letters and phone calls home had abruptly stopped, but it wasn't until Devon police contacted him that he realised how serious the situation was. He said his family's strong Christian faith kept their hopes alive for Daniel's safe return and they were "asking God to sort the whole thing out".

Nute said his son last phoned the family from Magnetic Island on the morning of Saturday 26 July, his younger sister's birthday.

"It would have been Saturday evening here and Dan was in a bar," Nute said. "All the family was at home and we each had a chat with him. It was a long conversation and he told me his plan was to travel a little further north to Cairns, but he didn't mention Cape Tribulation. He was then going to work his way back down the coast to Sydney before coming home. He was treating all this as an adventure in what we call a 'gap year' before university."

With the help of experienced local guides, Fraser and Ben Nute spent a long day on an emotional pilgimage to Mt Sorrow where they searched in vain for Daniel. A Queensland Rescue helicopter continued to sweep the many peaks and valleys of the mountain range but the missing backpacker could not be found.

Police announced they had already followed up several possible sightings of the man between Cooktown and Miriwinni, near Babinda, south of Cairns. Later, police received a report that Nute had been seen walking on the seldom-travelled Bloomfield Track north of Cape Tribulation on the day he went missing. Another possible sighting was reported from Wujal Wujal Aboriginal community. Police also alerted fishing fleets around Cape York Peninsula in case Nute had boarded a boat to work as a deckhand. Interpol had been advised and efforts were being made to locate any international backpackers who may have spoken to the missing man in north Queensland.

But police, search authorities and old hands in the region all agreed on one thing - if Daniel Nute had indeed climbed Mt Sorrow on 29 July, the time had long passed when he could be expected to survive in such inhospitable and unforgiving terrain. If he went up the mountain, they said, he was still there and may never be found.

On Saturday 30 August, airlines in Perth were placed on alert to watch out for Nute who was booked on a 9am flight back to the United Kingdom. But Nute failed to make contact and police revealed he had not used his bank account since his disappearance.

In September a flurry of possible sightings followed a story on Nute that was featured in the highly-rated "Australia's Most Wanted" television series, but the new leads led nowhere and police admitted they had reached a dead end in their investigation. A final search by Special Emergency Response Team officers in deep ravines and gulleys beyond Mt Sorrow yet again found no trace of the missing man.

Experienced north Queensland bushmen spent many days assisting police on several searches of Mt Sorrow and surrounding terrain. They describe the area as a dangerous wilderness of huge boulder "fields" and impenetrable scrub where an injured person or a body could be just a metre or two from searchers and still not be seen.

Former National Parks ranger and Vietnam veteran Pat Shears said the thickly-vegetated mountainous country was extremely harsh and allowed for no mistakes when bushwalking. Shears and a police team were dropped by helicopter into the Roaring Meg Falls area on a difficult three-day search, walking along creeks and gulleys back to Cape Tribulation in a fruitless last-ditch attempt to locate any sign of Nute.

Shears, who lives at Cape Tribulation and knows the country intimately, is one of a number of local bushmen who believe the British backpacker easily reached the peak of Mt Sorrow and then decided to walk on further until he became hopelessly lost.

"If you're young and fit you can reach the lookout in less than two hours, so you see an opening and think I'll go a bit further and then what happens you end up in a creek and follow that, but in that country the creeks go in all directions, so you end up in big trouble," Shears said.

"There are boulders in there so big that if you fall down a

THE FATAL VOYAGE

Manfred Weissensteiner – Cairns Magistrate's Court, March 1991. Photo: The Cairns Post

Susan Zack

Hartwig Bayerl

THE WHEELIE BIN MURDER

Michiko Okuyama – murdered and dumped in a wheelie bin.

Michiko Okuyama Memorial

DEATH IN THE HINCHINBROOK CHANNEL

Ken Scotton

Brett Scotton

Ken Scotton's vessel "Peppermint"

John Saibura

WHERE IS PATANELA?

Patanela – vanished from the high seas

Skipper of Patanela, Ken Jones and wife Noreen – on board when vessel disappeared.

WHERE IS PATANELA?

Ted and Marie McCarthy – reported sighting of Patanela off North Queensland coast.

Alan Nicol, Patanela's owner

Patanela crewmen, Michael Calvin and John Blissett, missing with mystery ship.

DARK JUSTICE

Kelvin Condren – railroaded for murder.

"TRIAL BY TELEVISION FRAMED ME FOR MURDER"

Ernest Arthur Knibb enters court on trial for murder.
Photo: Russell Francis

Scriptwriter Miranda Downes
– died at Buchan Point but
was it murder?

"TRIAL BY TELEVISION FRAMED ME FOR MURDER"

Buchan Point Beach

Cairns detective Bruce Gray (left) with 60 Minutes reporter Ian Leslie. Photo: Russell Francis

THE KILLING OF JASON TYLER

Pamela Walsh with a photo of her murdered son Jason Tyler.

MISSING ON MT SORROW

Missing person poster

Fraser and Polly Nute outside Mossman Court House.

A LONELY PLACE TO DIE

Angela Mealing – murder or suicide?

Behana Creek

Shrine at death scene Behana Creek. Note tree stumps after police removed trees for scientific testing.

Adrian Deemal leaves Coroner's Court – last person to see Angela Mealing alive.
Photo: The Courier-Mail

THE LAST DIVE OF TOM AND EILEEN LONERGAN

Tom and Eileen Lonergan

Jack Nairn and Tom Colrain.   Photo: Russell Francis

THE LAST DIVE OF TOM AND EILEEN LONERGAN

Dive Instructor, Karl Jesienowski outside Cairns Court.

Divemaster Harald Klose (L) and Senior Dive Instructor George Pyrohiw (R), leave court.

Eileen Lonergan's Parents, Kathy and John Haines.

WHO KILLED RACHEL ANTONIO?

Rachel Antonio – missing, presumed murdered

*Robert Hytch
– innocent of murder.
Photo: The Courier-Mail*

NATASHA RYAN AND THE MONSTER OF ROCKHAMPTON

Serial killer, Leonard John Fraser, flanked by detectives.
Photo: The Courier-Mail

Murdered schoolgirl, Keyra Steinhardt

Police informant, Allan Quinn.
Photo: The Courier-Mail

Natasha Ryan, before her disappearance.

Natasha Ryan celebrates her 19th birthday with mum Jennifer on the same day Leonard John Fraser was found guilty of killing three women. 9 May 2003.
Photo: The Courier-Mail

NO JUSTICE FOR THE MACKAY SISTERS

The Mackay sisters Judith and Susan in 1970.

*Murder suspect, Arthur Stanley Brown in 1999.
Photo: The Courier-Mail*

crevice, you go down a long way and you get stuck, and you rot away and die. Mobile phones don't work in there and he'd just get weaker and weaker, thinking he'd filled out the safety form and somebody would find him. There's no doubt in my mind that's what happened."

Shears said he searched for a backpack or some clothing wedged in a tree or rocks that would indicate where Nute was but he could find no evidence that could pinpoint the route he had taken.

"I told his parents I'd keep searching but all I'd find would be his backpack. Well, we couldn't even find that. He's up there for sure but we'll probably never know where."

Shears criticised the safety regulations of his former employer, the Queensland National Parks and Wildlife Service, which is a division of the Department of Environment. He said the official bushwalkers safety form was inadequate and not enough attention was paid to the possibility a walker may get lost and go unnoticed for days, or - as was the case with Nute - even weeks.

"I was a ranger for seven years and back then resorts and other accommodation places kept dates and times of any guests who went bushwalking, and they'd let us know if anybody was late getting back," Shears said.

"I made it my business to check every night to make sure everyone was back and if not I gave them until 11 o'clock the next morning to come out before we started a search. It worked well, but the bureaucrats changed the system and the ranger station is now unattended for long periods of time and nobody bothers to check if somebody is still out there. Human life should come before any other jobs that rangers are required to do."

In September 1997 a handwritten memo from the Brisbane office of then Minister for the Environment Brian Littleproud was faxed to Peter Hensler, far north regional manager of the National Parks and Wildlife Service in Cairns. The memo referred to a recent story in The Courier-Mail newspaper "implying" criticism of the department's rangers over Nute's disappearance. The memo, in part, read: "With the best will in the world and the best system we cannot ensure everyone's whereabouts and/or safety - a problem I imagine exists in all wilderness areas. We can't force people to tell us where they are."

The Courier-Mail's story on 9 September quoted an Environment Department spokesman as saying there was a "slip-up" on the occasion of Nute's disappearance and as a result "we are reviewing procedures in all national parks in that region so it doesn't happen again". The spokesman was quoted as saying walkers were supposed to leave a "chit" when they returned from a walk and if the ranger station wasn't open they could leave the note at "an appropriate place nearby". The spokesman said a "substantial" number of people failed to do this when they returned from hikes.

"In this situation, because of some misunderstanding, it was thought he (Nute) had returned with a group of other backpackers but later it was found he had not."

On 16 September a memo from Peter Hensler to Regional Director Lindsay Delzoppo recommended that "based on the experience gained from Mr Nute's recent disappearance at Cape Tribulation, (ranger) centres that are responsible for long walks in isolated locations (should) adopt a policy of making walker safety a responsibility of the walker and not the Department." Hensler also recommended that senior investigations officer Michael Chep investigate and report on "the circumstances relating to the perceived inaction by Department of Environment staff in not reporting Mr Nute being overdue from his walk to Mt Sorrow within the Daintree National Park after he had filled out a Departmental Bushwalker Safety Form."

The internal correspondence confirmed what everybody connected to the case already knew. Not only had Daniel Nute's disappearance gone unnoticed for three weeks by staff at PK's Jungle Village, but Department of Environment rangers completely missed his failure to return as well.

Department investigator Michael Chep's report delivered several weeks later was blunt and to the point. Early in his report Chep emphasised that on the day of Nute's "apparent" walk to Mt Sorrow, the Italian tourists who were also on the mountain left a note advising of their return but Nute did not. Chep noted there were no follow-up actions by staff to ascertain if Nute had returned.

Chep pointed out that Nute had written his home address "Devon, U.K" on the safety form, instead of an Australian contact to be used in an emergency, but it was not unusual for international visitors to do this as the form did not specify which address was required.

"It seems useless to have such a form and have no apparent follow up action as to whether the person who completes the form, which (then) becomes an accountable departmental record, can still be accounted for," Chep wrote.

The report stated that if the safety form system was dropped and the onus of personal responsibility for safety shifted to hikers, then backpacker resorts such as PK's Jungle Village would bear the brunt of media and public reaction if somebody went missing.

Chep had a reputation in north Queensland as a tough, no-nonsense wildlife investigator who enforced the law in national parks without fear or favour. In his report on Nute's disappearance he raised the possibility that the young Briton may not have climbed the mountain at all. "It could be argued that NUTE did not go to Mt Sorrow and therefore found no reason to submit the bushwalker safety form indicating that he returned safely," the report stated.

Chep criticised the Cape Tribulation ranger base as a "relatively small, often unrecognisable" station that is often left unattended while staff carry out patrol and maintenance duties and was therefore "ineffective" as a centre to educate tourists on behaviour and safety matters in the national park.

"The actions of ranger staff after the apparent disappearance of NUTE in failing to account for the whereabouts of NUTE can not be considered as appropriate. It would seem that management did not have a strategy in place to ensure follow up action after the completion of a bushwalker safety form."

Chep recommended that the safety form be redesigned to ensure a local contact address is nominated and safety responsibility be jointly managed by the department and tourist accommodation enterprises.

Chep concluded: "I do not believe that making bushwalkers responsible for their own safety enhances the ideals of the Department of Environment, especially for this particular area of the State of Queensland where visitor use is increasing at an astronomical rate."

In June 1998, almost a year after Daniel Nute went missing, a 19-year-old Swiss tourist survived three days lost in the Mt Sorrow region, narrowly avoiding a tragic end to his Cape Tribulation visit.

Pat Shears said the hiker's survival was due to good luck and not good judgement.

"He somehow headed north and stumbled down one of the creeks onto the road where someone picked him up and brought him back, but he was incredibly lucky to make it out of there."

Four months later two British backpackers repeated the mistake by walking past the Mt Sorrow lookout into dense terrain and becoming hopelessly lost. Glenn Hill, 28, and Sean Bates, 27, from Darlington in northeastern England, were found by a Queensland Rescue helicopter crew after wandering lost for 45 hours in the rain and cold. They were spotted from the air after lighting a fire in a clearing on Duncan Flats, about five kilometres east of Roaring Meg Falls.

The two men, who claimed they were both experienced bushwalkers, called on the Department of Environment to close the trail, claiming it was unsafe. Bates said the pair had been following marker tags on their hike up Mt Sorrow when they lost the track and followed a creek, expecting to emerge on the coast. The creek, however, flowed in the opposite direction, leading them further into the wilderness. The men ate chocolate and drank from the creek, sheltering from the rain under rocks and trees.

"There were times when I thought we weren't going to make it," Hill said.

The men said they were "surprised" authorities allowed people to walk in such a dangerous area, adding it wouldn't happen in England.

But the Department of Environment's Lindsay Delzoppo rejected the criticism as unrealistic, saying European visitors were used to formed paths and boardwalks and did not understand that bushwalking in Australia was a different experience in a different environment and great care must be taken. He said a sign warning hikers they had reached the summit of Mt Sorrow was to be erected in the near future.

Pat Shears was also involved in the search for Bates and Hill and said it was a classic case of hikers walking too far after reaching the peak and then getting disoriented in the maze of gulleys and boulders.

"These two blokes told the police that if they had the right information they wouldn't have gone so far," Shears said. "They'd been told it would take three hours to get to the top and they made it in two and a half, so they thought 'this can't be it' and kept going. I thought they'd be heading towards Roaring Meg Falls so I advised the helicopter pilot, and that's where they were."

The air and land search for Bates and Hill, involving a helicopter, 40 State Emergency Service personnel, police, rangers and local volunteers cost almost $30,000.

In February 1999 Fraser Nute returned to north Queensland with his wife Polly, determined to find a clue to their son's mysterious disappearance. The couple were strengthened by their belief that Daniel was still alive, and that their faith in God would ensure he survived to eventually be reunited with them. They said members of the family had experienced "very significant dreams" that told them Daniel may not have hiked up the mountain at all, but instead had been kidnapped and held against his will somewhere in the wilderness of Cape York Peninsula.

"I've had dreams of meeting Daniel somewhere in the rainforest, and sometimes of being reunited with him back in England," Nute said. "The incredible thing is these dreams are not mine alone but our other three children experience them too." He said two of his children, Emily and Ben, who both lived away from home, had identical dreams to his. "The three of us have dreamed very specifically about Daniel's return in very similar circumstances on the same night, but we've only realised this when we've compared notes days later.

"You can't engineer such things as this. It's absolutely stunning. I wake up in the night and think how extraordinary this is."

Nute said his other daughter, Mary, dreamed that Daniel was being held in "some sort of captivity" and he was very distressed, but was eventually found by the family.

"Daniel told Mary in the dream that two things sustained him during his time in captivity. He repeated the Lord's Prayer constantly, and he read a tiny card she had sent him with the 23rd psalm from the Bible on it, which he carried in his wallet."

He said Daniel shared his family's deep Christian convictions and was very resilient, "somewhat of a survivor", and that would help him through whatever crisis was before him.

"This is an extraordinary mystery that does not make sense, but God reveals mysteries we can't understand. God is in control of this."

Polly Nute said a family friend's six-year-old son had said God told him that Daniel would come out of a cave but would be a long time coming home.

"Then the idea of a cave or cavern started to emerge from the dreams and thoughts of people around us," she said. "Five of our friends over a single weekend told us they felt God had given them the word "cave". That could mean physical captivity or mental captivity, certainly some kind of imprisonment.

"We've wondered whether he might have disappeared into some kind of a secret cult, and although we have nothing to go on, that's a possibility."

In March a coronial inquest into Daniel Nute's disappearance was told the National Parks and Wildlife Service's previous "trip sheet" safety system was seriously flawed and a replacement program that put the responsibilty for safety back onto bushwalkers was just as bad.

Senior Constable Symon Punter, who took part in the searches for the missing backpacker, was critical of the self-registration procedure at the Mt Sorrow ranger base, which he said was unsatisfactory and compared poorly with other systems, such as the one used by the Coast Guard.

"Daniel Nute filled in the trip sheet but there was no follow-up when he didn't return, and we learned this was quite normal," Punter told the court. "Tourists became complacent about the trip sheet and it gave bushwalkers a false sense of security because they thought they would be safe. Subsequently we were unable to find Daniel."

Punter said his investigations revealed that nobody sighted Nute on the mountain and there was no confirmation he went there after filling in the trip sheet.

"We can only assume that Daniel did in fact walk up the mountain that day."

He said the National Parks and Wildlife Service changed the system after Nute disappeared and three other bushwalkers went missing in the same area but were all found alive.

Ranger Hans Niewenhuizen confirmed there had been changes to the form since Daniel Nute disappeared and the Department of Environment no longer took responsibility for a bushwalker's safety.

"You still fill in the trip sheet, but it's become more complicated," he said. "You must notify a friend and give contact details because we don't take responsibility. The person filling in the form must take responsibility."

Niewenhuizen said there was no printed information available about conditions on the Mt Sorrow track, but rangers pointed out to tourists it wasn't an easy walk.

"I wouldn't personally allow single walkers to go up there, a buddy system would be better."

Responding to a suggestion from P.K's Jungle Village's solicitor, Leeanne Bou-Samra, that the track should be closed down, Niewenhuizen replied: "How? Put a fence around it? They'd just go around that. There's a number of ways to go up there and then we'd never find them."

Niewenhuizen said up to 200 bushwalkers a month used the Mt Sorrow track in the tourist season, but "that's only the people we know of". He said the track was rarely used by the public in the wet season.

Niewenhuizen gave evidence that on the day Nute went missing the ranger base was extremely short-staffed and the ranger on duty had many other "chores" to do as well as man the base. He said three rangers looked after the Cape Tribulation area and because the base was only manned part-time "we check it as we go past to see what's going on."

Niewenhuizen said while Nute "looked like a walker" the Italian tourists "looked like city people" so he advised them to only walk part-way up the mountain. "I believe they did that, but I wasn't there when they came back."

The ranger said the system had problems but there were not enough staff available to check on every tourist who goes on a bushwalk.

"We can't follow up everybody (because) there's simply not enough time and not enough people on the ground," he said. "We can't undertake to look for you if you don't come back, that's what it boils down to now."

Niewenhuizen told the inquest he had lived in the area for 24 years and had been involved in four searches for missing people on Mt Sorrow.

Christopher Richard Hopkin, a receptionist at P.K's Jungle Village, tried to claim privilege from giving evidence but Coroner Ross Risson ruled that he must answer the questions. Hopkin testified that Daniel Nute booked in to the resort on 28 July 1997 for a five-day stay but police weren't notified about his absence until August 20, even though his tent was still pitched in the camping area.

Hopkin said the resort hosted about 60 campers a day at that time of the year and although tents were regularly abandoned by backpackers, they were "not checked immediately" by staff. Hopkin said backpackers moving on often just leave their tents erected and throw what they don't want inside and leave without notifying resort staff.

"When they hit Cape Tribulation it's the end of the line for some and when they're heading off to catch a plane they don't worry about a $60 tent."

Fraser Nute told the inquest: "Having listened so far it would seem we are simply discovering an unfortunate series of errors at P.K's and the ranger station, but our intention is not to point the finger, or apportion blame, but to establish where our son is and what happened to him.

"We happen to believe he could well still be alive, and as Christians God has told us that, but I have no material evidence to establish that."

The lessee of PK's Jungle Village, Peter Kaye, said notes were left on Daniel Nute's tent in an attempt to contact him, but the nature of the resort meant backpackers were constantly on the move and very difficult to locate.

"We can't track people down. Some people just jump on a bus and we have no check on them at all."

The inquest was adjourned and resumed on 4 May to hear further evidence.

Store manager Paul Loeven testified he spoke to a young backpacker at Wujal Wujal Aboriginal community, north of Cape Tribulation, about the same time Daniel Nute disappeared.

"He said he was from Devon and I've been there, so that was familiar and we spoke for about 20 minutes. When I saw the photo of Daniel in the newspaper I didn't have any negative feelings, but even though I wasn't 100 per cent sure it was the same person, it could have been him."

Loeven said the man had not mentioned Mt Sorrow or that he'd been on a particular walk, but he talked about working on conservation projects and on a cattle station.

"I told him he should contact the DPI (Department of Primary Industries)."

Loeven told the inquest he had recently met Fraser and Polly Nute and told them the man he had spoken to commented about how low prices were in the store.

"His parents confirmed that Daniel would have commented on that."

At 2pm on 21 May 1999, almost two years after he disappeared on Mt Sorrow, Daniel Nute was officially declared dead.

Coroner Ross Risson ended his findings with the solemn words: "I have concluded that Daniel Fraser Nute perished on or about July 29, 1997, and because of the environment, including feral animals, it is unlikely that any trace of Daniel will be found."

Risson said Nute had become depressed in Darwin after arriving from Indonesia and splitting up with his girlfriend. Later, working in Alice Springs, he was accused of unauthorised use of a mobile phone and placed on probation. On 18 March 1997, in what Risson called a "curious incident in Canberra" Nute allegedly reported to federal police a sum of money had been stolen from him, but later admitted the claim was false. A police source later confirmed Nute made a complaint to a Beat Squad office in Canberra that his "bumbag" had been "ripped off" his waist as he walked along the street. After questioning he allegedly confessed he lied and made the story up for "insurance reasons". The police source said this is not an uncommon ploy among backpackers travelling on a budget.

In his findings Risson said it was "not possible to be 100 per cent certain he (Nute) went up Mt Sorrow" but "there was no evidence he would want to hide" for any reason.

"The tragic fashion of Daniel's disappearance highlights the deficiencies of the trip sheet system. Changes have been made and recommendations have been made to improve the safety for walkers. I do not intend to make any recommendations.

"Subsequent to Daniel's disappearance others have been lost on Mt Sorrow (but) happily all have been recovered."

Risson said despite police investigations into several possible sightings of Nute, none had been confirmed as fact.

"Whatever responsibility PK's at the Jungle Village site (had) the evidence is clear he was last sighted at the ranger station. There is no evidence he returned to PK's.

"The check of the tents is purely commercial to ensure visitors pay the proper amount due for their stay at the resort."

Risson found there was insufficient evidence to charge any person in relation to Nute's disappearance.

Fraser and Polly Nute were back in England when the coroner handed down his findings. Although critical of the manner in which it was conducted, they were resigned to the fact the inquest would conclude their son was dead.

"The inquest all along was going to be as much about national park ranger practices and policies, as about the disappearance of our son," Fraser Nute said.

"It did strike me as bizarre that for a major, important hearing, there were only two and a half hours left in the afternoon, and then they have to adjourn and come back after the weekend or in this case several weeks time.

"We don't feel it would help to expose the situation, or right the wrong, or deal with the incompetence and threaten to sue. That wouldn't achieve anything, and so we forgive those people for their incompetence, but that doesn't mean we excuse it. When you forgive somebody, you're not saying they were right in what they were doing and you can't exercise critical judgement on the whole situation."

The Nutes rejected the possibility that Daniel deliberately chose to drop out of contact with them and assume a new life elsewhere.

"No, there is no question of that, I have absolute certainty of that, but there are so many unanswered questions, that's the mystery," Fraser Nute said. "There's stories of people who go missing and then they turn up years later. Yes, loss of memory, that is a possibility.

"A hard-nosed cop will think we are desperate people clutching at straws, but this is our son and because we know him he might be out there making a bit of money. OK, he hasn't accessed his bank account, but it would be in his temperament not to touch that, but to make money as he travelled. He's quite shrewd, keen on making money - there's a bit of an entrepreneurial streak about him."

Nute said he believed Paul Loeven's evidence in particular was very credible and this had reinforced the family's conviction that Daniel was alive and for some unexplainable reason hadn't contacted them.

"The young man who spoke to Paul fits Daniel's physical description and sounds very much like him in speech and manner as well, so we believe this could be a genuine contact with our son."

He said the coroner's finding was only one man's opinion and there was no material evidence to prove Daniel had disappeared on the mountain.

"If the name Mt Sorrow means anything to us at all, it's because Jesus is described in the Bible as 'a man of sorrows and acquainted with grief'. There's something very special about the fact that Jesus knows what we're going through.

"We still have hope and confidence that we will see Daniel again and in a quite remarkable way we can trust God to resolve this, because at the end of the day it's God's responsibility, and that takes a strong load off us."

CHAPTER NINE

A LONELY PLACE TO DIE

Did Angela Mealing commit suicide at lonely Behana Creek, or was she taken there against her will and murdered?

It was Saturday 1 April 2000, and Angela Maree Mealing was looking forward to enjoying a party with her friends that night. She had a sleep in the afternoon and was woken by her mother at 3pm and asked if she wanted to go to a rugby league football match and watch her cousin play. She said no and went back to sleep. Later she bought a pizza and when her brother Arron came home from basketball she teased him with the takeaway food, a ritual the close siblings often shared together. Arron left for work at about 4.30pm, and sometime after that the 17-year-old with the striking green-blue eyes left the family's White Rock home on the southern edge of Cairns to catch a bus into the city.

The teenage girl was her usual outgoing self that day, and there was nothing in her behaviour that suggested anything unusual was happening in her life. Her office administration studies at TAFE college were going well and and she was earning an income from her part-time job in a Japanese restaurant. She was, according to her family and friends, acting normal and appeared to be happy.

Mealing was to meet her friend Leonie "Yabby" Wood at a house in the Cairns suburb of Mooroobool. It was a housewarming get-together for a group of ATSI (Aboriginal and Torres Strait Islander) teenagers whom Mealing "hung out" with, even though her mother disapproved of the company. Wood had been mates with Mealing - whose nickname was "Rugz", because her friends said she dressed like a "rag lady" - since they were both 13-year-olds together in school.

Wood saw nothing unusual in Mealing's behaviour that night either. She was the same feisty, no-nonsense personality everybody knew and admired. At some point Mealing went to the nearby Balaclava Hotel, bought a cask of wine, and returned to the party. They were just a group of friends enjoying a few drinks together and having a good time. No-one could predict the dark events that would unfold later that night.

It was only when Ashley Baira arrived around 9 o'clock that trouble began to brew. Mealing had recently met Baira and the two had started seeing each other, but she kept the liason secret from her mother and the rest of the family. At the party a dispute soon erupted between Baira and another girl who was previously involved with him. It's believed the girl was upset that Baira was with Mealing. This led to a slanging match and Baira was ordered to leave because of his bad language - but he refused to go unless Mealing left as well.

"Eventually Angie left with him and that was the cause of what happened next," Leonie Wood later said. "It was a fight over him."

Mealing and Baira then briefly visited another teenage gathering at a nearby home before several females from the first party followed the pair to a nearby footbridge over Chinaman Creek, a route that connected residential Mooroobool to busy Mulgrave Road. Mealing was suddenly set upon and punched repeatedly until Baira intervened and stopped the assault, leading her away towards brightly-lit Mulgrave Road. Mealing was distressed by the attack and complained to Baira about his female friends, demanding he do something about their behaviour. But on a traffic island in the middle of Mulgrave Road, the tall, strongly built Baira lost his temper and punched Mealing in the face, a blow that knocked her to the road surface, cutting her mouth and head on a concrete edge of the island.

Angela Mealing's night of fun and laughter had turned bleak and menacing.

At about 11.30pm the pair walked south along Mulgrave Road towards Earlville, where a party was in full swing at the business premises of Solomons Carpets, with revellers spilling out into the driveway. As Baira and Mealing drew closer, Baira was recognised by an old schoolmate, David Roberts, who was celebrating his twenty-first birthday. Although he was "pretty drunk" Roberts asked Baira about Mealing's injuries, and Baira allegedly confessed he had punched her in the mouth after she had been bashed by some girls. Someone else from the party asked Baira why he had blood on his shirt, but he refused to comment further.

Mealing was taken inside by several female partygoers who cleaned her injuries and tried to calm her down. Deborah Laurie saw that both Mealings's lips were puffy, she had a deep cut on the top of her head, and blood on her face, arms and clothes. Although Mealing's voice was slurry, her eyes were focused and she didn't appear to be drunk. She refused offers to call police or be taken to hospital but silently mouthed "get me away from him", indicating Baira outside. She told the women she had no money but didn't want her mother to see her in that state.

After attempts to get Mealing over the back fence failed, she was taken through the office and let out the front door of the showroom, which was out of Baira's line of sight from where he was standing in the driveway. Deborah Laurie whispered to her: "Run for it, make a reverse charge phone call and get someone to come and get you."

It was around 20 minutes past midnight when Mealing left, heading south on Mulgrave Road. Half an hour later, when Baira realised Mealing had gone, he went looking for her. Security surveillance tapes show him walking south for a short distance, then heading back towards Cairns.

Angela Mealing didn't make it home that night, and her family and friends never saw her again.

It didn't take long for serious concerns to emerge for the girl's safety. Her mother, Jacqueline Shadforth, had felt the first twinges of alarm on Saturday night. Her daughter had left home without leaving a message to say where she'd gone. By late Sunday morning, Shadforth had found out from Angela's friends about the party and a witness informed her of the subsequent assault by the young females. Shadforth was worried and phoned the police. By Monday, the seriousness of the situation was enough for Detective Senior Sergeant Glenn Terry of the Cairns CIB to declare: "A young girl disappearing off the face of the Earth is of grave concern for her family and for police."

Media coverage of Mealing's disappearance led to a bus driver coming forward to tell police the girl and a youth were last off his bus near her home in Dundee Close, White Rock, at about 11pm on Saturday. He said Mealing had a cut lip and bruises on her face. However, police investigations later found that although the driver had recognised Mealing from previous occasions on the bus he was mistaken about seeing her on the Saturday night.

A massive search of the White Rock area by detectives, uniformed police and State Emergency Services volunteers failed to find any trace of the missing teenager. Leonie Wood and other friends who had been with Mealing at the Mooroobool party appealed to the public to help police solve the puzzle of what had happened to their friend.

Several days later the search for Mealing took a dramatic turn when police probationary constable Adrian Deemal informed detectives, including members of the Brisbane Homicide Squad, that he had picked the girl up late on the night she disappeared and driven her to Gordonvale, a sugar town 25 kilometres south of Cairns.

Deemal, a 39-year-old former diesel mechanic and father of two, had recently been on leave, but had taken part in the search for the missing girl when he returned to work. The trainee officer had been in the Police Service for two years and was mainly involved with traffic operations and other non-investigative duties.

His startling revelation came as a complete shock to investigators who were struggling for a lead to the girl's whereabouts.

Deemal told detectives he had been driving south along Mulgrave Road on his way to Edmonton at about 2.15am on Sunday when he saw Mealing in a dishevelled state, staggering along the road outside the Cairns Golf Club - a distance of two and a half kilometres from the Solomons Carpets showroom and about half-way to her home in White Rock. He said he stopped his vehicle under a street light and, after a brief conversation, she got in the car. He said her lips were covered in blood and she was disoriented. When he turned the car's interior light on he saw the cut on the top of her head. She explained her boyfriend had bashed her and they had a conversation about her injuries before he did a U-turn and headed back towards the city to take her to hospital for treatment.

But according to Deemal, Mealing refused to go to hospital and asked to be taken to Gordonvale instead. Deemal said he turned the car around when they were about one kilometre from the hospital and headed back out of the city. He said he dropped Mealing off in Riverstone Road, about 150 metres from a service station on the corner of Riverstone Road and the Bruce Highway. He told detectives he then drove through Gordonvale and back to Cairns.

Deemal, who is a member of a prominent north Queensland Aboriginal family, said he'd had a fight with his wife over marital problems and had left their Mooroobool home on Friday, sleeping in his car at The Pier Marketplace carpark that night. The next day, Saturday 1 April, Deemal said he booked into the Adobe Motel on Sheridan Street under an assumed name because he didn't want his wife to discover his whereabouts.

But after detectives re-enacted his movements to check time sequences, Deemal changed his story and volunteered a different series of events. At an interview on Friday 7 April, Deemal insisted on the presence of his solicitor Bebe Mellick before answering questions. In his new version of events, Deemal told police he cancelled a booking for a boat he had hired for a fishing trip on Saturday, and was reimbursed with a $300 deposit which he partly used to book a room in the Adobe Motel that morning. He said he went to sleep on the top of the bedcovers in room number 15 until about 3.30pm and then went out for a sandwich and to buy a six-pack of beer at a Freshwater hotel. Back at the motel, Deemal said he had a couple of beers in the bar before driving to Edmonton where he had several more beers with his brother. At about 10.30pm he said he left and drove to his cousin's house at Matilda Close, Woree, and watched a rugby league football game.

Deemal's wanderings then allegedly took him into the city where he parked in Lake Street and briefly visited the My Bar night club before walking down Spence Street to the Underdog Hotel and then the Sports Bar Saloon. Deemal said he didn't see anyone he knew, so he returned to his car and drove to The Pier Marketplace and sat in the car park. He said by this time it was 1.15am, and he stayed there for another 30-45 minutes.

The only problem with that scenario was that video tapes taken from a security camera stationed at the Sports Bar club doesn't show any vision of him when he was supposed to be there. Neither do video tapes taken from a camera positioned at the top of the escalator leading to My Bar show him at the night club.

Deemal couldn't explain to police why he didn't appear on the video tapes.

Deemal's second version of events then has him driving south on Mulgrave Road and encountering Angela Mealing. While driving back to Cairns with her, Mealing allegedly told him her father was in jail for murder and she lived on the streets. She said she wanted a drink and Deemal drove to the rear of a city motel known to sell after-hours takeaway alcohol, where he purchased a six-pack of beer. According to Deemal it was then about 3.10am and he drove to a quiet spot in Upward Street, about one kilometre from the hospital, where they each drank half a stubby of beer. He then drove Mealing to Gordonvale because, as he explained to police, "I didn't want her wandering around on her own". He said he was back at the Adobe Motel and in bed by 4am.

Police asked Deemal how close he thought the time estimates of his movements thaty night were, and he replied he might be 30 minutes out, but his recall would be "pretty close".

But Deemal's time-keeping was out by two hours. Security tapes and witnesses had him buying the six-pack of beer at 1.04am and a packet of cigarettes at a nearby service station in Sheridan Street a few minutes later. He couldn't explain the difference in time.

It didn't take police investigators long to work out Deemal didn't drop Angela Mealing in Riverstone Road as he claimed he did. Careful examination of 24-hour security video tapes taken from two cameras mounted at the Shell service station showed no sign of Deemal's red Toyota Lexen sedan in the area that night. Just to make sure the cameras covered the exact spot, police did a re-enactment of the scene with another vehicle. The result was clear. If Deemal had dropped Mealing off in Riverstone Road that night, the tapes would show his car. They didn't. When confronted with this evidence, Deemal couldn't explain to police why his car wasn't in the footage.

Asked why he didn't come forward earlier given the wide media coverage, especially as he had taken part in the search for Mealing when he returned to work, Deemal told police he hadn't made the connection until a description of her clothing "pricked his memory". He also said he was embarrassed by the fact he was having problems with his wife and had booked into a motel under an assumed name the night he picked up the teenager.

However, a search of Deemal's home uncovered a newspaper article detailing Angela Mealing's disappearance, prompting a police officer to later remark: "It was difficult to believe he did not know of her disappearance."

Although police impounded Deemal's car for DNA tests and the Adobe Motel room was sealed off for scientific examination, detectives were careful to emphasise Angela Mealing's disappearance was still officially a missing persons case and Deemal was a "witness helping with the investigation", and not a crime suspect. The forensic tests proved negative. There was no evidence that the missing girl had been in Deemal's car and there was no evidence from his clothes that linked him to her. The police were back to square one in their search for new leads.

Deemal, however, was placed on "recreational leave".

With a team of detectives headed by Brisbane Homicide Squad chief Detective Inspector Graham Rynders working around the clock on what was now called Operation Hawthorne, there was little doubt in anyone's mind that Mealing wasn't coming home. Far North Region Crime Co-ordinator Inspector John Harris came as close as he could to confirming his worst fears: "Let's hope we are not looking for a body (but) it's a possibility," he said. "It's been a week and experience tells us that it doesn't look good."

Meanwhile a massive search continued around Gordonvale with particular attention being paid to creeks, bushland and canefields in the area. Wet weather hampered search efforts and further frustrated police in their now-desperate hunt for evidence that could lead to Mealing's whereabouts.

Jacqueline Shadforth canvassed friends and acquaintances of her missing daughter in a personal campaign, hoping someone could provide a clue to the puzzle. She door-knocked the

Mooroobool area and distributed posters showing the girl's photo and description. Police dressed a mannequin in clothes similar to those worn by the teenager and placed it on Mulgrave Road, near where she was last seen, hoping it would jog someone's memory and provide a breakthrough.

On 19 April, the day after Adrian Deemal was interviewed by detectives for the third time, a Brisbane newspaper revealed the probationary officer had previous convictions for violence against a woman. The newspaper said court records showed Deemal was convicted twice in 1999 for breaches of a domestic violence order. He had also faced a charge of assault causing bodily harm, involving allegations he placed a knife to a woman's throat, but the charge was later dismissed when the complainant failed to appear for a court hearing.

Police questioned Deemal for several hours in a renewed attempt to piece together Angela Mealing's last known movements. Deemal's solicitor Bebe Mellick said his client denied any knowledge of the teenager's disappearance and was helping police in every way he could.

"He's a quiet, unassuming man and he doesn't like all this publicity," Mellick said.

On Friday 12 May, Angela Mealing's family gathered to mark the missing teenager's eighteenth birthday. It was an occasion of despair and fading hope as the family struggled with the reality of a future without her. Jacqueline Shadforth's surprise birthday present for her daughter was to be an $11,000 package of tickets and accommodation to the Sydney Olympic Games she had won in a national competition.

"It was going to be a trip of a lifetime for her and Arron, but if Angie's not here Arron won't go, so the tickets are meaningless if she doesn't come back," Shadforth said, adding: "Your life is like roses until something like this happens, and then it turns black."

Two days later, on Sunday 14, a man and his son travelling through the area on a trip from the Northern Territory to their home in New South Wales, stopped near a bridge at Behana Creek, on the Bruce Highway south of Gordonvale, to see if they could catch any freshwater prawns for fish bait. Instead, they found a wallet and a foul smell and promptly notified police.

The next day a police team arrived and began a systematic search of the creek and its banks. They soon found human remains. There wasn't much left, just a skull and a few scattered bones, a shirt and a backpack containing a hairbrush and a handful of other personal items. Although there was no scientific proof that this was Angela Mealing, experienced detectives at the scene had no doubt their search for the missing teenager was over.

Her remains were found just five metres from a track that skirts the edge of a canefield and 50 metres upstream from the bridge. They were scattered in a peaceful sun-dappled glen at the base of majestic hardwood trees where birdsong can be heard over the muffled sound of traffic passing on the bridge.

Behana Creek is picturesque, but it was a lonely place for Angela Mealing to die. The creek is a rainforest-shrouded waterway that meanders from its source high on a mountain range down through fields of sugar to the beaches of the Great Barrier Reef. It's a place you don't expect death to visit, and it's hard to imagine the terror Mealing must have experienced there on her last night alive.

Behana Creek is eight kilometres from where Adrian Deemal said he left Mealing in Riverstone Road, Gordonvale.

There was a bizarre and chilling aspect to the death scene that police didn't reveal until several days later. Above her scattered remains, in a slender tree that was little more than a sapling, hung a noose fashioned from synthetic, clothesline-type rope. On the trunk of the tree, and on a smaller one beside it, were scratched the words: "I'm sorry mum be strong not your fault Ang". A heart symbol was scratched beside the message.

Police later conceded they had missed finding the noose on their first day inspecting the death scene. On the second day a police photographer looked up and saw the rope hanging in the tree. A clump of hair and traces of flesh were found on the noose. The rope was frayed and in poor condition, with a vine partly growing around it, signifying to police it had been in the tree "for some time".

Police later staged a re-enactment of a suicide attempt at the scene, using an officer of "roughly the same size and weight" as Mealing. Although the police team had forgotten to bring a rope, it's claimed an officer found a handy length "in a matter of minutes" a few metres away. The police experiment concluded that it was "relatively easy" for a female to stand on a branch and fashion a noose higher in a tree, but "very difficult if not impossible" to carry a limp body up a tree and place it in a noose.

Although the evidence at first suggested a macabre suicide, homicide investigators drew no conclusions, speculating the scene could have been an elaborate set-up to hide a murder. Although tight-lipped about details, detectives felt the suicide factor did not quite add up and their suspicions kept Operation Hawthorne open to the possibility that Mealing may have been taken to Behana Creek against her will and murdered.

It was a conundrum that frustrated police as they grappled with the known facts of the case, the evidence at the death scene, and their own gut feelings.

There was, of course, no doubt that Mealing died a violent death. But did this teenage girl who loved life really submit to some dark compulsive force and commit suicide in that lonely place? Or was she kidnapped and perhaps terrorised sexually before her life was taken away in those final, terrible hours?

Mealing's family and friends immediately rejected the suicide theory. In spite of their grief, they spoke out defiantly, insisting Mealing had never shown such tendencies. They pointed to obvious anomalies in the suicide scenario, weak links that would also be evident to investigating detectives. How did she manage to walk eight kilometres along the Bruce Highway, well-used by north-south bound motorists even late at night, without being seen? To do so she would have first passed the brightly-lit, 24-hour service station on the busy intersection of Riverstone Road and the highway. But, like Adrian Deemal's car, she is not shown on security video tapes of the area.

And why would she walk so far, in such a distressed state, to end her life at Behana Creek, when secluded areas of bushland and canefields completely surround Gordonvale? She would have crossed the bridge over the Mulgrave River 800 metres south of the service station, and no doubt looked into its dark waters as she contemplated suicide. Why didn't she walk down the track to the river and along its gloomy, tree-lined banks - an obvious and very convenient place to hang herself? Why did she continue walking along the highway past canefields, around the base of the landmark peak known as The Pyramid, past the local garbage dump shielded from the highway by bushland, then past several more canefields and side roads, until she reached Behana Creek?

Behana Creek is a most unlikely place for a young woman to commit suicide - especially by hanging herself from a small tree barely 75 centimetres in diameter. How did the tree - a flexible sapling the police removed for forensic testing - support her weight? How did the solidly-built female - who couldn't climb over a two-metre fence at the back of Solomons Carpets to escape Ashley Baira's unwelcome attention - climb up there in the first place, somehow attach the rope, place her head in the noose, and then drop? Despite the police re-enactment, it would have been an extremely awkward and difficult exercise. Nearby, a much stouter tree curves out over the creek, with ample room on the bank to attach a rope and swing out over a sheer drop to the water several metres below - a much easier option for a suicide attempt.

And if Angela Mealing did take that eight-kilometre walk along the Bruce Highway from Gordonvale without being seen it must have been a remarkable example of sheer chance. After all, Gordonvale police had no trouble spotting another female walking alone on the Mulgrave River bridge at 1.45am that same night.

Police officers Kane Johnson and Ronald Williams were in a patrol car when they stopped to talk to a barefoot woman with "shoulder length, curly hair" who told them she had been to a party in Gordonvale and was on her way home to Innisfail - a distance of 64 kilometres. A long walk home for a lone female with no shoes, but, according to Williams, it was an action "not entirely out of character for that area". The officers said the woman had no facial injuries and was not agitated in any way, but they got the impression "she didn't want to talk to police".

Further questions were asked by Mealing's family. Where did she get the rope? She certainly didn't have it earlier in the night at the party, or at Solomons Carpets showroom celebrations. And she didn't have a knife, so what did she use to carve her final message in the tree?

Police said a "metal strip" found under Mealing's backpack was at first thought to have been used to scratch the message, but tests ruled that theory out and police had "no explanation" for the presence of the strip. They said household garbage was found strewn in the death scene area and Mealing could have found the rope by chance among the debris.

Mealing's aunt Julie Arnol said her niece had never been to Behana Creek before, and the family didn't believe she went there willingly the night she went missing.

"She certainly didn't go out of the house that night to kill herself."

Arnol said the family believed Mealing was raped and murdered, but she would have resisted her abductor to the end.

"She would not have submitted quietly but would have fought hard. She would have threatened to tell her mother and go to the police, and that's why she was murdered."

Natalie Burke, 24, who was a close friend and confidante of Mealing, said she had known the teenager for eight years and thought of her as a younger sister. Burke said Mealing would "tell me everything, whether I approved or not" and suicide would be the last thing on her mind. "She was a normal, responsible teenager who saw the best in everybody."

Burke had no doubts that Mealing was murdered and the suicide message was a fake, because she always signed her name "Angela", never "Ang".

"If it is her writing she was forced to do it by someone else," Burke said.

Two days after Mealing's remains were found, Adrian Deemal was suspended from duty on full pay for "being untruthful" to police investigators during their search for the missing teenager. Police insisted he was "definitely not" a suspect and gave him 14 days to appeal the suspension.

Bebe Mellick said his client had not lied to investigators when he first approached them but had "withheld certain information" to avoid embarrassment to himself and his family. He said Deemal had then initiated a second interview to correct the situation.

The investigation into Mealing's death took a strange turn when a sports bra top and a massage-type sandal belonging to the teenager mysteriously appeared at the death scene after it had been previously searched by police several times. The items were found by Julie Arnol and other relatives during an emotional visit to place a cross and flowers at the site in Mealing's memory.

"We went there to make the place look nice and Dean, my son, called out 'Mum, come and look at this', and there was the top she had been wearing the night she disappeared hanging in a tree," Arnol said.

The sandal was found in a hollow cavity of a tree root.

Police were adamant the top and sandal weren't there when they had earlier examined the scene and must have been placed there later by a "person unknown".

Homicide Squad detective Graham Clark later said it would have been "impossible" for police to miss the clothing when they scoured the area for clues.

"My belief is Angela was wearing the bra the night she died and it was placed in the tree by someone who found it downstream and didn't want to get involved. I can't explain it any other way."

The find was a further bizarre link in an already convoluted chain of questions about clothing worn by Mealing on the night she disappeared.

Police revealed a bloodstained white Nike shirt found in Mealing's backpack was similar to one that several witnesses thought she was wearing the night she disappeared. But her skeletal remains were found in a sky blue, three-buttoned, collarless shirt that her family and friends were unable to identify. Police concluded that either somebody at the carpet showroom party had given her the shirt, or she had somehow acquired it after she left and headed along Mulgrave Road on her own.

Although an autopsy failed to identify a cause of death due to decomposition, a forensic examination of Mealing's remains showed no obvious signs of trauma to the jaw, skull or any other part of the recovered bones. In late May the remains were formally identified as those of the teenager.

On 7 June, 600 people attended Angela Mealing's funeral at St Monica's Cathedral in Cairns. Father Kevin Lewis told the packed congregation the tragedy of the teenager's death was compounded by the fact there was nobody there to help her when she was desperately in need.

"The fact is nobody took Angela safely home that night and that's why we're at this funeral today," he said. "We are each other's neighbours whether we like it or not."

Later, a police escort led a procession of mourners to a ceremony at the White Rock Crematorium.

That night, Adrian Deemal collapsed on a Cairns street and was taken to hospital with an "alcohol-related" illness. Solicitor Bebe Mellick would only say his client had been admitted overnight with a stomach complaint. A close relative of Deemal's said the suspended police officer had been under a lot of stress and "was drinking too much". The relative said Deemal had moved out of his home and was difficult to contact.

Deemal was formally sacked from the Queensland Police Service on 19 June following a disciplinary hearing before Deputy Police Commissioner Ron McGibbon at police headquarters in Brisbane. Deemal, whose dismissal was for lying to police investigators, did not attend the hearing.

Soon after his sacking, Deemal left Cairns and started work at a remote mining location on Cape York Peninsula.

Also in June the powerful Queensland Crime Commission conducted its own inquiry into the Mealing case but refused to reveal its findings, except to say "the results of the QCC hearings will be passed to the Queensland Police Service".

The Commission's "star chamber" style of investigation is believed to have included secret interviews with Deemal, his wife and family, and the people who attacked Angela on the night of her disappearance.

Legislation prevents any publication of evidence or identification of witnesses who appear before the closed-door hearings, and the QCC has a policy of neither confirming nor denying speculation about the nature of its investigations.

Crime Commissioner Tim Carmody said it would be "inappropriate" for him to say why the QCC was in Cairns.

"This is to preserve the integrity of its investigations and to protect the privacy of witnesses (and, in some cases, their safety). It is also, more generally, intended to avoid lending weight to rumour or giving rise to false hopes, unrealistic expectations or unjustified suspicions," Carmody said.

Throughout the police and QCC investigations, Jacqueline Shadforth maintained a steadfast belief that her daughter did not commit suicide and demanded her killer be found and brought to justice. While grief had caused her health to suffer, Shadforth was outspoken in her views and refused to be silenced by the passage of time and the gradual winding down of inquiries into Angela's death.

Shadforth made it plain on many occasions she didn't believe Deemal's story.

"Angela had no reason to go to Gordonvale. She had been bashed and she would have been walking home because she had no money. She wasn't far from home and safety.

"Every morning I wake up and think of that horrible place, if she was out there injured and suffering, and if we might have been able to save her had we known she was there."

Shadforth is adamant that the assaults on her daughter led directly to her death and she has publicly called for police to lay charges against the teenagers involved.

"Angie was distraught and vulnerable after they bashed her, and it affected her judgement - that's why she got in that car.

"There's no way she would do that normally. She was almost home and would have kept walking. I believe Angie was taken out there, raped and murdered, and as far as I'm concerned, everyone who assaulted her that night is an accessory to her murder and should be charged."

But Shadforth was told by senior police that without a complainant there is no evidence to charge any person with assault and there was nothing more the authorities could do.

"That's not good enough and I'm not going to stand for it," she said. "I know at least one of the offenders has admitted to the assault, but I'm told because Angie is dead there is nothing that can be done. They are the cause of her missing the bus home and of the state she was in that night. If they had left her alone she would have come home.

"I'll take civil action if I have to. They are not going to get away with this."

In desperation, the angry mother appealed to the Member for Mulgrave, Warren Pitt, to take up the issue with Police Minister Tony McGrady.

Pitt, a former teacher who once taught Angela Mealing, said he had a personal interest in the case and understood Shadforth's grief and frustration.

"It disturbs me that a number of people have allegedly signed statements over their involvement in the attacks on Angela, which is surely an admission of guilt, and if such admissions have been made, they should pay the penalty," he said.

"Mr McGrady has told me that police have decided not to lay charges, but I'm not satisfied with that answer, so the Minister has promised me a full report on the matter. If no charges can be laid as a point of law, one would wonder why that exists and why it can't be changed. In this case, the law defies description."

On 15 November 2001, a coronial inquest into Angela Mealing's death opened briefly in Cairns before being adjourned until April the following year. During the hearing, Coroner Ken Lynn accepted more than 20 exhibits, including video tapes, clothing, maps and photographs.

After the court adjourned, Lynn was accompanied by Crown solicitor Bill Isdale, investigating officer Detective Senior Sergeant Graham Clark and solicitor for Mealing's family, Ross Norman, to the Behana Creek site where the teenager's remains were found.

Outside the court Jacqueline Shadforth told reporters she hoped the inquest would help resolve the mystery of her daughter's death and bring justice to the family.

"I've cried every night since this happened and I know I can never get Angie back but the inquest might tell us the truth about how she died," she said.

Shadforth said she was not confident the law was capable of justice because of its present structure, but she intended to campaign for legislative changes that would allow police to prosecute the people who assaulted her daughter.

"I'll fight until the end and every bastard involved will pay for it," she said.

On 2 April 2002, on the second anniversary of Angela Mealing's fateful last walk, the inquest into her death resumed. On day one, the court heard evidence from detective Graham Clark, who outlined the police investigation into the case, including Adrian Deemal's conflicting stories about his movements on the night, and his failure to fully explain his actions.

The next day Deemal claimed privilege and refused to testify on the grounds such evidence might incriminate him.

Showing no emotion before a public gallery packed with Mealing's relatives and friends, Deemal briefly told the court he had been a probationary police officer for two years at the time of the girl's disappearance and death.

"I was not fully trained, a trainee at the time, doing traffic duties and office duties," he said.

Deemal said he was currently employed as a machinery operator.

Counsel assisting the coroner Bill Isdale asked Deemal if he knew a person known as Angela Mealing.

At this point Bebe Mellick intervened and claimed privilege for his client.

Isdale told the court the purpose of an inquest was to ascertain the evidence and a cause of death, and whether someone should be charged with murder or manslaughter.

"Technically I could stand here all day and ask questions but it would be futile, a useless exercise," he said.

Jacqueline Shadforth told the court her daughter was a happy, well-adjusted person who had never shown any suicidal tendencies, and had always turned to her for help when it was needed. She said she had never seen the blue shirt found with her daughter's remains and was sure it didn't belong to her.

Shadforth said her daughter "could hardly tie her shoelaces" and would be incapable of tying the noose and attaching it to the tree at the death scene.

"She had no knowledge of ropes and was not athletic enough to pull her own body weight upwards," she said.

In an emotional address to the court, Shadforth said her daughter should have been delivered home by Deemal on the night she disappeared.

"Why did he drive Angela straight past her home with blood all over her? He was a policeman with the authority to take her to hospital. She was nearly home."

Shadforth said police had given her daughter's poems, lyrics and artwork to a psychiatrist to be analysed, but most of the work was copied from popular songs and some came from her friends. Shadforth said a drawing with references to good and evil was actually a school assignment.

Barrister Jim Henry, counsel for Mealing's family, said the artwork studied by the psychiatrist was only part of a much broader body of work, most of which comprised "hopeful and optimistic topics".

"The psychiatrist might have focused on quite gloomy subjects," he said.

In a phone link-up to Brisbane, Senior Sergeant John Kranenburg, a rope expert with the Major Event Planning Department, said he had studied the various knots on the noose and although the arrangement was not sophisticated it would perform its purpose "very, very well". He said the noose was tied in such a way "the loop would tighten when pulled", but would need "a degree of trial and error, good luck, or pre-existing knowledge", to achieve.

"Some knowledge or thought was put into tying the knots," Kranenburg told the court.

The second witness to claim privilege on the grounds his evidence might incriminate him was Ashley Baira, the man who admitted to police he had assaulted Angela Mealing on the night she disappeared.

Before claiming privilege, Baira told the court he had given police a false version of events when he was first interviewed about his involvement with Mealing.

"I was frightened when I gave the first statement after she went missing. They (the police) were talking rough to me. I was scared then - I was doing community service, and I was worried about her, wondering what happened to her. The first time I told them I took her to a bus stop, but I lied - she took off from the party."

At this point, when advised by Coroner Lynn that he could claim privilege from further questioning, Baira promptly did so.

Nicole Roberts testified she was at the Solomons Carpets party when Baira and Mealing turned up outside the showroom. She told the court Mealing had wanted to get away from Baira without him knowing.

"She just kept repeating she wanted to go home," Roberts said.

The court was told a witness saw a red vehicle drive out of Behana Creek and head back towards Gordonvale late at night "on or about" 3 April, the day after Mealing disappeared.

Barry Malcolm Campbell, a waste transfer station supervisor, said he had been shopping in Gordonvale and was heading south to El Arish to start work at midnight when he saw "what looked like a red sedan, similar to the one in the paper" come out of the dirt road alongside Behana Creek, just as he crossed the bridge.

"It was dark and I couldn't see people inside or the number plates."

Campbell said he came forward after he read about the missing girl, hoping the information might help police. He told the court he was at first "fearful for my life" but was persuaded to tell his story to the authorities.

"I didn't want to get involved but when it came on TV, a friend said you should tell police and he phoned up (the police)," Campbell said.

Deemal's cousin Audrey Deemal testified she was with Deemal until just before midnight on the night Mealing disappeared. She said she and her niece Sacheen drove with Deemal to his brother Harold's place in Edmonton at 8.30pm to pick up some clothes and then returned home. She said they all watched a game of football on television and Deemal left about 11.45pm, returning to the house early next morning when he went to sleep on a couch. She told the court her cousin mentioned to her on 7 April he'd had "dealings" with the police over the missing girl but didn't tell her anything further.

She gave evidence no red car was cleaned at the house in the days that followed Mealing's disappearance, contrary to claims made by a neighbour who had contacted police.

In his closing submissions Jim Henry said the evidence had not proved "the matter of when, where and how" the teenager's death had occurred, and "there was every reason why an open finding would appear to be consistent with the standard of proof required".

On 3 May, Coroner Lynn handed down an open finding into the death of Angela Mealing.

In his finding, Lynn said even though "hanging or strangulation" could not be ruled out as the cause of Mealing's death, the decomposed state of her remains meant the actual cause could not be conclusively determined.

"There remain unanswered questions and I am not satisfied it was caused by hanging," he said.

Lynn said that although Deemal's different versions of his movements meant his statements were unreliable, there was no evidence any harm had come to Mealing in his car.

"That raises the question of where Deemal drove the deceased and what occurred between the two," he said. "Deemal has not told the whole story of the circumstances of his time with her.

"Why he came forward and told so many lies remains unexplained."

Lynn said evidence suggested Mealing was looking forward to the future and that her state of mind was not consistent with an intention to kill herself.

He said evidence from witnesses revealed Mealing had been drinking at the party earlier on in the night and was a "bit drunk" but not staggering as Deemal told police she was when he picked her up.

"The inference is Deemal stopped to pick her up for some other reason," he said.

In his finding, Lynn said a "cryptic" message found on a tree at the death scene that said: "I'm sorry mum be strong not your fault" was carved by someone using an unknown implement. He suggested a significant time would have been needed to carve the message and if Mealing had still been alive at daybreak it was possible she did it herself, but that could not be determined with certainty. There was an inference, he said, suggesting an unknown person or persons fabricated the final message "and if that happened death could have occurred at an unknown place."

"If someone knew her whereabouts (that night) we might not be here today," he said. "It may be that more useful information has not been forthcoming about the final movements of the deceased."

Lynn concluded that although the cause of Mealing's death was unknown there was insufficient evidence for anyone to be charged with any offence.

The open finding was both a victory and a loss for Jacqueline Shadforth and her family. On the one hand it meant there was no proof that her daughter had committed suicide, but on the other hand it also meant there was no actual proof she had been murdered.

Shadforth said she intended to keep asking questions and appealed to anyone with more information to "come forward to clear their conscience so they can sleep at night".

"I will keep fighting for the truth and never give up until the murderer is caught," she said.

CHAPTER TEN

THE LAST DIVE OF TOM AND EILEEN LONERGAN

They were left behind on the Great Barrier Reef and were never seen again, but what really happened to the Lonergans during that long night alone at sea?

It was a postcard perfect day at the dive site called Fish City when American scuba diving enthusiasts Thomas Joseph Lonergan and Eileen Cassidy Lonergan went missing on the Great Barrier Reef. The water was crystal clear and dead calm as the couple prepared for a third and final dive before the tourist charter vessel *Outer Edge* would begin the 38 nautical mile home journey back to Port Douglas.

The Lonergans, from Baton Rouge, Louisiana, were looking forward to their exploration of Fish City's coral "bommie" - a subsurface coral outcrop - measuring about 80 metres by 20 metres, just off the northwestern tip of St Crispin Reef, the first of a string of "ribbon" reefs that stretch north along the edge of the continental shelf. A short distance from the shelf, the ocean drops dramatically into the deep waters of the Coral Sea.

This is a busy part of the Great Barrier Reef for the tourist industry. Just over two nautical miles north from Fish City, in the Agincourt Reefs group, large catamarans berth at a giant two-storey pontoon owned by Port Douglas company Quicksilver Connections where several hundred tourists swim, snorkel and scuba dive daily. Nearby, a helicopter platform is permanently anchored. Another three nautical miles further north, an even bigger pontoon provides a marine playground for 450 visitors at a time.

But *Outer Edge* is a smaller vessel and Fish City - named by the crew for its abundance of marine life - was an ideal location for its more intimate complement of 26 passengers.

It was just after 2pm on Sunday 25 January 1998, when *Outer Edge* owner Geoffrey (Jack) Nairn gave the eager group a dive site brief, and divemaster Harald Klose announced the dive plan. Nairn was relief skipper on his boat that day, filling in for regular skipper Marcus Knight who was busy moving house that weekend. The dive plan was clear and concise. At Fish City, the dive depth was to be 12 metres and the duration of the dive strictly 40 minutes. Earlier in the day, *Outer Edge* had visited two other dive sites and Fish City was to be the easiest and most enjoyable of all. Everybody was keen to go. At 2.20pm the divers entered the water.

Underwater, it was peaceful and serene. There was a neutral, or "slack" tide, with virtually no current, and the water was a warm 29 degrees. The divers marvelled at the bommie pinnacle which rises from a depth of 20 metres to a metre below the surface, and they swam around it, eagerly inspecting the coral organisms and other marine life. Visibility was 15 metres and the divers felt they were swimming in a fish tank. This was what people paid for and at Fish City they were getting their money's worth.

Dive instructor Karl Jesienowski, a qualified marine biologist and Class 5 skipper with over 4,000 dives experience, escorted a group of resort (inexperienced) divers around the site. He called the conditions "absolutely idyllic", and all the divers were clearly visible and comfortable.

Tom and Eileen Lonergan were diving as a buddy pair and there was no reason for concern. Tom was 34 and Eileen 29, they were both physically fit, confident scuba divers with their own professional equipment and over 80 dives each to their credit - 45 of those logged in the past year. They had arrived in Queensland 10 days before on a three-month visa after serving three years as volunteer teachers with the US Peace Corps in Fiji and Tuvalu.

The Lonergans had been together since they were students at Louisiana State University. Tom Lonergan had graduated with a degree in chemical engineering and then served four years in the Air Force in Albuquerque, New Mexico. Eileen Lonergan received a degree in geology from the University of New Mexico. The couple joined the Peace Corps in 1994 and Fiji was the first in a string of countries they intended to visit on a scuba dive odyssey that, as well as Australia, would include Indonesia, France and Hawaii, before returning home to America.

Jesienowski, who had chatted with the couple throughout the day, said they were the ideal buddy types, and he rated their experience highly.

"On the whole they were in the top five per cent of the type of divers you feel confident in letting into the water," he later said.

At 2.45pm, English tourist Bryan Brogdan swam past the Lonergans on his way to the surface. Tom Lonergan pointed to a starfish and a giant clam and Brogdan gave the "OK" signal in return. Brogdan, an experienced scuba diver who uses a dive computer, said he was out of the water at 3.05pm.

With the divers back on deck and cleaning up, assisted by Jesienowski, Harald Klose and dive instructor George Pyrohiw, Jack Nairn was almost ready to take *Outer Edge* home. The other crew member, Katherine Traverso, who was acting as a divemaster and part-time hostess that day, was busy recording dive profiles.

Brendan Vidian, a Cairns systems analyst, said he asked Nairn for permission to jump off the bow of the boat for one last swim and was told to make it quick. Nairn later denied giving his express permission to do this, but in any case restaurant manager Simon Townsend joined Vidian and the pair dived into the water, swam back to the stern and clambered on board.

After helping Klose and Pyrohiw clean the scuba gear, Jesienowski was asked to go overboard and manually recover an environmentally sensitive anchor from a coral head because the vessel's winch wasn't working. While he was underwater removing the anchor, taking care not to damage the coral, and then waiting on the surface for the anchor and line to be stowed, Fish City was peaceful and Jesienowski saw no signs of activity below. He was the last person back on the boat and estimated between 55 and 65 minutes had elapsed since the divers first entered the water.

Jack Nairn scanned the water's surface for several minutes as he idled the boat's engine. Everything appeared normal and, sometime around 3.30pm, 25 minutes after the last diver climbed back on board, the skipper steered *Outer Edge* away from Fish City and headed for Port Douglas.

The trouble was, Tom and Eileen Lonergan weren't on the boat. It was two days before the Louisiana couple was reported missing and 60 hours before a search got under way.

Norman Stignant, a tour bus driver who was due to drive the couple back to their hostel in Cairns, wasn't worried when they failed to appear after *Outer Edge* returned to Port Douglas because he said tourists are often late, or "jump on another bus" without telling anyone, but he went looking for them anyway. When he couldn't find them he phoned the bus company before returning to Cairns with his other passengers. Corinne Scharenguivel, an administrative clerk for BTS tours, took Stignant's call, and later told a coronial inquest she immediately phoned *Outer Edge* and told a man whom she believed to be Jack Nairn that "we can't find the Lonergans".

The next morning was Australia Day, a national public holiday. *Outer Edge* went back to the reef on its daily run, the crew unaware anything was amiss. On board was the Lonergan's dive bag, but even if the crew noticed it had been left unclaimed overnight, they wouldn't have been concerned. Forgotten or lost property left behind on dive boats is a common occurrence and raises few eyebrows in the industry. Eventually the gear is claimed and that's the end of the matter. Karl Jesienowski remembered there were two pairs of shoes left over when the passengers disembarked in Port Douglas on Sunday, but he thought they belonged to Kathy Traverso and George Pyrohiw, or that they had accidentally been left behind.

At Fish City that day the dive went ahead as normal. The Lonergans were nowhere to be seen, but then nobody was looking for them. Although divers found abandoned weight belts on the sandy bottom of the dive site, that alone was not enough to suggest anybody had been left behind at sea. Later examination failed to link the weights to the missing Americans.

Another 24 hours went by. Late in the evening of Tuesday 27, Nairn phoned Gone Walkabout Hostel owner Barry Weyman, where the Lonergans had been staying in Cairns, and asked if he had seen them. He hadn't. They owed Weyman 10 days rent and all their belongings were still at the hostel. Weyman was alarmed. He told Nairn he "deemed" the Lonergans were missing and he was going to call the police.

But Nairn asked Weyman to let him do it and at 8.15pm that night Nairn phoned police. By then Tom and Eileen Lonergan had been missing at sea for more than two days.

Karl Jesienowski was having a birthday drink in a Port Douglas bar when Harald Klose, ashen-faced, walked in and asked him to come to the office. At the *Outer Edge* office were Nairn and operations manager Tom Colrain. They waited until senior constable Stephen Burgess arrived from the Mossman police station. Burgess was in no mood to play games and had a tape recorder secretly rolling in his shirt pocket.

The covert tape, played to the Cairns coroner's court in September, was a confusion of comments on safety procedures, personal responsibilities and uncertain recollections of events on board the *Outer Edge* on 25 January. Nairn is heard telling Burgess that after discovering the Lonergans' bag that night and looking through it, he thought: "Jesus Christ, it's got a wallet and papers in it."

Jesienowski remembers the moment with clarity: "It transpired rather quickly and I thought, 'Oh God they've been left behind'."

Burgess wasn't happy when nobody could remember who did the crucial last head count at Fish City. Nairn is heard to say he didn't do the head count but he accepted full responsibility. He said he remembered two people jumping off the bow of the boat and saying to George Pyrohiw, whom he presumed was doing the count: "Did you get those people who jumped in the water?" Nairn then said to Burgess: "There's a possibility they were counted twice and that's why 26 were counted."

The tape also recorded Burgess asking Pyrohiw on a telephone hook-up if he did the head count, adding the warning: "Don't start making stuff up. I know people start worrying about their own backsides, but honesty will be the best policy in this case (because) lives are at stake here." Pyrohiw denied he was responsible for the last head count. Nairn is heard saying to Pyrohiw: "Two guys jumped in the water and I asked you to do the head count. Nobody's trying to pin anything on you but we've got to do the best we can.

There's two people out there and we've got to go and find them."

Three days later Pyrohiw changed his story and admitted to police he had carried out the head count. It became clear the two men who jumped in the water had been counted twice.

But the search for the Lonergans didn't start until the next morning - 60 hours after the couple went missing. Five Royal Australian Navy divers searched the sea bed around Fish City from the deck of *Outer Edge*, this time skippered by Marcus Knight, who had visited the area more than 1,000 times on the tourist boat. A massive aerial sweep involving 15 fixed-wing planes and three helicopters, co-ordinated by AusSAR (Australian Search and Rescue) in Canberra, covered 7,000 square nautical miles of Great Barrier Reef waters over the next few days. Water police and a task force of 10 detectives, backed up by uniformed officers, scoured the coastline north and south of Port Douglas. As well, tourist charter boats, professional fishing fleets and recreational reef users were on the lookout for the couple. It was the largest missing person search ever undertaken in north Queensland.

At 4pm on Friday 30 January the large-scale search was officially called off by AusSAR and handed back to local authorities.

Karl Jesienowski criticised the search plan, emphasising the Americans could still be alive, but the search was wrongly focused to the south and west of Fish City when in fact the prevailing currents flowed in a northwesterly direction. He told police the couple was well equipped to survive as long as a week or possibly longer in such mild conditions - that overnight squalls would have provided them with water, and they could either be stranded on a shallow reef or drifting north towards the coast. Jesienowski also felt the Lonergans had a good chance of swimming to shore with the aid of a "flooding" tide that was prevalent for the first few hours after *Outer Edge* departed Fish City. To prove his point, Jesienowski allowed himself to drift with the current in similar conditions, covering three nautical miles towards shore in one hour. He felt that if the Lonergans were still in the water, either alive or dead, they would be afloat and visible somewhere in the search zone. Jesienowski publicly stated he believed the search was incomplete and should be resumed.

"The Lonergans could still be alive and desperately awaiting rescue," he told reporters.

Jesienowski enlisted the aid of internationally renowned filmmaker and underwater explorer Ben Cropp, who agreed the search had been focused in the wrong direction. Jesienowski was further troubled by the fact that the coast guard had apparently not been activated and emergency messages had not been broadcast on VHF marine radio to alert the many local fishing and pleasure vessels that used the area.

Significantly, St Crispin Reef played host to several boats during the critical time of the Lonergans' disappearance, yet nobody on board any of them was aware that a life-and-death drama was unfolding in the calm waters around their vessels.

Cairns resort owner Robert Prettejohn anchored his 13-metre cruiser, *Sula*, inside St Crispin Reef - about two and a half nautical miles south of Fish City - at 10.35am on 25 January, and he didn't leave until 11.30am the next day. He was on a pleasure cruise with family and friends, swimming and relaxing in an area of the Great Barrier Reef he has frequented for 30 years. Prettejohn is an observant and conscientious skipper, and that night, as always, he listened to the national emergency channel on his radio. There was nothing unusual on the broadcast to interest him. It was an "exceptionally clear, calm night" and the lights of the large tourist pontoon at Agincourt Reef to the north shone brightly. Prettejohn said the *Sula's* cabin lights were on until 11pm and should have been visible "quite clearly" from the Fish City dive site.

Prettejohn also took note of an unusual amount of debris in the water, which he reasoned had been carried north on the tides from recent floods around Townsville. When he heard news of the missing Americans on his car radio later that week he telephoned the Mossman coastguard and "informed them of my observations - the search should be conducted to the north". Prettejohn was upset that he was anchored within sight of Fish City but was unable to help the Lonergans. "We weren't able to do anything because we didn't know," he later told the coroner's court.

Prettejohn wasn't the only experienced mariner within helping distance on that fateful night. Just half a nautical mile to the south of *Sula*, tucked in behind St Crispin Reef, the 12-metre beche-de-mer fishing boat *Wy Knot* arrived at 5pm on Sunday 25 and stayed all night. Skipper Andrew Curven observed *Sula* and a vessel called *Sea Rover*, plus another two boats in the area during his stay. Curven described conditions as "dead flat, a brilliant glass-out ocean, with the anchor line loose in the water all night." He said an anchor light - located on the mast - was on during the night, as was a reading light.

But the 22-metre scientific research vessel, *Harry Messel*, was even closer to Fish City - barely one nautical mile away on the northwest flank of St Crispin Reef on the morning of Monday 26. Skipper Allan Reif said there was only a slight breeze and the seas "were like glass". Five divers spent the day completing scientific work on the northeastern tip of St Crispin Reef, including a circumnavigation of the entire reef riding manta boards - underwater sleds that are towed behind surface craft. Around mid-morning, Reif saw a large yacht "no less than 40 feet (12 metres) in length", and a charter dive vessel in the area, but didn't identify them. The night before, the *Harry Messel* had all its navigational lights on and was "lit up like a Christmas tree", but anchored well to the south off Opal Reef. Reif told the coroner's court that the *Harry Messel* stood eight metres high on the water and would be visible "quite clearly" from 6-7 nautical miles away.

A pleasure craft named *Pursuit* was also present that night, fishing on the eastern side of St Crispin Reef.

The reef was a busy area by any reckoning that night, yet a number of experienced mariners and their crews saw no sign of the Lonergans during the several hours of daylight left after *Outer Edge* departed on the afternoon of Sunday 25, nor were the Americans - who would obviously be distressed and making attempts to attract attention - sighted the next day.

Apart from the known boats in the area that night, and the large tourist pontoon within sighting distance of Fish City, there is also a clump of rocks on the extreme northern tip of St Crispin Reef, just over one nautical mile in a straight line west of the dive site. These rocks protrude from the water almost two metres at low tide and half a metre or so at high tide and, although difficult to see from water level, are, according to experts, easily within swimming distance. This rocky outcrop was an overnight haven for the Lonergans if they had chosen to swim for it. Even closer was a fisherman's beacon - a steel post with a reflector on top - that could have been reached for support.

So what did Tom and Eileen Lonergan do after they surfaced and found that *Outer Edge* had gone and they'd been left at sea? Karl Jesienowski helped navy divers search the Fish City site and found no broken coral or signs of human distress that would point to an answer. He reported logs and other floating debris - also later confirmed by Robert Prettejohn and other witnesses - in the immediate area, which the Lonergans could have used for support if they'd needed it, even though their wetsuits and buoyancy vests would have kept them afloat indefinitely.

There was much subsequent speculation and debate about whether they waited until nightfall and then in desperation attempted to swim the 2.3 nautical miles across the deep channel separating Fish City from the tourist pontoon, and were swept away by the strong incoming tide and treacherous currents. If so, as Jesienowski reported, they would certainly be carried in a northwesterly direction, and could have remained afloat for days.

At the coronial inquest in September, scuba dive specialists gave their opinions on the Lonergans' chances of survival if they attempted the difficult channel crossing in an effort to reach the pontoon and safety.

Queensland Workplace Health and Safety diving inspector Christopher Coxen, a qualified PADI diving instructor whose task was to investigate the safety aspects of the Lonergans incident, said he could swim the channel in five hours, but his training would tell him to wait at Fish City at least three hours for the boat to come back looking for him. Coxen said to make the crossing a very good swimmer might dispose of all equipment to increase speed, or retain the gear and move slower. He suggested a swim of one nautical mile in one hour would be "doing quite well". Coxen said he would ditch his scuba tank and weights and inflate his bouyancy vest to use less energy to stay afloat. When asked by counsel assisting the coroner, John Bailey, if he would consider taking his wetsuit off in an emergency to "sprint for it" Coxen said that fell into the "what if spectrum" and ten people would give variable answers. He said he couldn't think of any good reason to dispense with a wetsuit "unless speed was the essence".

Coxen also gave evidence that after the disappearance he issued four improvement notices to Outer Edge Dive requiring the company to tighten their system of record keeping and head counting. He said his investigation into the incident concluded that individual crew members were not specifically delegated important procedures such as head counts.

"The evidence I gathered indicates it was not the first time a head count had not been done prior to the boat leaving the final dive site," he said.

Ben Cropp told the court he was a self-taught scuba diver with more than 10,000 dives to his credit and if he was in the Lonergans' predicament he would take his bouyancy vest off and swim with it under his chest, heading for the nearest reef, rather than the pontoon. He said no experienced diver would discard the vest. "It's a life support and I wouldn't let it go. No, they would have kept it until they were dead."

Cropp said if the Lonergans had tried to cross the channel the odds were by nightfall they'd be swept out to sea by the rushing tide, and then back in again. "Anything that goes out comes back in again - always to the northwest."

Cropp and Jesienowski were right about that. Eleven days after the Lonergans' disappearance, a buoyancy vest belonging to Tom Lonergan was found on a remote stretch of beach near Indian Head, 10 kilometres north of Cooktown - precisely in a northwest direction from St Crispin Reef. The vest - unbuckled and undamaged - was clearly labelled "Tom Lonergan, Peace Corps, Fiji".

The discovery gave rise to speculation that the Lonergans had made it to shore and were still alive somewhere in the crocodile-inhabited wilderness of Cape York Peninsula. North Queenslanders had a field day with the possibilities the find opened up. For a start, there was a great deal of scepticism in the dive industry over the near-perfect condition of the vest, after it had supposedly drifted more than 100 kilometres through a maze of reefs, sandbars and exposed rocks without sustaining even minor tears. Then there was the fact that the vest was unbuckled - meaning it had deliberately been taken off. One theory was that the Lonergans - or Tom on his own - had left the vest on the beach as a signal for searchers to keep looking. Or maybe it was a red herring, deliberately put there to throw searchers off the track. Why the Lonergans would do that was another matter.

Port Douglas dive shop owner and scuba instructor Grahame Connett raised the question of why the vest had deliberately been undone and discarded when it offered so much bouyancy at sea. Speaking to reporters, Connett said the find posed many unanswered questions in the minds of local people about the Lonergans incident, including the possibility they had had faked their own disappearance.

"There is definitely a problem with these two experienced divers disappearing underwater," he said. "It's all a bit convenient in my book, the vest just wouldn't come off by itself."

The police weren't having any of that, though, with Acting Chief Superintendent Col McCallum dismissing the notion of a staged disappearance as "pure speculation". He said the vest had been sent to Cairns for scientific examination, but it appeared to have been on the beach no longer than 24 hours. McCallum said no footprints had been found anywhere near the vest and police considered the chances of finding the Lonergans alive "extremely remote".

In a bizarre twist to the Lonergan mystery, a postcard from Cairns dated 19 January, arrived at the home of Tom Lonergan's parents in Baton Rouge, Louisiana, telling them a "hurricane" had passed over north Queensland. Elizabeth Lonergan said her son's message was enthusiastic and it was obvious he was enjoying himself. She said it was painful to read the card but comforting to know they had been in their son's thoughts.

Police released details of another postcard, this one sent by the Lonergans to friends at the dive company Scuba Bula in Fiji, complaining about high costs and poor diving conditions on the Great Barrier Reef. The postcard, sent on 23 January - two days before their fateful Fish City dive - described a previous dive trip off Cairns as a "big mistake". The couple wrote that the sites they visited - Hastings Reef and Michaelmas Cay - were very shallow, with a lot of dead coral and poor visibility.

"Mediocre diving at best and $99 a piece (sic) for the whole trip (Sa!). We'll try again up in Port Douglas," the postcard read. Sa is a fijian word that roughly translates: "I can't believe it."

The Lonergans wrote on the postcard: "This city is NOT for serious divers. We had to sit through a 15-min lecture on how to put on your mask and fins (?!?)."

Jonathon Wilson, an American teaching in Fiji, told a newspaper journalist Tom Lonergan could often be cynical and sounded depressed with the thought of returning home to America.

"They told us they didn't want to go back to Louisiana to the rat race and the dog-eat-dog world over there," Wilson was quoted as saying. He said Lonergan was a highly intelligent man who wanted to complete a marine biology course at the University of Hawaii before returning home.

On Sunday 8 February, Special Emergency Response Team (SERT) police officers found a scuba-diving fin marked "Eileen L" on the beach at Indian Head. The SERT team members and water police worked warily from a launch because of the risk from estuarine crocodiles in the area. The next day, a second buoyancy vest with the words "Eileen Lonergan, Peace Corps, Fiji" clearly written across its front surface, was discovered at the high tide level. Both the fin and vest were undamaged, showing no tears, teeth marks or bloodstains. Police also found a State Emergency Services marker buoy which had been dropped in the water at St Crispin Reef on 28 January. They also reported debris that was believed to have drifted north from the Townsville floods.

Questions were raised about the logic of a swim flipper finding its way so far north when experts agree these fins do not float on the surface.

Two days later a diving suit hood marked with Eileen Lonergan's name was found on the beach.

Searchers also found a black scuba tank at Cape Bedford, north of Indian Head, but there was no evidence to prove it belonged to either of the Lonergans.

On Saturday 14 February, three weeks after the Lonergans embarked on their last dive cruise, north Queensland police officially called off the search for the missing couple.

Cairns police chief Col McCallum did his best to hose down speculation the Lonergans were still alive, telling journalists he was satisfied the couple were left behind, that they did not fake their own disappearance, but ultimately did not make it to shore and perished at sea. He discounted "dozens" of sightings reported to police since the Lonergans disappeared, including reports from the Northern Territory and New South Wales, but said that was a normal reaction, citing for example the fact that hundreds of reported sightings of the three Beaumont children, who disappeared from the Adelaide suburb of Glenelg in 1966, had occurred over the years

However, a police media spokesman from Brisbane said senior police were "not totally convinced" the Lonergans were lost at sea, but it would be left for a coroner to decide what actually happened.

The discovery of a second unmarked scuba tank at Indian Head by residents of the Hope Vale Aboriginal community sparked renewed search efforts by a police team that yet again scoured the remote beaches for some sign of the Lonergans, or at least their remains. In the following weeks two wetsuits - one torn and frayed - were also found, but evidence suggested they had been deliberately discarded by tourists or accidentally lost overboard from a larger vessel.

In early March, senior detectives travelled to Fiji and interviewed friends and associates of the Lonergans in an attempt to piece together the Louisiana couple's last weeks before leaving for Australia. One intriguing aspect of their visit was to question Fijian authorities about a possible link between the Lonergans and Milton Windsor Harris, an American insurance scam artist who faked his death by "disappearing" off a Cook Strait ferry in May 1985, only to emerge four years later alive and well in Auckland.

After his "disappearance" Lloyds of London refused to pay out a nearly $4 million insurance policy when investigators discovered Harris had tried the trick a few days earlier by "falling" from a Kangaroo Island ferry in South Australia. On that occasion his plan was thwarted by rescuers who pulled him from the sea.

Harris hailed from the Lonergans' home town of Baton Rouge and like them, was a member of the First Uniting Methodist Church and had also served time in the US Peace Corps.

But Queensland police said although they were interested in the Harris case they had found nothing suspicious in the Lonergans' insurance policies and ruled out any connection.

In a startling public statement on 8 March, the state government announced charges under Workplace Health and Safety legislation would be laid against both Jack Nairn and Rye Holdings Pty Ltd, Nairn's family company that operated Outer Edge Dive.

Industrial Relations Minister Santo Santoro said he had received Crown Law Office advice that a prima facie case existed against the two parties and they would be charged for breaches of safety under the legislation.

Although the police investigation was yet to be completed and no coronial inquest had been held, Santoro defended his jump-the-gun announcement - which he described as an "unusual step" - with the explanation that because of the high level of public interest in the case it was necessary to help end "alarmist (and) unhelpful" speculation over the incident.

But Jack Nairn was unimpressed with the news, stating neither he nor his company had yet been charged with any offence and his legal rights to a fair trial in the future could already have been jeopardised by Santoro's comments.

"This course of action hasn't helped any of the parties involved and if the company is being charged, or I'm being charged, then we have the right for those charges to be identified now, and not at some time later on," Nairn said.

Public opinion was on Nairn's side, especially in Port Douglas, where Santoro's action was seen as a political publicity stunt that had damaged Outer Edge Dive's credibility before Nairn had even been formally charged.

On the last day of March, Eileen Lonergan's parents, John and Kathy Hains arrived in north Queensland as guests of the Queensland Government. According to Premier Rob Borbidge the invitation was extended to the family as a "gesture of goodwill' and the government was willing to pay "transport costs" for the visit.

"It is quite appropriate for governments to exercise a degree of compassion, particularly taking into account the circumstances resulting in the disappearance," Borbidge said.

On 1 April, the Hains, accompanied by their son John Jnr, held a memorial service at St Crispin Reef to farewell their daughter and son-in-law. The family placed floral wreaths in the calm waters where the missing couple was last seen and prayed quietly. At a media conference two days later, John Hains Jnr said it had been very important for the family to visit the reef where his sister disappeared because it was a way of saying goodbye.

"We came to Queensland fully realising that we will never see Eileen and Tom again," he said.

The mystery of the Lonergan's disappearance took a dramatic new turn when the skipper of a Quicksilver Connections tourist vessel that visits the company's Agincourt Reef pontoon told police the passenger head count was three too many on its return trip to Port Douglas the day after the Americans went missing.

Mike Rose, skipper of Quicksilver V, said the vessel was chartered solely by a party of 288 Italian tourists that day, but the head count came to 291, and he remembered hearing a male American accent on board as the boat headed home. He said a surplus of "two or three" was not considered "out of the ordinary" for large passenger numbers. It was only if the head count was under the required tally, or "five or six over", was there cause for concern.

In another development, a Quicksilver maintenance worker reported seeing a black and pink wetsuit snagged on coral in the close vicinity of the Agincourt pontoon. Eileen Lonergan was wearing a similar wetsuit when she and Tom dived for the last time at Fish City.

Rose said he hadn't reported the head count discrepancy to police earlier because he did not consider it important enough, but had he known about the wetsuit sighting he would have come forward.

Outer Edge Dive operations manager Tom Colrain wrote in a

statement to his solicitor after the Lonergans went missing that Tom Lonergan had persistently questioned him about Agincourt Reef on 24 January, asking repeatedly if the vessel would visit that particular reef the next day. Colrain reported he became exasperated with the American's questions.

"He asked me at least three times, and I remember thinking to myself what a pest this guy was, and how many times do I have to tell him where we're going?" Colrain said.

Lonergan also upset tourism consultant Gaile McLean with his questions about Agincourt Reef. McLean, who worked for the Cairns Visitors Information and Booking Centre, said Lonergan insisted - despite her assurances to the contrary - that Quicksilver boats visited the Ribbon Reefs chain to the north of the company pontoon, and not Agincourt Reef.

"Finally I got my back up and told him I didn't care what anyone else said, Quicksilver went to Agincourt Reef," McLean said. "He was such a smart alec, he thought he knew it all."

The Quicksilver revelations fuelled long-standing speculation that the Lonergans could have waited until *Outer Edge* left Fish City, then swam the 2.3 nautical miles across the channel to the giant pontoon and hidden in its superstructure overnight, before mingling with tourists the next day and returning with them unnoticed to Port Douglas.

Police said the new information would be investigated, even though the long-overdue police report to the coroner would be further delayed.

On 28 June, five months after the Lonergans went missing, a private charter boat crewman found a weathered dive slate wedged in mangroves at Archer Point, 20 kilometres south of Cooktown. The slate revealed a faint, handwritten plea for help, purportedly written by Tom Lonergan. It was dated 8am, 26 January. Strangely, details of the message were released to the media by relatives in Louisiana - not by Queensland police.

The sometimes illegible message on the slate included the faded words: "Anyone...can help us...we have been abandoned...Agincourt Reef by MV Outer Edge...please help us...to rescue us before we die..."

After weeks of forensic testing, however, a police spokesman would only say the writing on the slate was "more than likely that of Mr Lonergan" but conceded that did not prove the couple was dead.

"It doesn't matter if the handwriting is theirs or not (because) that won't tell us whether it's a fake disappearance or not," he said. "We don't know for sure when it was written or under what circumstances or why."

If the slate did indeed belong to Tom Lonergan and did carry a desperate plea for help, it also clearly means he and his wife had survived 18 hours in the water, time enough, according to many experienced scuba divers, to make it to safety - either to the Quicksilver pontoon at Agincourt Reef, or the rocks on St Crispin Reef, or one of the boats in the area.

Dive Queensland president Wayne Inglis said there were past instances of divers being abandoned and swimming much greater distances to safety.

"But we are expected to believe the Lonergans couldn't swim to the Agincourt Reef pontoon in very good conditions."

Inglis said he also found it strange that the couple had not written a last message to their loved ones back home if they thought they were about to die.

Cairns scuba dive expert Col McKenzie said it was unlikely the Lonergan's dive slate would wash so far to shore because that type was designed to sink before obscuring a diver's vision.

"I am ninety-nine per cent sure this should have sunk to the bottom and not been washed up," he said.

Australian Institute of Marine Science researcher Peter Wolanski told the inquest the slate would not float, however it showed no marks consistent with being dragged along the sea bottom.

Two police officers at the inquest gave evidence the slate had been immersed in water to test its bouyancy, but because it had been found with the usual strip of rubber and marker pencil missing, the slate did not float.

Preliminary inquest proceedings into the disappearance of the Lonergans finally got under way in the Cairns Coroner's Court on Wednesday 22 July. The atmosphere in the courtroom was abuzz with tension and expectation, with Australian and American media representatives spilling over from the press table and forced to compete for space in a packed public gallery.

Perhaps the most compelling revelation to emerge from the case was a "death wish" entry in Tom Lonergan's diary and the fears expressed in his wife's own diary that she could become caught up against her wishes in his disturbing vision of the future.

The existence of the Lonergans' diaries had been known for several months, but carefully kept under wraps by police, with only brief and selected excerpts released by the families hinting at their broader content. The diaries had been at the centre of constant speculation as the police conducted their investigation, but had never been available for public scrutiny. Only much later, at the inquest, and then at Jack Nairn's trial, were the diaries examined as evidence - but even then, only selected entries were released to the media by the court.

On 3 August 1997, when the couple lived and worked in Fiji as teachers, Tom Lonergan wrote in his diary: "Like a student who's finished an exam and is merely waiting to hand it in and go, I feel as though my life is complete and I am ready to die."

The diary entries paint a picture of a close and loving couple who paradoxically struggled with the direction of their lives and Tom Lonergan's bleak vision of what lay ahead.

In February the same year he wrote of how he thought others saw him: "From other people's points of view my personality is, at times at least, obnoxious, overbearing, presumptions (sic), intrusive, irreverent to the point of insensitive, self centred......and generally offensive. As reality would have it, my pure intentions are misunderstood. My words are misconstrued. My actions are mistaken for something they are not."

Lonergan wrote of how he had failed to live up to his family's expectations by "eloping" with Eileen and being absent from family events in New Orleans. He wrote despairingly of a fading memory and his belief that at the age of 25 the brain's full capacity had been reached and "it's after that time the trouble starts". The entries darkened progressively: "I have no clue what I want to do or what I should do with the rest of my life. As far as I can tell from here, my life can only get worse. I've peaked and it's all downhill from now until my funeral."

On 27 October he wrote: "I've had enough of casting pearls before swine. I don't want to waste any more of my breath."

On 4 November: "It makes it seem like we joined the Peace Corp (sic), quit our jobs, came 10,000 miles and put up with all the shit for nothing."

And on 15 December: "It's clear to me now, that not only does it get much worse than this, it hardly in fact gets any better."

Eileen Lonergan's diary reveals how she hated teaching with her "zero management classroom skills". She complains how sugar cane-cutting dust, sinus blockage, her neighbours - in fact "everything" - gave her headaches. "My jaw is often clenched amazingly tight. I must be psychologically preparing myself for life back in America."

In her diary Eileen Lonergan records her fears for her husband's life and how she struggled with the philosophical meanings of their long discussions together in Fiji. Her entries sometimes graphically mirror those of her husband's.

On 12 August she wrote: "As we walked and talked, Tom bared his soul. His fears and anxieties about an uncertain future. His unhappiness about present and recent past. His understanding of himself and the world, which makes him certain that he has reached his peak in life and can only go downhill from here.

"How can I explain it? He's happy with the way things have gone in his life, his experiences being with me, but he feels he's done all he wants. From here on is only repetition. He doesn't know what he wants to do with his life. He knows he can't stand to do anything for an extended period of time.

"He thinks he is nearly ready to die, which is not the same as being suicidal. It seems to be a mixture of feeling his life is completed, and feeling he ought to get out while the going is good and not spoil it by staying too long.

"That and fear, fear of pain of all kinds. The body that fails of boredom. Fear of a life that seems to have no meaning and is not going anywhere. Fear of the failing memory. Part of me wants to tell him, 'Your life isn't over, it's hardly beginning.' and part of me knows he's right.

"For as long as I have known him, I have known of his inability to stand one job for long. He's always looking to escape his job, the place he lives. I have known of his hard, cynical, perceptive view of reality that makes life harder to bear. In his personality it matters not where we live or what he does, he's discontent (sic). He's passed, I hope forever, the suicidal phase, but he hasn't found the inner strength to take whatever pain and joy life presents and take whatever he can from life."

In her diary on 15 October Eileen Lonergan wrote: "Our lives are intertwined now. We're hardly true individuals. When I go out among people here without him, I feel alone and vulnerable. Where we are now goes beyond dependence, beyond even love. Together we are not really Eileen and Tom but some new entity and almost individual in its own right."

On 9 January 1998, just 16 days before she disappeared with her husband, Eileen Lonergan entered these thoughts in her diary: "A couple of nights ago Tom explained to me in great detail why he feels his life is over and he is ready to die. Mostly he is afraid. He is afraid of the emptiness that faces him regarding jobs and career. He feels he has no particular skills, talents or desires and has only a sense of confusion over the what to do next issue. He hopes to die a quick, fairly painly (sic) death and he hopes to have it soon. He wishes to be free of this sorry world so that he can move on to the next one which he has been promised will be much nicer.

"I had to correct him when he said he hoped that we will die soon together, so I would not be left alone...huh...better alone than dead.

"When he finished I told him my own philosophy was very different, that I hoped to live to be ridiculously old, that I love my life and I'm terrified of death. He said, 'If you are so afraid of dying, if you love your life, why do you risk diving?'. It's because I love my life that I dive."

"And so now I hold in my hands a very uncertain future indeed. Tom's not suicidal but he's got a death wish that could unconsciously lead him to what he desires and I could get caught in that. 'You have a death wish. I believe this wish may very well lead you to be in the right place at the right time to get what you want.' I may get caught in that since we remain physically together so much of the time it's a risk I take. Just as he formed his death wish to include me and I fought it off in dreams, I formed my life wish to include him. Whose will is stronger?"

The diary entries were described as "chillingly prophetic" by Detective Sergeant Paul Priest at the inquest but he said later he became convinced that the message on the recovered dive slate was a "dying declaration that Tom and Eileen didn't want to die, they were saying come and rescue us". Priest, who led the investigation into the couple's disappearance, told the court it was obvious to a layman that Tom Lonergan could not anticipate being left behind at sea and it was also obvious that a slow death by thirst and dehydration, and possibly being attacked by sharks, would not be a painless death, as referred to in his diary.

Priest said he had concluded that the flawed head count and failure to mobilise an early search for the Lonergans had led to their deaths.

"There's overwhelming evidence to suggest it is not a murder-suicide," he said.

Priest told barrister Graham Houston, counsel for Jack Nairn and the Outer Edge Dive company, that the diaries had not been examined by a psychologist or other experts because "everyone has a right to personal privacy".

Houston requested complete copies of the diaries to have them analysed for an expert opinion but was refused permission by Coroner Noel Nunan who pointed out the diaries had been accessible to lawyers for two months and he, Nunan, didn't want "copies floating around the place (because) personal information will get out".

There was absolutely no doubt in Ben Cropp's mind what happened to the Lonergans. The internationally known filmmaker has spent a lifetime documenting marine life and he believes they were both attacked by tiger sharks and killed within 24 hours. Cropp graphically described to a hushed court how tiger sharks move into the edge of the Great Barrier Reef at their normal feeding time every day around 3.30pm, and how they would then have circled the Lonergans until the first bite, after which a feeding frenzy would finish them off. This scenario was not speculation, he told the court, but straightforward logic.

"If you're in the water long enough a tiger shark will find you - dead or alive, you wouldn't last too long out there," he said. "Tiger sharks are pretty horrible feeding machines when they make up their minds.

"Dehydration and despair, and then delirium, could have killed them off first. They would have been dead before the search started."

Cropp predicted parts of the Lonergans' wetsuits would eventually be found washed up on one of the beaches around Cooktown, but disputed a wetsuit found at Indian Head belonged to one of the Lonergans.

"I see wetsuits on the beach all the time and this one is a tourist's suit, not one an experienced diver would use."

Tom Lonergan's sister, Nancy Lonergan, and her husband Jim Weir, were visibly distressed as they listened to the veteran mariner's evidence.

Outside the court, Weir said he felt Cropp's evidence made sense.

"It's pretty tough, but we want to hear the opinions of the experts," he said. "We don't believe we will ever know what happened to them, but we think they were left at sea."

But many old hands in the dive industry scoffed at what they called Cropp's "grandstanding for headlines". Most simply don't believe sharks would devour the American tourists completely without leaving some evidence. Some say you can swim within the Great Barrier Reef for days without even seeing a dangerous shark. They point to the fact that both the Lonergan's buoyancy vests, Eileen Lonergan's flipper and dive hood were all found without the slightest evidence of a shark attack.

Former *Outer Edge* skipper Marcus Knight gave evidence at the inquest that it was not uncommon for tourists - especially those who used dive computers - to disobey the recommended dive times and stay underwater for longer periods of up to 15 minutes. He said the practice wasn't encouraged and definitely not acceptable if it "interrupts the program of the day".

Knight said the skipper of a vessel was always the designated lookout and was often the only person left on board while dives were in progress. He said head counts were carried out first thing in the morning and before the vessel left each dive site, but sometimes "they don't add up".

"People are moving around the boat and you may have to do the count two or three times," he said.

Knight gave evidence that two qualified divemasters were required if more than eight certified divers were in the water, but Katherine Traverso was the only one on board that day, leaving *Outer Edge* one divemaster short.

Apart from the tiger shark scenario, there was no shortage of theories to explain the Lonergans' disappearance, including a faked drowning by the couple, a murder-suicide carried out by Tom Lonergan, and of course the inevitable conspiracy theory - that the Lonergans were covert US government agents who had been kidnapped and executed for security reasons.

If the Lonergans managed to fake their own drowning and then disappear it was a masterful exercise. They haven't used their bank accounts and, as far as can be ascertained, they haven't left Australia by conventional means. Nevertheless, there were 23 alleged sightings of the couple, including a report from a Port Douglas bookshop proprietor who claimed she sold the Lonergans maps of the Northern Territory on the day after their disappearance, a sighting by a Darwin woman who told police she served the Americans drinks in a hotel on 29 January, and one from a Victorian postmaster who reported that a man "with glasses and an American accent", whom she believed to be Tom Lonergan, had made inquiries about a passport in May.

But in spite of barrister Graham Houston's pleas at the inquest that he be allowed to call certain witnesses, who were not "cranks and losers", to give evidence on the subject of sightings, Coroner Nunan refused the request. He called the sightings "far-fetched" and based on misinformation. Solicitor Rob Davis, counsel for the Lonergan families, went further, suggesting the sightings were in the same category as "Elvis Presley and flying saucer" sightings.

The murder-suicide theory created an uproar at the inquest when Houston raised the issue while cross-examining navy diver Brett

Daniels, who took part in the search for the Lonergans at Fish City on 28 January. Houston asked: "If one diver wants to kill another diver underwater, how would that be achieved?" There were gasps from the public gallery and members of the Lonergan families sat in stunned silence as counsel assisting the coroner John Bailey leapt to his feet, protesting that the theory was "wild, unsubstantiated speculation", adding: "I'm not sure navy divers are trained to be assassins." Davis joined in the verbal barrage at Houston with: "This is really outrageous stuff, I hope my learned friend is going to produce more evidence on this point, except disgusting, slanderous allegations calculated to attract the press."

Houston pressed on, referring to the passages in Eileen Lonergan's diary where she wrote of her fear of her husband's death wish, submitting his question was entirely legitimate. Nunan replied he saw no reason to believe Eileen Lonergan feared she would be murdered, but: "She feared she would be led into a dangerous situation, perhaps because of his outlook."

Solicitor Philip Bovey, representing Katherine Traverso, submitted to the court that Houston's questions "should be allowed, it's as simple as that."

Finally, Daniels answered that one diver could kill another by turning off the air, pulling the air hose out of the diver's mouth, or by holding that person underwater.

Karl Jesienowski gave evidence at the inquest that he later remembered seeing two pairs of shoes left on the dock after *Outer Edge* had returned to Port Douglas from Fish City on 25 January. He said "no bells rang" in his mind, even though the shoes were sitting on concrete at the Port Douglas Marina on a very hot summer day. Jesienowski said he assumed the shoes belonged to crew members still on board the dive boat cleaning up.

"It didn't occur to me it was significant," Jesienowski said. "This has been very hard for me, a very traumatic experience."

The coroners court was again the stage for controversy when Outer Edge Dive operations manager Tom Colrain stormed out of the witness box during a bitter legal row over his refusal to give evidence.

A clearly reluctant Colrain had entered the witness box after Jack Nairn and Outer Edge Dive former employees George Pyrohiw, Harald Klose and Katherine Traverso had all successfully claimed privilege from giving evidence on the grounds they might be incriminated.

Graham Houston put it to Coroner Nunan that his client faced the "peril and possibility" of being convicted on criminal charges and also offences under the Workplace Health and Safety Act if directed by the court to answer any questions other than his name and address. Nunan twice told Houston to "sit down" when the barrister spoke of "star chamber" tactics during the row. The coroner refused to grant privilege until he was satisfied Houston had a legitimate legal argument for the request. At one point Colrain jumped up, shouting he was "bloody sick of this" and attempted to leave the court, only returning to his seat when told to do so by Houston.

Houston argued that privilege was a cornerstone of the legal system and everyone had the right to remain silent.

Nunan eventually agreed to grant Colrain privilege but suppressed publication of the legal argument leading to his decision.

In another intriguing courtroom revelation, Tom Lonergan's sister Nancy gave evidence that her brother, who was 15 months older than her, had very poor eyesight and was not a good swimmer. She said "Tommy" took one swim lesson as a child and "didn't like it'. In fact, she said, he hated swimming.

Lonergan, a dental hygienist from Covington, Louisiana, said she had tried to talk her brother into competing in a triathlon with her, but he backed out, protesting "No way" when he found out swimming was involved.

She testified that during an eyesight test as a child Tom Lonergan was asked to read a chart on a wall "10 feet" away, but could not even see the chart properly, declaring to the eye specialist: "What chart?"

She denied suggestions that her brother and sister-in-law were having problems with their relationship and said neither of them would have left the other in dangerous circumstances.

On Friday 11 September, after five days of evidence, the inquest was adjourned until early October, when Noel Nunan and inquest lawyers proposed to visit Fish City and see for themselves the dive site where the Lonergans disappeared. Nunan made it quite clear during the week's proceedings that he expected Jack Nairn to be charged with manslaughter due to criminal negligence. It was also clear that the skipper and owner of the ill-fated Outer Edge Dive boat would face the charge alone.

Conditions at Fish City on 1 October 1998, were not nearly as good as they were eight months earlier when the Lonergans and other *Outer Edge* divers slipped smoothly into the glass-flat sea for their last dive of the day. In fact, Noel Nunan, accompanied by an entourage of lawyers faced stiff 25 knot winds and a 2.5 metre swell when they donned their snorkelling gear and bobbed about in the choppy water to see what they could see. Graham Houston and Philip Bovey were notably absent from the party. Nunan declared he was making the trip to find out if it was possible to see the Quicksilver pontoon and the rocky outcrop at St Crispin Reef from water level at Fish City. It's unlikely he saw anything but sea and sky, given the rough conditions on the day, but in any case he declined to comment after the trip other than saying he would take his experience into consideration before reaching a final decision on the outcome of the inquest.

At the conclusion of the inquest on Friday 9 October, Jack Nairn was ordered to stand trial for unlawfully killing the Lonergans. When asked by Nunan if he had anything to say, Nairn spoke for the first and only time in a clear firm voice: "Yes, your worship, I'm not guilty of this charge."

As expected, the other crew members on board *Outer Edge* that fateful day were not charged with any offence, although it was considered all except Karl Jesienowski had breached dive regulations.

In his findings Nunan rejected any suggestion the Americans had faked their disappearance, or that their deaths were the result of a murder-suicide, ruling that they either drowned or were taken by sharks.

Nunan said it was obvious the Lonergans were "young, idealistic and in love with each other", but the diaries revealed that "despite enjoying life, he was apprehensive about the future and recognised he had a restless nature".

He said that Tom Lonergan "felt his body and mind, particularly his memory, would soon begin to deteriorate. He could accept death. He was introspective and had the occasional dark or pessimistic thought like most people do."

But he found that the Lonergans often overstayed their dives and evidence from a dive company in Fiji verified the couple "were always the last ones back on the boat".

"In retrospect their habit of pushing their time to the limit was risky behaviour, especially when they put their lives in the hands of the relatively inexperienced relief crew of the *Outer Edge*," Nunan said.

"Arguably the Lonergans contributed to their own deaths by overstaying their last dive."

He said that Jack Nairn, as skipper and lookout on board the boat that day, should have been aware of the Lonergans' habit of returning late from previous dives, and, coupled with the failed head count and long delay in reporting the couple missing, it was evident Nairn should be held accountable for the tragedy.

"When one combines the severity and number of mistakes made by Mr Nairn with the magnitude of the risk of death that was likely to result from his defaults, I am satisfied that a reasonably (sic) jury properly instructed could find him guilty of manslaughter caused by criminal neglect. Whether the litany of errors and failure to heed warning signs is elevated to criminal negligence is therefore a question to be considered by twelve of Mr Nairn's peers."

But such a conclusion can be seen as flawed, given such a difficult combination of known facts, uncertainties and speculation the Lonergan case presents. Nunan's neat and straightforward conclusion was not accepted by many observers of this complicated and bizarre disappearance. Indeed - especially in Port Douglas, where many locals make a living from ferrying tourists to the Great Barrier Reef - questions were still being asked about troublesome gaps in the official version of what happened to the Lonergans.

There is no doubt the Americans were left behind. There is also no doubt the head count was wrong and the dive book on the return journey was incomplete. Everybody in the industry at the time knew faulty head counts on dive boats were a fact of life. Many people have been left behind over the years. Fortunately most have been picked up in time to avert a disaster. As Ben Cropp told the inquest: "It's a common, common thing for divers to be swept away and picked up by other boats. I've picked up people and taken them back to their boats."

Unfortunately, 16-year-old Victoria Bryant, who died when left behind on a snorkelling trip to Green Island in 1993, was not so lucky.

But, as Noel Nunan pointed out, Tom and Eileen Lonergan were guilty of human error too. Their dangerous habit of overstaying their dive times was an undeniable risk factor. Regardless of the varying estimates of how long they were underwater at Fish City, and exactly when *Outer Edge* left, the fact remains they stayed down too long. One of them at least must have known this, and noticed there were no other divers around. Where were they then? Karl Jesienowski didn't see them when he manually retrieved the vessel's anchor. That means they must have been out of sight on the other side of the bommie. Why? Were they hiding? And if they weren't there, it can only be concluded they had deliberately swam away from Fish City. If they were nearby, at least one of the pair must surely have heard *Outer Edge*'s engines as the vessel idled for a considerable time before departure.

If Tom Lonergan was as experienced as his dive log suggests, with more than 80 dives to his credit, it's unlikely he would take his buoyancy vest off when faced with the prospect of a long night at sea, and he would surely realise that by staying put, the chances of being picked up the next day were extremely high. One much-discussed theory suggests the Lonergans would have removed their vests and placed them under their chests for better manoeuvrability while swimming. But Tom Lonergan's sister said he could barely swim and his eyesight was extremely poor. If that was the case, he would have to depend on his wife for survival.

Regardless, they had both been in unfamiliar waters many times in their travels and commonsense would dictate - if they chose not to remain where they were - they would head slowly for the exposed rocks that Eileen Lonergan should have seen just one nautical mile across the dead calm waters at St Crispin Reef. It was just after 3.30pm and nightfall wasn't until 7.30pm. They had four hours to make it to safety.

But apparently they didn't take that option. Instead, Tom and Eileen Lonergan simply disappeared.

It must be considered at least a possibility that when Tom Lonergan surfaced and saw that the boat had gone, the moody thoughts of death recorded in his diary now flashed into his mind and he seized the opportunity fate had miraculously presented to him. Was this his "right place at the right time" Eileen had eerily written about in her diary? Did he somehow persuade his wife to join him, to wait for the outgoing tide, and then ride out to 500 metre-deep water just beyond the reef, discard their buoyancy vests, and descend into oblivion? Did Eileen Lonergan, although fearful, refuse to leave him out of love and loyalty until, exhausted and spent, she gave up and died with him?

All the experts agree that if the Lonergans were swept the other way, on the incoming tide, they would have drifted northwest towards landfall in the Cooktown area. But if so, why weren't they spotted during the massive air and sea search that followed their disappearance? Even though the search was delayed, they should have been seen - alive or dead. And if Ben Cropp is right and they were attacked by tiger sharks, why weren't at least parts of their savaged and bloody wetsuits found on the beach, along with the other items of their equipment?

It must also be possible that Tom Lonergan deliberately stayed down too long at Fish City, somehow distracting his wife until he knew the boat had gone and then, when they surfaced, persuaded her that they were doomed, and that a quick death together was better than a long, agonising wait for their inevitable end in the loneliness of the open sea. Tom Lonergan had cynically criticised the Queensland dive industry. Perhaps he suspected and gambled the head count system was poor and might fail, and there was a chance they might be left behind. He may have overstayed his dive time to see if he and his wife were missed, and when they were not, decided to carried out his death wish on the spur of the moment.

But why weren't the Lonergans missed on the trip home? Out of 24 passengers who had dived and socialised together with the couple all day, why didn't somebody say: "Hey, wait a minute, where are the Americans?" After all, Tom Lonergan was an inquisitive, talkative person, who was usually remembered by people who met him. An amateur video taken by one of the passengers on the outward journey shows Lonergan chatting to Jack Nairn in the vessel's cabin. Karl Jesienowski remembers conversing with the Lonergans on the way out and between dives during the day. Why then wasn't their absence noticed, either on the boat or on the wharf at Port Douglas when the passengers disembarked?

Jack Nairn spent 13 months on bail before he faced a jury, pleading not guilty to manslaughter.
On Monday 8 November 1999, Justice Stanley Jones instructed a jury of seven men and five women in the Cairns Supreme Court to ignore publicity over the case and begin the trial with an open mind. He told them not all the evidence presented at the inquest would be admissible at the trial and they should start with an "information blackout" of anything they had heard beforehand.
The 13-day trial included testimony from dive instructor George Pyrihow, then living in Melbourne, who told the court he was asked to do a head count at Fish City by Jack Nairn. "I walked around and counted 24. I told Jack there were 24, and he said there were two in the water - two plus 24 is 26, so I went back in the galley. I didn't see them in the water, but I saw them get back on board while I was inside serving drinks."
Under cross-examination by Jack Nairn's counsel, Brisbane barrister Tony Glynn, Pyrihow admitted he had lied to police about the head count, agreeing with the suggestion he had done so to protect himself.
The court also heard the Lonergans' last dive details were not entered in the log book at Fish City because Katherine Traverso and Harald Klose had each thought the other would fill the names in, so

nobody noticed the Americans were not back on board. Traverso - who at one point fled the courtroom in tears while a video of the outward trip was being played - said dive logs were not always completed and she couldn't remember who had direct responsibility for the log that day.

Questioned by Crown prosecutor Tom Wakefield about her responsibilities as a divemaster, Traverso testified that the Lonergans had requested permission to dive separately from the group at Fish City and under Workplace Health and Safety regulations, certified divers were ultimately responsible for their own safety once they entered the water.

"We are required to advise them about currents and marine hazards, (and) obviously we are required to bring them home," she said.

Traverso told the court the sound of a boat's engines underwater was "very loud" and even a flushing toilet can be heard, but agreed with Wakefield that dive hoods the Lonergans were wearing could affect their hearing.

Traverso said *Outer Edge* was not in a hurry to leave Fish City because Jack Nairn had a reputation for taking his time after the last dive of the day.

"Jack was passionate about the reef and it was difficult to get home," she said.

Justin Wunderwald gave evidence that as *Outer Edge* motored away from Fish City he sat on the rear deck looking back over the dive site for a considerable time but saw no sign of human activity.

Another *Outer Edge* passenger, Andrew Williams, testified he swam past the Lonergans, who were almost directly under the boat as he was about to surface five minutes before the end of the planned 40-minute dive.

"I was about 10 metres from the boat and you could look up and see it quite clearly," he said.

Certified diver Richard Triggs said conditions at Fish City that day had been "the best I've ever experienced, no current, visibility was excellent", and he estimated a person in the water could be seen "at least" one kilometere away from the deck of the boat. Triggs said he recalled the Lonergans were using their own equipment and on the last dive Tom Lonergan donned a wetsuit hood, which Triggs thought was "out of the ordinary" for such hot conditions. He estimated the boat left Fish City 15-20 minutes after he and his wife left the water.

Australian Maritime Safety Authority senior search and rescue officer Brian Willey told the court a radio emergency beacon somewhere south of St Crispin Reef had been activated at 5pm on 26 January, and a Royal Flying Doctor Service aircraft had been despatched to search the area for the source of the alarm. After 30 minutes the signal was found to be coming from the Cairns wharf. Earlier in the trial, Willey had given evidence that AMSA had searched the St Crispin Reef for two fishermen in separate dories on 26 January 1998.

"I was mistaken when I said the dories were missing in that area, the incident actually happened in Torres Strait on previous days," he said.

On Wednesday 17 November, eight days into the trial, Justice Stanley Jones, together with the entire jury, prosecution and defence lawyers - and Jack Nairn - took a day off from courtroom dramas to visit Fish City on board the cruise boat *Hooker Too*. Although Nairn was not skipper that day, he guided the boat to all three sites visited by *Outer Edge* and explained features of the reefs that had been highlighted in court. It's not known whether the day's outing helped the judge, jury and lawyers understand more intimately the physical background to the tragic events of 25 January 1998.

Two days later Jack Nairn gave evidence for the first time about the disappearance of Tom and Eileen Lonergan. Nairn, clearly nervous but calm, quietly told the court both Katherine Traverso and George Pyrohiw had informed him all the divers were out of the water before he steered *Outer Edge* away from Fish City. Nairn said he was in shock when the covertly taped police interview took place after he learned the Lonergans were missing, but he did not dispute the transcript of what was said during the interview.

"I was really floored. I believe I was in a state of shock," he said.

Nairn said he bought the Outer Edge Dive business in June 1997 and sold it in January 1999 "because of these proceedings".

Nairn said the duties of lookout were shared at Fish City on 26 January by himself and Harald Klose, but the ultimate responsibility rested with the skipper.

Nairn reiterated he had asked George Pyrohiw if all the passengers "including the two in the water" had been counted and Pyrohiw had replied: "Yes, we have 26." Nairn then said he asked both Katherine Traverso and Harald Klose if a head count had been done and they both confirmed all the divers were on board. Nairn denied he had been told the Lonergans were late out of the water on previous dives.

Defence counsel Tony Glynn told the court the head count had been delegated to the most experienced member of the crew, George Pyrihow, and that once, on a previous occasion, Pyrihow had told Nairn to "keep his nose out of it because dive matters were his business".

Glynn said his client was a victim of circumstance.

"Mr Nairn is a man who finds himself plucked from obscurity as a small business owner (and) cast in the role of a villain who caused the death of two passengers."

In his closing submissions Glynn said that while the Lonergans had not been found and had not contacted their families, there was no direct evidence they were dead.

"The Crown has to satisfy you, and satisfy you beyond reasonable doubt, that Mr and Mrs Lonergan are dead. It is not up to Mr Nairn to prove they are alive," he said. "Just because they are missing, you can't presume they are dead. How do you get lost, how do you disappear - if you don't want to - from a boat that size?"

Glynn said seven witnesses had claimed they had seen one or both of the Lonergans since their disappearance.

"These witnesses are different to the people who see Martians or Elvis Presley, but I don't say all the witnesses are correct - a number might have made a mistake. The Crown has to satisfy you every one of them is wrong, but if you think even one of them might be right then you cannot convict my client, because they might be alive."

Glynn told the jury that the dive log was not Nairn's responsibility and he wasn't a qualified divemaster or dive instructor, but he had trained employees on his boat to fulfill those roles. He said Nairn could not be held accountable for the fate of the Lonergans, who remained underwater for 70 minutes - half an hour beyond the designated dive time of 40 minutes..

Glynn said the plea for help on the recovered dive slate was "purported" to be written at 8am on Monday 26 by Tom Lonergan but if the couple had been swept away by currents he would have said so on the slate.

"There was no current to sweep them away. One thing you can say is that they were somewhere where they were left (the night before). Where were Mr and Mrs Lonergan? Where had they gone?" Glynn asked the jury.

"They were alive 18 hours later and in pretty good condition if the writing is genuine. If you think to write on a dive slate - truly a cry for help - why not a direction for help? Not a word. Is it a cry for help, or a piece of evidence meant to be found?"

Glynn said despite a thorough grid search over three days for the couple and some of their equipment washing up on a beach, and despite a number of boats anchored in the area at the time, their bodies had not been found.

"Aerial searchers saw domestic buckets in the water, but no bodies. What are the chances they would have been missed, dead or alive. They were able to write a coherent message the next day - what chance both would abandon their buoyancy vests? Where were the bodies?"

Glynn raised the issue of the controversial entries in Tom and Eileen Lonergans' diaries, stressing he was not advancing theories of either a murder-suicide or a double suicide.

"Both of these theories have exactly the same problems as the Crown case - where are the bodies?"

Glynn said the diaries portrayed a loving couple in a "closely bound partnership" that could mean if one was to disappear the other might feel bound to go as well.

"They show Tom Lonergan as a man who thinks his life is over, who wants a big change in his life to give it some meaning. His is a study of a discontented man, a picture of a man looking for a new life, a man who wants to avoid returning to the trappings of his old life."

Glynn said if the Lonergans staged their disappearance it could have either been feigned or it could have been decided on the spur of the moment.

"It is not for the jury to decide which, but you must be satisfied they are dead. When you weigh up all the evidence, you acquit this man of all the charges."

Crown prosecutor Tom Wakefield in his concluding address said as master of the vessel, Jack Nairn, was responsible for all facets of the operation and "the buck stops here". He said Nairn was guilty of negligence "so bad", it could be described as criminal negligence.

"It may be that Mr and Mrs Lonergan made a wrong decision. Perhaps they swam the wrong way, but that was forced on them. You would expect them to be missed and the boat would return."

Wakefield referred to the contentious diary entries as "what people record, their innermost thoughts constructed in dramatic ways. They are nothing more than that."

He asked the jury to put aside any sympathies they might have for Jack Nairn and deliver a verdict according to the evidence that the Lonergans were left behind at Fish City and their deaths were caused by "omissions" that amounted to criminal negligence by the skipper of *Outer Edge*.

In his directions to the jury Justice Stanley Jones said although there were no bodies, the suggestion that the Lonergans had faked their own deaths had "very cruel consequences for their families and also for Mr Nairn and his family."

He said that to find Nairn guilty the jury must believe his actions had been reckless and showed disregard for the life and safety of others.

On Wednesday 24 November 1999, the jury took less than three hours to find Jack Nairn not guilty of the manslaughter of Tom and Eileen Lonergan.

Extraordinary scenes followed the verdict. Jack Nairn's father, Ian, burst out "Thank God, thank God" and wept unashamedly in the public gallery. Next to him, Outer Edge Dive's operations manager Tom Colrain also cried. After a few moments, John and Kathy Hains, who sat through the trial, embraced Ian Nairn, and whispered words of comfort.

Justice Stanley Jones, his voice shaking at times with emotion, complimented the jury members on the way they carried out their task, before extending the court's sympathy to the Hains family. To Jack Nairn, he said: "Only you would know what this has cost you. You're free to go."

Stepping down from the dock, Nairn, his eyes damp with suppressed tears, entered the gallery, shook hands with John Hains and told him he was sorry. Nairn was then embraced by Kathy Hains, before he returned to his defence team. He left soon after with his wife and father, asking reporters for privacy.

Outside the court, John Hains told a media throng that the family accepted the court's decision.

"I'm a little disappointed but the court did what it was supposed to do and that's the end of the matter," he said. "We've always prayed for Tom and Eileen and we'll continue to do so, and we'll pray for Jack Nairn's family and himself."

John Hains also ruled out long-standing rumours that the family would take civil action against Jack Nairn any time in the future.

"That was never our intention," he said.

For Jack Nairn, still facing Workplace Health and Safety charges over the Lonergans incident, there were no winners to come out of his courtroom ordeal. Although he was free, he had not won. Nairn had lost his business and had managed to pay his legal bills only with the help of his family in Western Australia. He knew he would long be known as the skipper who left the Lonergans at sea, but he had to get on with his life. He had to start again.

Nairn refused to discuss the tragedy and subsequent legal drama at length, except to say he believed he had been made a political scapegoat and suffered harsh treatment at the hands of the government of the day. Nairn also said comments made at the inquest by counsel assisting the coroner, John Bailey, hurt him greatly. Bailey referred to the Outer Edge Dive operation as having a "slipshod, devil-may-care operation".

Nairn said one single factor puzzles and disturbs him the most: Why did the Lonergans remain underwater for 70 minutes - 30 minutes over the designated dive plan? That's the question that continues to mystify observers of this tragic sea drama that made newspaper headlines around the world. It's a conundrum, that, if solved, would perhaps explain everything else about this intriguing mystery.

On 2 May 2000, in the Cairns Industrial Magistrate's Court, personal charges against Jack Nairn for breaches of the Workplace Health and Safety Act were dropped. However, Nairn's family company, Rye Holdings, was fined $27,000 for failing to keep an accurate logbook of the number of people who dived at Fish City on the day the Lonergans disappeared.

Magistrate Bruce Schemioneck said the company was not a "cowboy operation" and although a timely guilty plea had been entered, he was compelled to impose a fine for the "deterrent value".

The fine was in addition to an estimated $350,000 Nairn said his family had paid out in costs associated with his manslaughter trial.

"The Supreme Court took my business, my house, my car, and probably the future education of my children, and it's a struggle to keep going," he said.

Nairn said he was not bitter over the fine handed down, but still believed the decision made at the coronial inquest to charge him with manslaughter was wrong.

Jack Nairn was left with one more legal hammer hanging over his head. Eight weeks after his manslaughter acquittal, Tom Lonergan's family served a writ for damages against Rye Holdings in Western Australia, where the company is registered. The writ, seeking unspecified damages, was lodged by Tom Lonergan's parents and a sister.

Nairn said he had no money left but he would defend his dignity and integrity with whatever resources he could muster.

"I understand how the (Lonergan) family feels about this, I have a family of my own, but there is nothing more certain than I will stand up for myself, and I have to deal with it the best way I can," he said.

"I would give them money if I had it, but I'd feel very sorry for them if this was about money. All this has caused financial ruin and personal pain and suffering for my family and I don't look forward to this matter prolonging the pain."

But in January 2001 Nairn breathed a deep sigh of relief when the news came through that Tom Lonergan's parents had dropped all legal action against him. Once again, the embattled dive boat skipper faced the media, declaring at last he would now be able to resume his life without the threat of more court appearances.

Nairn said he didn't know why the Lonergan family abandoned the writ, but said it would have been a futile action in any case, because he would have been unable to pay any damages.

"They didn't give a reason and it doesn't really matter. The reality is I've been to hell and back over this and nothing was proven against me."

Nairn had survived the tragedy that changed his life, but the legacy of the missing Americans will be in his heart forever. The burden of responsibility will always be his. As he privately said on several occasions: "I've got broad shoulders and I've got to carry this alone. I was the skipper that day."

But Nairn judges himself more harshly than his peers in the dive industry who watched the drama unfold in disbelief, knowing among themselves that Nairn was in the wrong place at the wrong time, and what happened to him could easily have happened to any one of them.

"It was a case of 'there but for the grace of God go I'," said one.

Another: "Jack didn't order a head recount - and that was the only thing he did wrong. It's as simple as that."

Even though a jury found Jack Nairn was not responsible for the deaths of Tom and Eileen Lonergan, that verdict, and the trial itself, failed to shed any conclusive light on the mystery of what happened to the Lonergans.

In the minds of many people there are questions about that final, fateful dive at Fish City that still remain unanswered. And there are those who can't forget the chilling words Eileen Lonergan wrote in her diary about her husband's state of mind, just 16 days before the couple disappeared.

"I had to correct him when he said he hoped that we will die soon together, so I would not be left alone...huh...better alone than dead."

CHAPTER ELEVEN

WHO KILLED RACHEL ANTONIO?

She was waiting for the movies to start and then she vanished. But if she was murdered, where is Rachel's body?

On Saturday 25 April 1998, Bowen schoolgirl Rachel Joy Antonio was looking forward to seeing the movie *Good Will Hunting* at the local beachfront theatre. It was Anzac Day and like any normal teenager on a weekend, the 16-year-old high school student had asked her mother if she could go out that night, enjoy the movie, and get a lift home with one of her friends or a parent afterwards. Failing that, she would catch a taxi home. The cinema was less than 10 minute's drive away from her home near the centre of town. It was a reasonable request and Rachel's mother, Cheryl, agreed. The only trouble was, the family car had a blown headlight, so Rachel had to be dropped off while it was still daylight, well before the movie was due to start at 7pm.

At 5.45pm Rachel stepped from the car directly across the street from the art deco-style Summergarden Theatre twin cinema complex. She told her mother she intended to stroll along Queens Beach to fill in time until the movie started. It was a natural inclination. Rachel was a member of the Bowen Lifesaving Club and joined the club every Sunday on beach patrol. She was a dedicated outdoors girl and the beach was her second home.

Rachel made her way to the stinger safety net, 500m from the theatre, where she met two Mormon church missionaries who held a conversation with her about 6pm. They later reported she appeared to be in a "reflective" mood. Shortly after that she was seen standing outside the tennis courts in Murroona Street near the movie theatre by two men leaving a neighbouring lawn bowls club.

The men asked her if she was all right. She said she was, and moved a few steps away in the opposite direction.

Rachel Antonio then vanished.

When she didn't turn up by 9.30pm, her parents weren't overly concerned. Cheryl and her husband Ian, a local council worker, knew their daughter would phone if there was a problem getting a lift or a taxi home. But as the night drew on, their apprehension grew. Rachel would never stay out without contacting them. But they didn't phone Rachel's friends to see if she was with them, nor did they notify the police - and their car's faulty headlight kept them from driving the streets late at night. It was 6am before Ian Antonio set out in search of his daughter and it was after 9am before Cheryl phoned police.

Rachel Antonio was not overnighting with her friends. She was missing. The owner of the Summergarden Theatre, Benito De Luca, knew Antonio by sight and he was adamant she was not at the *Good Will Hunting* session on that Anzac Day night. He said it was a very quiet night at the theatre and only 12 people attended the 7pm session. Over the next few days, police, State Emergency Service volunteers, worried locals and a contingent of soldiers from Townsville searched the entire Bowen district for Antonio, including all rivers, waterways and dams, but failed to find a single clue to her whereabouts or her fate. The search was hampered by heavy rain over the two days following the teenager's disappearance, effectively erasing potential evidence such as footprints and tyre marks on and around Queens Beach that could have provided police with important leads.

The small north Queensland town was thrown into turmoil by Antonio's disappearance. The slim, year 11 student, with the long brown hair and brown eyes, was well-liked by locals and popular with her peers. As well as her involvement with the surf lifesaving club, she was a promising long-distance runner and a member of the air cadets. She had marched with the cadets in the Anzac Day morning parade through the streets of Bowen. She was close to her two older siblings, John, 24, and 22-year-old Christine, and apparently had a loving relationship with both parents. What had happened to her? Had she been abducted, or murdered, or - for reasons of her own - simply run away from home?

Bowen's 8,500 or so residents felt the chill wind of fear once again. The normally quiet coastal town had already been rocked by two recent murders, both of them still unsolved.

Just five months earlier, on 13 November 1997, retired schoolteacher Herbert Edward Murray, 73, was found murdered on Pennsfield Station, a 730-hectare cattle property 15 kilometres north of the town. Murray, a horse trainer and recently appointed Bowen Turf Club secretary, had been slain by a single gunshot to the head.

The World War II veteran and grandfather of seven was a widely respected and admired member of the Bowen community and had been managing the cattle property when he was murdered. Murray's car, a faded blue 1990 Commodore sedan was missing from the property when his body was discovered. Police believe Murray may have picked up a hitchhiker who later killed him and stole the car.

In March 1998, police found the car abandoned in an inner-city Townsville street following an anonymous tip-off. Detectives were at a loss to explain how the vehicle, widely publicised in a state-wide murder hunt, could have gone unreported for at least three months in busy Mitchell Street, North Ward.

Less than three weeks after Murray's killing, Dianne Mary Angwin, 50, was stabbed in the chest by an intruder who broke into her town unit about 1am. She died on the way to hospital in a neighbour's car. Police believe her killer could be a local who was known to the deceased woman.

And now Rachel Antonio was missing, presumed dead. Police were now investigating three murders. Homicide squad detectives from Brisbane joined north Queensland investigators in a bid to hunt down the killers of Murray and Angwin, and to find Antonio either miraculously alive, or - the most likely scenario - her body.

Police soon had a suspect in their sights but they weren't saying so publicly. Shortly after Antonio's disappearance detectives seized a white Ford Falcon from a 25-year-old local man during a raid on his home. Clothing, a hubcap, a vacuum cleaner and a wheelie bin were also confiscated for scientific tests. It was a breakthrough in the case, but the investigating authorities were cautious. They would only confirm the man was an "associate" of the missing girl.

Chief investigator Detective Inspector Dennis Bauer, confirmed rumours that the "associate" of Antonio attended a birthday party the night she disappeared but left the function "for a considerable period of time" before returning. Bauer told reporters witnesses had come forward and provided police with information regarding the man's movements and that was being "followed up" by invesigators.

But people like to talk, especially in small towns, and journalists who had flocked to Bowen saw the emergence of a picture that seemed to tell a story that was not totally based on rumour and innuendo. Too many people were saying the same things, albeit only with the assurance their names would not be used in the media, and those things began to add up to what was considered a reasonably accurate version of events surrounding Antonio's disappearance.

According to reports from eyewitnesses, Rachel Antonio's still unnamed "associate" had left his brother's 18th birthday party at the family's Rose Bay home shortly before 7pm to pick up a bag of ice and hire a video five kilometres away in Bowen. He was absent for approximately 50 minutes and when he returned he was not wearing the same T-shirt and had then changed into other clothes. The "associate" told partygoers his car had broken down and he removed his shirt because he'd got it dirty trying to start the engine.

Antonio's friends told police they believed she had been in a relationship with the "associate" but he had broken it off before her disappearance. In October, police spokesman Brian Swift confirmed a "more than platonic" relationship had taken place, but refused to name the man involved. Swift said the relationship had been confirmed by four witnesses who had come forward independent of each other with new information. He said the relationship had been kept secret from Antonio's parents but there was evidence the couple had been seen embracing on several occasions. Police also received a profile report from a Brisbane psychologist that suggested the last person to see Antonio would have been known to her and able to make her comfortable and relaxed in his presence. Swift also said police were interested in evidence that a man had purchased a pregnancy test kit from a Bowen pharmacy before Antonio disappeared, but there was no evidence the teenager was pregnant when she went missing.

In mid-December 1998, the Queensland Crime Commission used its special authority to hold hearings into the Antonio case after certain witnesses declined to be interviewed by police during their investigation. Under the commission's legislative powers, individuals face contempt charges if they refuse to give evidence at closed hearings.

On Thursday 30 December 1998, eight months after Rachel Antonio mysteriously and dramatically disappeared, police finally charged their prime suspect with her murder. He was - as everybody in Bowen already knew - the missing teenager's "associate", Robert Paul Hytch, a labourer and former captain of the local surf lifesaving club.

Hytch's lawyers were successful in a bail application to the Supreme Court and Hytch remained free to await a committal hearing. In a statement to the court at the application, Detective Sergeant Mark Inmon of the Bowen CIB revealed Antonio had lied to Hytch, telling him she was pregnant with his child, after he had ended their relationship in favour of another woman. Hytch had then allegedly coerced Antonio into taking a home pregnancy test but she had faked a positive result using urine from a pregnant friend.

Outside court, a small band of Hytch's supporters gathered bearing placards that read: "Rachel phone home," and "No body, no murder".

At the committal proceedings in the Bowen Magistrate's Court in May, Cheryl and Ian Antonio said they didn't believe their daughter was involved in a relationship with Hytch, but several witnesses gave evidence to the contrary.

Bowen resident Sandra Ross testified she had seen Antonio sitting on the beach with Hytch leaning over her as if they were about to kiss, and barman Brendan Reid said he had seen the couple in conversation outside the North Australian Hotel just before Christmas 1997. Reid said Hytch later told him he was "sort of seeing her".

Bowen Lifesaving Club member Hagar Quirke told the court Hytch and Antonio often left training together for periods of time and were often seen flirting with each other.

Mormon missionary Clinton Walker testified that Rachel Antonio had spoken to him and a colleague about an hour before she disappeared. He said Antonio questioned him about life after death and wanted to know if people go to hell if they committed suicide. It was revealed that a friend of Antonio had committed suicide a few months earlier.

The court heard Hytch allegedly told police he did not arrive at the video store until 7.40pm on the night Antonio disappeared - 40 minutes after he left the party at his parents' home. He claimed his car broke down but could not explain to police how he fixed the problem, nor could he explain what happened to the dirty T-shirt he said he discarded and left on the radiator.

Senior Sergeant Gary Wright gave evidence he inspected Hytch's vehicle 11 days after it allegedly broke down and despite a build-up of dust and grease under the bonnet, he could find no indication the engine had been worked on recently.

"I would have expected to find some marks if it had been touched in the past month or so, but I found nothing," he said.

In a startling revelation to the court, Cheryl Antonio testified that 10 months before her daughter disappeared, she had been stalked for weeks by a man of "Turkish" appearance. She said the man followed her daughter home and to a fun run, walked past the house twice, and protested "I do nothing" when confronted by her.

Detective Senior Constable Paul McCusker told the court 51 alleged sightings of Rachel Antonio had been reported to police since she disappeared but none had been confirmed and most were proven to be cases of mistaken identity.

In November 1999, Robert Hytch, then 26, faced trial in Townsville's Supreme Court charged with the murder of Rachel Antonio.

One of the prosecution's trump cards was the fact that several drops of blood that were found on a sandal worn by Hytch on the night Antonio disappeared had a DNA profile consistent with the missing teenager.

The prosecution claimed that Hytch had left his brother's birthday party for a secret meeting with Antonio near the movie theatre, where he lured her away and murdered her. It was alleged Antonio had falsely claimed she was pregnant in a bid to seek revenge against Hytch for dumping her for another woman. Antonio had allegedly told a friend that Hytch had got the woman pregnant. A week before she disappeared Antonio had told the friend: "I'm going to call Robert and ask if he's lying about her being pregnant (and) if he says yes, I'll tell him I'm not pregnant and that it was a lie".

The jury heard Antonio was planning to force Hytch into giving her $350 so she could leave Bowen. School friend Rebecca Bond testified Antonio had told her she intended to inform Hytch on 25 April that she was pregnant.

The police case was backed up by the two Mormon missionaries who said Antonio had told them during their long conversation with her that she was meeting her boyfriend at the movies. They claimed she even mentioned he lived at Rose Bay. Hytch denied a meeting was arranged or took place, but admitted phoning Antonio at 5pm that day to remind her about a surf patrol the next day.

The court heard Hytch told police Antonio had pursued him after he returned from a year-long visit to England in 1997 but he resisted her advances and remained "just friends". Hytch said while he was away from Bowen, Antonio had "chased" his brother Scott, but when he got back from overseas she turned her attentions to him.

"I told her no way, you're only fifteen, and stayed away from her (but) she still seemed pretty keen," Hytch told police.

The court also heard Hytch's mother, Sheila, claimed young men were "scared" to take Antonio home because she was reluctant to get out of the car and "couldn't be trusted".

Former manager of the Bowen Swimming Pool, Sidney Pate, denied he made phone calls to the Antonio and Hytch households late on the day Antonio disappeared. Pate had shut the pool 90 minutes early that day to see the 7pm session of *Good Will Hunting* at the Summergarden Theatre. Theatre owner, Benito De Luca, said as well as not seeing Antonio at the session, he can't remember seeing Pate either.

Pate said he was away from Bowen in May 1998 attending a swimming coaches' conference in Melbourne and visiting his family in Brisbane, but returned to "clean up some business" before returning to Brisbane to live in June. He denied any knowledge of Antonio's disappearance.

The court heard evidence of Hytch and Antonio "flirting" on the beach during surf lifesaving training drills and Antonio "playing around" with a man who drove a red sports car.

Defence counsel Harvey Walters told the jury of seven women and five men there was no proof at all that Rachel Antonio was dead and the Crown case relied solely on "small-town gossip" that she was having an affair with his client.

"How can you be satisfied beyond a reasonable doubt that she's dead?" Walters asked the jury. "The Crown do not have a body and do not have any idea of how - if she is dead - she died. There is no evidence of foul play, no crime scene and no murder weapon."

Walters suggested that Antonio had disappeared of her own accord, as "hundreds" of people in Australia do every year for reasons of their own.

"She's not a Jaidyn Leskie. She's old enough to take care of herself and at that age of adolescence where you can do silly, impulsive things."

Walters referred to evidence heard from witnesses who reported sightings of women fitting Antonio's description from all over Queensland since her disappearance.

"I concede they can't all be right, but can they all be wrong?"

But in his closing address to the jury, Crown prosecutor Jim Henry said it was ludicrous to suggest Antonio was still alive.

"She was not one of the problem children of Bowen, but someone planning to make something out of her life until she had it taken from her.

"The problem with murder cases is the best witness has been eliminated."

Henry said the circumstantial case against Robert Hytch was too strong for the accused to be not guilty of Antonio's murder.

"Could he be this unlucky? He said he's never been in a relationship with Rachel Antonio yet a myriad of witnesses have given evidence making it obvious they were (in a relationship)," Henry said. "He's not had a relationship with her, but of all the times he goes to get a video alone, is the same time Rachel was last seen waiting at Queens Beach. He's not unlucky, but guilty."

Addressing the jury, trial judge Justice Kerry Cullinane singled out the issue of provocation as a possible factor to differentiate between a verdict of murder and that of manslaughter.

He pointed out that if the accused "caused the death in the heat of passion, caused by sudden provocation, and before there is time for his passion to cool, and a person of ordinary characteristics and powers of self-control might similarly in those circumstances have lost his power of self-control and acted in the same way, then the accused would be guilty not of murder but manslaughter. It is for the prosecution to exclude provocation beyond a reasonable doubt."

On Wednesday 17 November, after hearing 15 days of evidence, the jury took five-and-a-half hours to find Robert Hych not guilty of murder, but guilty of manslaughter. Justice Cullinane remanded the former surf lifesaving club captain in custody until sentencing.

Hytch stood expressionless in the dock while members of his family cried behind him in the public gallery.

Later, Jim Henry said the verdict indicated "provocation manslaughter, or manslaughter in emotional circumstances" but the court had failed to take into consideration the accused man's total lack of remorse.

"We have a man who must know where Rachel's body is and we have a family who don't have their child's body," he said.

Outside the court Ian and Cheryl Antonio told a media gathering that their daughter had been murdered and her murderer had been let off with the lesser verdict of manslaughter.

"It should definitely have been murder. The legal system is wrong and needs reform," Ian Antonio said. "Not only did we lose our daughter but there's been 18 months of lies and cover-up."

The couple said the family could not move on with their lives until Rachel's body was found.

"We know she's gone, we know Robert's murdered her. We want to know where the body is so we can have a funeral," Cheryl

Antonio said.

Two weeks later Robert Hytch was jailed for nine years.

On 4 August 2000, Hytch's conviction was quashed in a unanimous judgement by the Court of Appeal and a new trial ordered.

Justice Bob Douglas said Hytch's appeal was based on the premise that the Crown, on the admissible evidence, had a weak circumstantial case.

"The jury was not satisfied Hytch killed Rachel either intending to kill her or do her grievous bodily harm," Douglas said. "The verdict of manslaughter appears to smack of compromise."

Court of Appeal president Margaret McMurdo and Justice Ken Mackenzie ruled the trial judge had not sufficiently explained to jury members how they could fully make use of evidence that Antonio intended to meet Hytch on the day she disappeared.

Mackenzie said although Hytch's appeal questioned the validity of DNA evidence, that was not a fundamental flaw in the Crown case, and the "deficiencies" of the evidence could be avoided in another trial.

Because Hytch had already been acquitted of murder by a jury, he could not be tried again on that charge, but could only be retried for manslaughter.

Six days later Robert Hytch was released from the Townsville Correctional Centre after Justice Kerry Cullinane ruled he could see no reason why Hytch should not be freed on bail pending his retrial. Hytch had spent eight months in jail as a medium security prisoner, spending five days a week working in the prison store.

Immediately after his release Hytch announced plans to marry Maree Young, 23, whom he proposed to when she was visiting him in jail. The couple said they became secretly engaged shortly after he was imprisoned.

In June 2001, at his second trial in the Townsville Supreme Court, Hytch was found not guilty of manslaughter.

Three years after Rachel Antonio disappeared, the man accused of killing her and disposing of her body, had been cleared of all charges relating to her death.

But that wasn't the end of the Hytch-Antonio saga. In October, Sheila Hytch was ordered to face court on perjury charges. It was alleged that Hytch lied at her son's second trial about his movements on the night Antonio disappeared. Crown prosecutor Peter Smid alleged Hytch's testimony at the June trial conflicted with statements she gave to the Queensland Crime Commission during its investigation into the case. Smid told the court that during the trial Hytch had testified that her son had left the family party to buy ice at her request, and at a time she chose, not a time of Robert Hytch's choosing. If that was the case, Robert Hytch, of course, could not have been part of an arranged meeting with Antonio. But Smid alleged the mother's testimony was "blatantly contrary" to evidence given at the Queensland Crime Commission hearing

The perjury charges against Sheila Hytch were dismissed in the Townsville Magistrate's Court three months later. Magistrate Ian Fischer ruled there was insufficient evidence for a jury to convict her.

In May 2003, north Queensland police announced a new search for the missing teenager would take place in a fresh bid to unravel the bizarre mystery.

Military equipment that utilises ground penetrating radar technology was planned for the search when it became available.

Regional crime co-ordinator Detective Inspector Richard Nikola would not reveal details of the proposed search and would not be drawn on the subject of further suspects in the case.

"I never talk about suspects," he said. "This is about the disappearance of a person and we haven't found a body."

Nikola said a new team of detectives had been assigned under the police Homicide Case Management System to "renew investigations and revist the case".

"This case has never been closed and I'm very keen to resolve the matter," he said.

Cheryl Antonio said she was pleased the search for her daughter's body was continuing and she hoped the police would be successful with their latest effort. She said the family had not yet learned the truth about what happened on that tragic night five years ago, but it was impossible to believe Rachel had voluntarily disappeared.

"There was no reason for Rachel to run away. She was happy at home, she was doing well at school and she had her life planned. We know Rachel won't turn up. She would always phone us if she was going to be late and let us know. She won't come back."

Cheryl Antonio said her family had no contact with the Hytch family, but in the small community of Bowen they sometimes crossed paths.

"If I see them in the street I just keep walking," she said.

The mystery of who killed Rachel Antonio remains unanswered. Now that Robert Hytch has been cleared of any involvement in her death, there appears to be no other suspects on the police blotter. Who else among her friends and acquaintances could be responsible for such a crime? Police investigators say there is no one who falls into that category. So it must have been a stranger, someone who whisked her away at 7pm on that Anzac Day evening. But why wasn't she seen with that stranger? People in small towns notice strangers with locals. They see and remember things - especially young girls with strange men. Nobody saw Antonio after 7pm. She simply vanished and left no clues to her disappearance. And, despite the most extensive and intense search of Bowen and its surrounding countryside and coastland, her body has not been found.

Bowen mayor Mike Brunker said although the community had largely moved on from the tragic events of Anzac Day, 1998, both families had supporters with strong personal views about what happened to the missing teenager.

"Opinions are still split in the community," he said. "It will always be a real mystery, similar I suppose to the Chamberlain case."

Brunker believes investigators may have taken the girl's disappearance too casually at first, perhaps thinking she had run away and would return or be found in a couple of days.

"There are all types of theories and one of them is the police probably didn't take this too seriously and the trail went cold," he said.

Brunker said one theory was that Antonio's body could have been thrown in a dumpster on a construction site and covered over with rubble.

"A skatebowl was being built near where she was last seen. If she was put in a dumpster at the site, her body could have ended up anywhere."

CHAPTER TWELVE

NATASHA RYAN AND THE MONSTER OF ROCKHAMPTON

Child sex killer Leonard John Fraser was on trial for the murders of four women when one of them, Natasha Ryan, dramatically reappeared after five years in hiding.

It was just after 2.30pm on Thursday 10 April 2003, twelve days into Rockhampton serial killer Leonard John Fraser's trial for the brutal murders of four women, when Crown prosecutor Paul Rutledge stood up and made a dramatic announcement that caused a national media frenzy and sent shock waves through the state of Queensland's judicial system.

Rutledge told the Brisbane Supreme Court that one of Fraser's alleged victims, Natasha Ann Ryan, had just been found alive and well after disappearing in 1998. Ryan was 14 years of age when she went missing and had long been presumed murdered.

Rutledge, in suitably theatrical tones, addressed Justice Brian Ambrose with the words that created a sensation in a trial already making daily headlines for its gruesome litany of violence, rape and murder.

"Your Honour, I am pleased to inform the court that Leonard John Fraser is not guilty of the murder of Natasha Ann Ryan," Rutledge said. "Natasha Ryan is alive."

It was a revelation that stunned the courtroom. Even Fraser, who obviously knew he had not killed Ryan, seemed shocked when the murder charge against him was officially dropped by the judge. Fraser slumped back in his seat, red-faced and wiping away tears.

Fraser, 51, who was currently serving a life prison term for the murder and suspected rape of nine-year-old Rockhampton girl

Keyra Steinhardt in April 1999, now had one less murder charge against him, but still faced charges of murdering Julie Dawn Turner, 39, Beverley Doreen Leggo, 37, and Sylvia Marie Benedetti, 19, all at Rockhampton between August 1998 and April 1999.

Despite several confessions made to a fellow prisoner and taped by prison authorities that he committed all the murders - including a confession that he killed Ryan and disposed of her body - Fraser pleaded not guilty to all the charges.

The trial was adjourned while lawyers, in particular defence counsel Adrian Gundelach, considered the legal implications of an alleged murder victim being discovered alive during the trial of her alleged murderer.

Immediate speculation surfaced that future defence strategies in murder cases where no bodies had been found could point to the Ryan reappearance as evidence that many missing people were not dead but had willingly disappeared for reasons of their own. Consensus in the legal profession strongly indicated the "Ryan factor" would be used to bolster defence arguments as often as possible, and probably with a great deal of success.

The Ryan drama also cast a cloud over the practice of secretly taping prison confessions to be used in court cases. Defence barristers could warn juries of the dangers of using circumstantial evidence to convict a defendant. There could also be complications when multiple murder charges are bundled together into a single trial.

Fraser's former cellmate Allan Quinn testified at the Rockhampton killer's trial that he had made up his mind to help police build a case against Fraser because he had seen Natasha Ryan's father on television appealing for help to locate his daughter.

Quinn, a convicted conman, was secretly wired by police to record conversations with Fraser in their shared cell. During their conversations over a two-year period, Fraser detailed how and where he had murdered his female victims. He also drew "mud maps" of the locations where they could be found. On one occasion Fraser told Quinn he had taken missing teenager Natasha Ryan to a party in an abandoned house on a rural property where he stabbed her to death under a mango tree before using a trench digger to bury her body nearby. He also said the teenager was pregnant to him when he killed her.

Detective Senior Sergeant David Hickey testified that while Fraser was leading police to the remains of his other three victims, Leggo, Benedetti and Turner, he pointed out a particular property halfway between Rockhampton and Yeppoon that he said police should investigate because they would find Ryan's remains there.

Before Ryan's spectacular reappearance, prosecutor Rutledge told the jury at Fraser's trial that, because of his own admissions, the case against the defendant was "overwhelming".

"At the end of the day there will be no doubt that he murdered Natasha Ryan, that he murdered Julie Turner, that he murdered Beverley Leggo and that he murdered Sylvia Benedetti," Rutledge said.

Natasha Ryan failed to return home from North Rockhampton High School on 31 August 1998 after she was dropped off by her mother that morning. Her family never saw her again until she was discovered by police four and a half years later hiding in a cupboard in the home of her long-time boyfriend, 27-year-old milkman Scott Black.

The runaway teenager was seen two days after disappearing from school by friends Ebony Loomans and Maioha Tokotaua at a Rockhampton cinema complex. The friends said Ryan played video games before being picked up by an unknown man in a yellow car. They said Ryan had talked about running away from home because she was pregnant and didn't want to get her boyfriend into trouble.

School social worker Ngari Anne Bean testified at Fraser's trial that Ryan had confessed to smoking marijuana and taking amphetamines and cocaine, and she was worried her baby might be deformed because of the drugs. Bean said Ryan was "extremely troubled" before her disappearance.

Incredibly, Ryan had eluded and deceived family, friends and police, and somehow remained unseen by all who knew her in Rockhampton - a community of 60,000 people. She stayed hidden despite knowing her parents had suffered for years, thinking she was dead - most likely murdered by a serial killer.

An anonymous letter finally tipped police off with a telephone number, leading them to a Mills Avenue address where they found the runaway teenager crouched and trembling in the cupboard after Black had tried to turn detectives away by denying she was in the house.

Ryan told police she had been with Black the entire time she had been missing and had lived almost entirely indoors fearing discovery. She claimed she had ventured outside only six times, under cover of darkness, smuggled to the beach by Black so she could walk barefoot in the sand.

Authorities later revealed that Ryan had ran away from home once before, in July 1988, and had been seen with Black before being found several days later. Friends said the 14-year-old had told them she was pregnant with Black's child. Black denied any involvement with Ryan's runaway escapade, but was later charged with wilful obstruction of a police investigation and fined $1000 after admitting he helped pay for a hotel room to hide the girl because he feared she was suicidal.

Despite Black's obvious close connection with the teenager, police somehow failed to find the two together when she disappeared the second time.

It was revealed that Black had dated Natasha Ryan's older sister Donna in 1998, before switching to the younger sibling.

In May 1999, not long after Keyra Steinhardt's body was found, Rockhampton police reported a female claiming to be Ryan had contacted them for a meeting but had failed to show up at the police station at the agreed time. The call was later dismissed as a hoax.

Black and Ryan had also lived at nearby Yeppoon, but neighbours at both addresses claimed they had no idea a woman had been with Black, insisting they believed he had lived alone. Black had lived the life of a recluse, returning home from his early morning milk run and shunning contact with outsiders except for shopping trips and an occasional trip to the pub. In a story that defies credibility, Ryan told police she hid in cupboards and wardrobes for long periods of time - sometimes for six hours - whenever members of Black's family were in the house.

Ryan's separated parents were shaken and confused by their daughter's back-from-the-dead performance. Her mother, Jennifer

Ryan, had given evidence during the first days of Fraser's trial. She told reporters she was "floored" by the "mind numbing" news which had left her both distressed and relieved at the same time. Natasha Ryan's father Robert, who had travelled from Bundaberg to attend the trial of his daughter's alleged killer, was at first too upset to talk about her bizarre self-exile, but told a media outlet that he had mixed feelings of hurt, happiness and confusion.

Two days after his daughter came back from the dead, Robert Ryan was reunited with her in Rockhampton. She was, he later told the media, "very beautiful, very pale, and very confused and frightened".

"Two years ago I had a memorial service like a funeral for my daughter," he said. "To do that and then find that she's alive...I'm a very mixed-up man and I'm trying to keep my composure."

Natasha Ryan told police that despite the anguish her parents had endured and the search efforts - estimated to have cost $500,000 - made to find her, she had remained in hiding "because the lie had become too big" - especially after Fraser had been charged with her murder in August 2001.

She also told police she and Black were afraid that if she came out of hiding Fraser would "get off with the other girls' murders as well" and she didn't want that to happen because she believed Fraser was guilty of the killings.

Ryan's exposed "big lie" had turned the working-class city of Rockhampton into a media circus with every major television network and print organisation furiously rummaging around daily for breakthrough stories. Ryan was a star at the centre of a feverish bidding war for her tell-all exclusive. Ryan's parents and Black were also wooed with offers. Finally the Ryan family called in celebrity super-agent Max Markson to negotiate a deal among the blue-chip bidders.

It was no surprise to observers when Markson brokered a cheque-book journalism contract with Kerry Packer's magazine and television empire. But Markson refused to reveal who would bank the cheque and denied reports the deal, involving interviews with *60 Minutes* and *Woman's Day*, was worth more than $200,000. Britain's *News of the World* tabloid also got a bit of the action, securing a staged photograph of Ryan huddled in the now famous cupboard for a reported $50,000.

Robert Ryan refused to take part in any media deals involving his daughter, and mother Jennifer, in a Rockhampton radio station interview, also denied making money from the story, saying the family had not signed any contract involving payment.

Natasha Ryan eventually told police she had phoned a telephone counselling service, Kids Help Line, on 10 March 2003, a month before Leonard Fraser was due to stand trial for her murder, telling the operator her name was "Sally" and asking that the police be contacted. She told the counsellor she had run away with her boyfriend several years ago and now that a man had been charged with her murder she wanted to go back to her family. She allegedly asked the counsellor to contact police. But the information was not passed on to police headquarters until three weeks later, and to continue the litany of errors and incompetence, the police officer who took the call failed to check the information and inform either homicide detectives or the missing persons bureau of the situation.

Queensland Police Commissioner Bob Atkinson was far from happy over the bungle.

"I have considerable concern about what appears to be a lack of action by a police officer in relation to a girl calling herself Sally who telephoned a youth counselling service," Atkinson said in a carefully worded statement. "I have spoken to the Crime and Misconduct Commission chairman Brendan Butler and he has agreed to a full investigation to establish whether the inaction amounts to misconduct."

In June the Crime and Misconduct Commission recommended the police sergeant responsible for the incident should be disciplined and the police communications centre should review its procedures to ensure a similar situation did not occur again.

The Natasha Ryan back-from-the-dead saga, arguably the best Queensland news story of the year, had degenerated into a daily media diary of what the 19-year-old was doing, where she was going, who she was seeing, and any other morsel of information that could keep the story rolling.

Her highly-paid 27 April appearance on *60 Minutes* was little more than a tearful sorry-mum-and-dad episode, blended with a declaration of love for Black that still apparently burned in her heart. There were no serious questions asked and the interview that went to air did nothing for the self-styled reputation of *60 Minutes* as a hard-hitting current affairs program.

The reputed $200,000 payout for Ryan's exclusive interview failed to impress either the police or the citizens of Rockhampton, who felt they'd been betrayed by one of their own, and the least they deserved was the complete truth about Ryan's four-and-a-half-year underground escapade. Volunteers who had given up their time and risked their safety in the many searches for the missing teenager were particularly angered by the teenager's apparent lack of remorse.

On 8 May rumours that Ryan and Black would be charged were confirmed when police lodged a sworn complaint in the Brisbane Magistrate's Court to commence proceedings against the couple in relation to false representations causing a police investigation. Police said a full brief of evidence was being compiled, which would then be referred to the Queensland Director of Public Prosecutions for consideration of all the evidence. It was also understood that police were considering the more serious charge of attempting to pervert the course of justice.

Black, meantime, continued his daily milk run, but refused to talk to the media.

In early May, almost a month after Ryan was found huddled in Black's house, the identity of the anonymous letter writer who tipped off police was finally revealed.

Rockhampton massage therapist Len Bauer said he decided to blow the whistle on Ryan's secret hideout after his friend and one-time employee Ben Elkins told him he knew where she was. Elkins, 22, a former boyfriend of the runaway, told Bauer he had spoken to Ryan on the phone several times after she had contacted him six months previously asking for his help. He said he advised her to contact a telephone counselling service after she told him she wanted to end her exile and go home. Bauer said he wrote the letter after discussions with Elkins because they both felt it was the right thing to do, and if they didn't act quickly, the opportunity for police to find her could be lost.

Elkins soon hopped on the dollar bandwagon, selling his story to Channel 9's *A Current Affair* for a rumoured $20,000. Elkins said Ryan had been phoning him for several months but he finally decided to act because she was "basically a prisoner" in Black's house and he was unable to convince her she should let her family know she was alive and safe.

In another strange twist to the bizarre story, police received Bauer's anonymous letter on 9 April, just two days before Scott Black was due to give evidence at Leonard Fraser's trial.

When Fraser's trial resumed four days after Ryan's reappearance, Detective Senior Sergeant David Hickey told the court police had conducted a covert surveillance operation on Scott Black's movements after the teenager disappeared, including a search of his home, but had found no evidence to connect him to the missing girl.

On 30 April, in a sensational appearance, Ryan was called as a defence witness in a packed Brisbane Supreme Court to give evidence at the trial of the man who, just three weeks previously, stood accused of her murder. Ryan, who was the only defence witness, testified she had never met Leonard Fraser, and the first time she heard of him was when he was charged with the murder of Keyra Steinhardt.

Under cross-examination by prosecutor Paul Rutledge, Ryan denied she had ever been pregnant and denied she had told school counsellor Ngari Bean or her friends Ebony Loomas and Maioha Tokotaua that she was pregnant.

Ryan told the court she had made no special plans to run away, but on her last day at school she walked out at lunchtime after an altercation with a teacher, and later walked to Scott Black's house, which he then shared with his parents and brother, and stayed in his room. She said she only left Black's room when his family was out and the house was empty.

Ryan testified she had run away from home on three separate occasions, including "one with Scott", but claimed privilege from answering a number of questions on the grounds they might incriminate her.

An undated note written by Ryan to Black told him of trouble she was having at home and of her intention to run away.

"I really need a friend to talk to at the moment, but I don't think that I will come back because I don't want to get you in trouble like the last time," the note read. "Maybe I will see you some day, but I just want to thank you so much for being there for me and being such a good friend." Ryan declined to say when she had written the note.

In his closing address to the jury, defence counsel Adrian Gundelach asked how a murder case could possibly be influenced by the evidence of "a foolish 14-year-old girl" who had run a way from home.

"It was a bit like being on a plane and the pilot coming over the intercom and saying cheerfully: 'An engine has exploded and I will put on a world-class liar to tell you the other three engines are all right...just ignore the smoke and flames," he said.

Gundelach told the jury the police case was based on a well-known liar, Allan Quinn, who fed Fraser information in jail and then trapped him into repeating it on tape to to help build a police case against him.

Prosecutor Paul Rutledge portrayed Fraser in his closing address as a man who had revealed his own guilt by a cunning manipulation of the truth, and the evidence pointed to the fact he had murdered all three women.

"He has twisted and turned his stories over two years," Rutledge said, describing the triple murder case as one with a "particularly dark shade about it".

Just after 6pm on Friday 9 May - on the same day Natasha Ryan celebrated her 19th birthday and one month after her sensational return to the land of the living - Leonard John Fraser, the monster of Rockhampton, was found guilty of murdering Sylvia Benedetti and Beverley Leggo, and guilty of the manslaughter of Julie Turner.

It's believed the jury decided on manslaughter instead of murder for Turner's death because of confusion over the way she was killed.

After a six-week trial the jury had deliberated for more than a day before deciding Fraser was guilty. The verdict took Fraser's gruesome tally of victims to four and ensured his entry into Australia's hall of infamy as one of the nation's worst psychopathic murderers and Queensland's first known serial killer.

Family members of the three women wept with relief in the public gallery as the verdicts were announced by the jury foreman. Fraser, dressed in a blue jumper and white jeans stood red-faced but impassive, yawning with his hands behind his head as the jury filed out of the court. The grey-bearded killer seemed only mildly interested in the verdicts and what they would almost certainly mean - a lifetime in prison with virtually no chance of parole.

At the same time, Natasha Ryan was at home celebrating her first birthday in five years with her mother Jennifer. Mother and daughter posed for photographs with a huge cake adorned with number 19 - Natasha's age - along with the numbers 15, 16, 17 and 18 - the four missing birthdays she had spent in hiding. Jennifer Ryan lit a symbolic candle that she had used to commemorate special occasions during her daughter's absence.

Perhaps Natasha Ryan also pondered the symbolic reality that, if she had not been discovered in time, Leonard Fraser would almost certainly have been convicted of her murder - on her birthday.

But, fortunately for the women of Rockhampton, Leonard John Fraser's evil reign of terror had finally ended.

Fraser was born in 1951 in the north Queensland sugar town of Ingham but moved to Sydney with his parents when he was six years of age. He dropped out of school when he was 14 and took his first tentative steps on the long road to murder in 1966 when he was sentenced to 12 months detention in a Gosford boys' home for stealing offences. That was innocuous enough for a streetwise 16-year-old testing his mettle against the strength of the law, but the next few years saw Fraser graduate to frequent court and jail appearances for a variety of offences that included car stealing, assault, street brawling and larcency. Still, no-one at that stage could have foreseen the terrible litany of sexual assaults and murders that officially started in October 1972 when Fraser savagely raped a 37-year-old French tourist while she was taking photographs in Sydney's Botanic Gardens.

The mother of two young daughters was visiting Sydney with her husband who was attending an accountant's convention when she was attacked from behind and beaten almost unconscious during the rape. The assault left the woman with a fractured cheekbone and sickening bruises and lacerations to her face.

For the time being Fraser got away with that horrific assault - his first known rape - and drifted north where he was convicted the following month in a Townsville court of living off the earnings of prostitutes.

Back in Sydney Fraser copped five years for robbery but only served 18 months jail time before setting out in June 1974 on a sexual assault rampage, raping one woman and attempting to rape two more. While being interviewed by detectives over the assaults Fraser unexpectedly confessed to the rape of the French woman. Apparently he experienced a rare touch of conscience, telling detectives he regretted the attack. That would be the one and only time Leonard John Fraser showed any remorse for his crimes. In December of that year Fraser was sentenced to 21 years for the sex attacks.

A Long Bay prison psychiatric assessment of the then 23-year-old labelled him a "classic psychopath" with no conscience or ability to control his impulses. Fraser told his psychiatric examiner that he often drank alcohol all day, had smoked marijuana and taken LSD, and engaged in homosexual affairs. He also claimed he belonged to an outlaw bikie gang and rode a stolen motorcycle without a licence. The report concluded that Fraser would "use anyone and anything" to achieve his aims without thought for other people, and "unfortunately there is no known treatment for this psychopathic state".

Despite that damning profile, Fraser only served seven years for his string of violent sex crimes, and in 1981 he headed back to Queensland where the following year he struck again in Mackay, assaulting a woman in her own home. The woman was lucky. She somehow managed to talk Fraser out of raping her. Incredibly, she apparently also talked him into letting her phone her husband. Fraser allegedly told the husband: "I hope you're not going to kill me - I just wanted to prove a point that somebody could break in and rape your missus."

Considering his record, Fraser was also lucky, receiving only two months jail for that offence.

Between 1982 and 1985 Fraser had a de facto relationship with a Mackay woman that was apparently trouble-free. A daughter was born to the couple during that time.

Fraser worked at the Mackay railway yards where he was treated with caution by workmates who thought he was "strange, somebody to be wary of at all times". When police arrived at work sometime in 1985 and led Fraser away, nobody was surprised.

"He didn't come back and we found out later he'd raped a woman," a former railway employee said. "We didn't bat an eye because it was no great shock to us. He was odd, there was something about him that just didn't quite fit in with normal life."

Fraser was convicted of raping a woman at Shoal Point, north of Mackay, after stalking her on a beach for several days. He was sentenced to 12 years at Rockhampton's Etna Creek jail.

At Fraser's trial, Justice Des Derrington told him he was a dangerous man who preyed on lone women, a violent sex offender who "failed to realise the enormity of the cruel and cowardly crimes you have committed." He said Fraser's victims would consider him "the equivalent of a filthy animal".

This time Fraser was forced to serve the full sentence and remained behind bars until January 1997. When he was released Fraser moved in with a woman at Yeppoon who had visited him in jail. The woman, who was terminally ill, was later admitted to a Brisbane hospital where it is alleged Fraser raped her in the hospital chapel. No charges were laid and the woman died a short time later.

In 1998 Fraser lived in Mt Morgan, earning money mowing lawns and doing odd jobs. He also earned a reputation as an oddball who prowled the district at all hours and was often seen talking to children after school. In June he started work at a Rockhampton meatworks where he met Julie Turner, who told relatives and friends she was thinking of sharing a flat with a man she called "Lenny" because he said he could give her a better life.

Turner was last seen sometime after 2am on 28 December at an inner-city Rockhampton nightclub. When she left the club in an intoxicated condition, Fraser was outside, lurking in the shadows, waiting and watching. He silently followed her across a bridge to the Rockhampton Police Youth Club, and when she stopped to light a cigarette he crept up behind her and struck her in the face with his fist. Julie Turner died that night at the hands of the man she had befriended. She was almost certainly raped as well.

The monster of Rockhampton's killing spree had begun.

Fraser's next victim was Beverley Leggo, who was last seen outside a bank in a Rockhampton shopping centre on 1 March 1999. Leggo was a friend of Fraser's intellectually impaired girlfriend, 19-year-old Christine Wraight, who had moved in with Fraser in November 1998. Fraser and Leggo had been friends since 1997, when they stayed at the same hostel in Mt Morgan. On the same day as she was last seen, Leggo accompanied Fraser to a swimming hole at Nankin Creek, northeast of Rockhampton, where he bashed her unconscious with his fists before strangling her with her black sports panties and a bra.

Leggo's handbag was found weighted down with rocks in the Fitzroy River on 1 April, leading police to believe she had been murdered and thrown in the river. A search, however, failed to find her body.

Next on Fraser's killing list was Sylvia Benedetti who was bashed to death on 18 April by the murderous psychopath in the Queensland Hotel, a derelict pub that was due for demolition a few days later. Fraser later admitted killing Benedetti with a block of wood after she resisted his sexual advances.

But Fraser had not yet been questioned by police for any of the three murders and he may have escaped detection, until, less than a week after he murdered Benedetti, he took the life of nine-year-old Keyra Steinhardt as she walked home from school on 22 April. The child's schoolbag, shoes and a hair comb were found in an overgrown allotment, the scene of her murder and abduction. Late that day Fraser was tracked down by police at his Rockhampton unit after they matched his red Mazda sedan with the vehicle seen by witnesses at the spot where Keyra disappeared.

The next day Fraser was charged with child stealing and remanded in custody. On 6 May, after two weeks of fruitless searching by hundreds of police, volunteers, and army personnel, Fraser led detectives to bushland about 100 metres off the Rockhampton to Yeppoon road where they found the decomposed remains of the schoolgirl. Fraser had callously dumped his young victim's body near a dry creekbed and covered it with grass.

At a committal hearing in November 1999, the Rockhampton Magistrate's Court heard there were witnesses to the murder of Keyra Steinhardt on a bush pathway near the Beserker Street State School she attended, but police weren't called until 20 minutes after she was killed.

Lynette Kiernan and her 15-year-old son Tyron said they were sitting on their verandah when they saw a man attack a young girl from behind in a vacant allotment opposite their house. They said the man knocked the girl to the ground, where he bent down and appeared to sexually assault her before dumping a "bundle" behind a clump of trees and hurriedly leave the scene. They saw him return in a red car and watched as he placed the "bundle" in the boot and drive off. Kiernan said she and her husband had seen the little girl "talking and singing to herself" on other occasions as she walked along the track from school. They had seen the same man near her the previous day and presumed he was her father. A man believed to be Fraser had also been seen standing next to the girl at a set of traffic lights after school on the day before she died. A prison officer testified he knew Fraser well, and had seen him on the same day and in the same area where Keyra disappeared.

Kiernan said she thought the "father" may have been disciplining the child when he stuck her, but she became alarmed and phoned police when the man returned and opened the boot. She later testified at Fraser's trial that she made an anonymous phone call to the CIB because "I didn't really want to get involved".

It was only the second week that Kyra's mother had allowed her to walk the 30-minute journey home from school.

Fraser's footprints and tyre tracks from his car were found at the scene of the attack. Keyra's blood was found on the ground and in the boot of Fraser's car. Five blonde hairs were also found in the boot and later DNA-matched to the schoolgirl.

Fraser's former girlfriend, Christina Wraight, told the court she had been with Fraser in his Mazda car when he dumped a "little person" in tall grass in the bush after removing it from the boot. She said Fraser had warned her not to watch what he was doing and later punched her for disobeying him. Later, at Fraser's trial, she said he appeared to be carrying a "blonde doll" wearing a green uniform.

Wraight somehow escaped Fraser's murderous rampage despite living with the killer for about 18 months. Her pet cattle dog was not so lucky. A former landlady claimed she caught Fraser having sex with the dog and promptly evicted him, later selling the house and moving away with her husband. Fraser killed the dog with rat poison and buried it in the same general area as his human victims. Police said he was visibly upset when he pointed out the dog's grave.

During committal proceedings into the murder of Keyra Steinhardt, Fraser was ordered to reappear at a later date on a charge of murdering Sylvia Benedetti. Police had charged him with Benedetti's killing after traces of blood taken from the boot of his car matched Benedetti's blood that was found sprayed on a wall of Room 13 in the abandoned Queensland Hotel. During a search of the condemned hotel police also found bone and tooth fragments and Benedetti's clothes hidden in a refrigerator. The woman's remains were later found half buried in sand at Yeppoon.

The string of cold-blooded murders was beginning to unravel for the cocky serial killer.

At his trial in the Brisbane Supreme Court for the murder of Keyra Steinhardt beginning in August 2000, Fraser pleaded not guilty to a crime Crown prosecutor called a "coldly premeditated attack" on an innocent child.

The court heard Keyra's remains were decomposed to the extent it was impossible to determine if she had been sexually assaulted, but there were no clothes on her remains except for a school jumper covering her head She had suffered a blow to the skull, inflicting a 40mm fracture, but it could not be established if the blow had been fatal.

The court also heard Fraser on a police tape offering to lead them to the girl's body in exchange for the lesser charge of manslaughter because he was "scared to go down on the big one (murder)". Fraser told police he couldn't explain how Keyra's blood came to be in the boot of his car and he had never seen the schoolgirl except for pictures of her in newspapers and on television after she went missing.

"I am not a child molestor (or) a child abductor and I am not a murderer," he said. But after leading police to her body Fraser said that although his mind was a "haze" he was probably responsible for killing the girl and he must have panicked afterwards and tried to conceal her body.

After he was charged with her murder Fraser offered an apology to the girl's parents.

"I'd like to say sorry to her mother and father. I know a lot of people won't believe me, but if you check my background it's not my go to harm a child," he said.

The court heard a tape recording of Fraser asking a fellow prisoner, who was about to be released, to dispose of a knife hidden in a peg basket in his flat, saying: "If I get caught with it, you know, I'm gone."

Brett Bignall, who had previously served jail time with Fraser, volunteered to be locked up with the accused man after he heard about the Keyra Steinhardt case. Police installed a listening device in a cell shared by the men in the Rockhampton watchhouse and recorded Fraser saying he wanted the knife to "disappear" before police found it.

"There's nothing wrong mate, I just want it away from there," Fraser said.

The court heard DNA tests confirmed blood on the knife belonged to the murdered schoolgirl.

Prosecutor Paul Rutledge told the court the covert tape recording clearly linked Fraser with the knife and the child's murder.

"The simple, brutal explanation was he had plunged that knife into the body of Keyra Steinhardt in her neck or upper chest," he said.

On Thursday 8 September, after a 19-day trial, Fraser was found guilty of murdering the schoolgirl in an attack that Justice Ken Mackenzie called a "parent's worst nightmare".

Paul Rutledge said Keyra had been the victim of a premeditated and sexually motivated attack that had resulted in her death. Fraser was subsequently sentenced to an indefinite term in prison -

effectively a life sentence.

At Fraser's subsequent trial for the murders of Julie Turner, Beverley Leggo, and Sylvia Benedetti - and of course Natasha Ryan, before she materialised unharmed from her secret life with Scott Black - the court heard of an elaborate plot by Fraser to blame the killings on a character he invented and named "Squeaky".

On 18 January 2001, Fraser wrote a "press release" purporting to come from Squeaky, which Fraser tried to smuggle out of the cell he shared with police informant Allan Quinn. But the so-called press release that was intended for the media went straight to detectives who were taping conversations between the two prisoners.

"I want you to air this to the world by the tabloids and the electronic media," the statement began. "I want you to understand that I am responsible for all of the murders in the Rockhampton area. You will never know my real name, you can refer to me as Squeaky. Now I will give you information on these murders that only the real culprit would know."

The statement outlined a curious blend of fact and fantasy that served only to tighten the police case against Fraser. By this time he had already led detectives to the remains of his last three victims and Squeaky's description of how they were killed tallied with Fraser's own secretly recorded confessions, as well as forensic tests carried out on the women's remains and clothing. Squeaky also detailed information that, as he claimed, could indeed be known only by the "real culprit" - such as the fact that Leggo had been strangled with her own underwear and a pair of sandals belonging to Turner could be found near where she had been murdered. One sandal and a bra were later found at the location.

Squeaky also "confessed" to the murder of Natasha Ryan, several rapes and another "30-odd" assorted crimes.

Fraser's mixed bag of truth and lies included an admission to Quinn that he had murdered a female backpacker and dumped her body in an abandoned wildlife park north of Rockhampton. A comprehensive police search, however, failed to find any evidence to back up the claim.

Detective Senior Sergeant David Hickey told the Brisbane

Supreme Court that Fraser continually switched stories, sometimes admitting to dumping the bodies of his victims himself and at other times blaming Squeaky. In one version, Fraser claims Squeaky took him to the burial sites after a drinking session and threatened him with a gun, warning him to keep his mouth shut about the graves.

And then, despite admitting to Hickey in taped interviews that he dumped all four bodies, he insisted that Squeaky alone had killed the victims.

" 'Til the day that I die, I still deny that I done murder," he told Hickey.

In November 1999, Fraser told Quinn: "The cops think I am a piece of shit but they don't realise what I've gone through in my life, what I have gone through that has caused me to kill those people. All the hate over the years (has) come to the fore and has ended with the murder of these people."

During Quinn's two-year undercover operation that recorded more than 150 hours of taped conversations with Fraser, the convicted fraudster gave up a personal chance of parole to continue his risky double life in the prison cell he shared with the convicted murderer. He did it for the relatives of Fraser's victims, he told detectives, and to atone for his criminal past. Whatever the reason, there is little doubt that if he had been unmasked as an informer, the age-old prison code would have dealt with him harshly and swiftly. Regardless of the fact that Fraser was considered a "rock spider" - jail terminology for a pedophile - for the rape and murder of Keyra Steinhardt, a police informant was even worse, and Quinn would have faced a bleak future had he been discovered.

After his conviction for the killings of Turner, Leggo and Benedetti, Fraser refused to submit to a psychiatric examination requested by his defence counsel prior to sentencing. Prosecutor Rutledge put his viewpoint bluntly, stating Fraser was clearly a danger to the community, adding: "We don't need a psychiatrist to tell us that."

Rutledge tendered victim impact statements from the families of the three slain women to Justice Brian Ambrose for his consideration before sentencing. He also tendered psychiatric assessments and sentencing remarks relating to Fraser's numerous offences over the past three decades.

Rutledge said the Crown would ask for an indefinite sentence for the three killings, including a 30-year minimum imprisonment term for the two murders.

On 13 June 2003 Justice Brian Ambrose sentenced Fraser to three indefinite jail terms and ordered he serve at least 30 years in prison before he is considered for parole. It was the first time in Queensland an indefinite jail sentence has been handed down for manslaughter.

Ambrose described Fraser as an incurable psychopath with a brutal sexual drive that drove him to kill females "from middle-aged women down to children".

A post-trial psychiatric assessment of Fraser concluded he was a "sexual sadist (whose) interest in sexual violence extends to children". The report stated he was resigned to a lifetime behind bars.

Prosecutor Paul Rutledge told the court Fraser "should never see the outside of a prison wall again".

Conceivably, though - despite a staggering total of four indefinite jail terms - the serial sex killer could be free again at the age of 81.

In the meantime Natasha Ryan was apparently intent on rebuilding her life in the Rockhampton community. The now-famous runaway girl planned to complete her education to Year 10 level by completing a five-month course at TAFE college.

Ryan visited Bundaberg in May to be with her father Robert and his wife and two children on his 51st birthday

Robert Ryan, who owns an electrical wholesale business, and who had maintained a low profile throughout his daughter's back-from-the-dead saga, told a journalist Natasha couldn't pose with him for a newspaper photo without special permission from her lawyer.

"I feel she can't open up," Ryan said. "She's been told what she can and can't do while she's here."

In June Natasha Ryan left her mother and stepfather's home and moved back into her former suburban hide-out with Scott Black.

The trial of Leonard John Fraser and the reappearance of

Natasha Ryan created a headline feast for Australia's media industry. It also became a milestone case in Queensland legal history. Fraser became the state's first convicted serial killer after one of his alleged victims turned up alive during his trial, and then appeared as a defence witness. The trial was described at one stage by presiding judge Justice Brian Ambrose as a "sideshow" because of the bizarre developments that occured throughout the court proceedings.

Although most people consider it unlikely that Fraser will ever again prowl the streets looking for victims, few will forget the monster who lived in their midst and turned Rockhampton into a city of fear.

And few will forget the secret life of back-from-the-dead runaway, Natasha Ann Ryan.

CHAPTER THIRTEEN

NO JUSTICE FOR THE MACKAY SISTERS

Two little girls were raped and murdered more than three decades ago but the death of suspect Arthur Stanley Brown means the killer's identity may forever remain a mystery.

The murders of the Mackay sisters in 1970 and the death of Arthur Stanley Brown in 2002 are inexorably linked by time and circumstance, but it now may never be known if Brown was indeed the heartless killer who raped and stabbed the two little girls at lonely Antill Creek in north Queensland.

Brown, 90, died in an Atherton nursing home on 6 July 2002 and was buried friendless in the town's cemetery. There was no public farewell or sympathy, and no media attention for the man who became the chief suspect in the brutal sex slayings of Judith and Susan Mackay more than three decades ago. Brown had managed to escape judgement after a jury failed to convict him and an ensuing two-year legal battle over his mental state bogged down in a mire of judicial wrangling that effectively guaranteed his freedom from justice.

With Brown's death, one of Queensland's most horrific crimes remains unsolved. Police now have no leads and must start again in a renewed attempt to prove, once and for all, who did rape and murder the sisters all those years ago.

At about 8am on 26 August 1970, seven-year-old Judith and her sister Susan, 5, set out from their Aitkenvale home on the outskirts of Townsville to catch a bus to school. The bus stop was only a short distance down the street. It was a normal weekday morning and the little girls were among hundreds of other children around the city on their way to school.

Although kidnapping and child sex crimes were rare in Australia at that time, the national psyche had been scarred by the strange disappearance of the three Beaumont children from an Adelaide beach in 1966. Parents across the country were suddenly alert and warned their children to beware of strangers.

Bill and Thelma Mackay were no exception and had taught their daughters not to get into cars with anyone they did not know. But the girls had walked to the bus stop many times and their parents had no reason to think that this morning was anything other than a pleasant winter's day in the sleepy northern city.

Tragically, Judith and Susan did not arrive at school that day. Later in the afternoon news spread throughout the city that the Mackay sisters had been abducted and grave fears were held for their safety.

Two days after the biggest search in north Queensland's history got under way, the bodies of the girls were found at Antill Plains, 25 kilometres southwest of Townsville, just off the highway to Charters Towers.

It was a discovery searchers had dreaded.

Susan's body was found laying on her back in the creek bed, dressed only in her underwear. Judith was about 70 metres away, face down and naked. In a grotesque gesture, the killer had carefully folded the girls' uniforms and placed them beside their bodies.

A post-mortem revealed the sisters had been sexually assaulted, stabbed and strangled.

Despite all their efforts, police investigations led nowhere. One of their strongest leads was the description of a man driving a vehicle believed to have been either a green or blue FJ Holden with an odd-coloured passenger door. Witnesses said the driver had olive or suntanned skin and described his hair variously as "thick wavy", "brown greying" or "dark woolly". They told police they had seen the girls in the car with the man on the day they disappeared. But neither the car nor its driver were ever located and the manhunt for the killer, although never shelved, wound down as time passed and all leads were exhausted.

Arthur Brown did not attract police attention when the sisters were murdered. He was a wiry, 58-year-old at the time and lived a quiet, unassuming life. He was employed as a carpenter with the Queensland Public Works Department, working as a maintenance man at a number of schools, including Aitkenvale State School, where the Mackay girls were pupils. Brown was an introspective man, neat and tidy to the point of being compulsive, and was known for his meticulous habits, such as ironing creases in his freshly-starched work clothes every day.

Brown was married to Hester Porter until her death in 1980. He then married Hester's sister Charlotte.

It was 28 years before the authorities showed any interest in Brown. In 1998 a relative, then living in Perth, came forward and told police Brown had sexually molested family members for years and had shown a macabre interest in the Mackay case.

Homicide detectives suddenly had a new line of inquiry and in December they moved in and arrested Brown for the 1970 murders.

In March 1999, after a five-day committal hearing in the Townsville Magistrate's Court, Brown was ordered to stand trial for the abduction, sexual assault and murders of the Mackay sisters. He was also committed on another 32 charges of sexual offences against four girls under the age of 14 in Townsville and Rockhampton between 1975 and 1977.

Defence counsel Mark Donnelly told the court Brown pleaded not guilty.

"My client categorically and unequivocally denies the charges," he said.

The court heard evidence from three witnesses who claimed Brown confessed to the killings.

Building manager John Hill testified he first worked with Brown when he joined the Public Works Department as a 16-year-old apprentice carpenter in 1975. He said he was a passenger in Brown's blue/grey Vauxhall sedan on one occasion as they drove past the Townsville police station when he remarked to Brown: "I wonder if the police will solve that Mackay sisters' murder?" Brown allegedly replied: "I know all about that. I did it."

Another witness, Richard White, gave evidence a man named "Ardie" Brown had told him in a Charters Towers hotel bar in August or September 1970 that he had "killed those two girls" and got away with it. Asked if he had seen the man again, White pointed to Brown in court and said: "That's him there."

White said he reported the incident to police but heard no more about it.

A former family friend, Merle Martin-Moss, testified Brown told her during a conversation in 1970 that he "could" have killed the two sisters.

Vietnam veteran Neil Lunney was one of several witnesses who gave evidence they saw two young girls with a man in a car that resembled a Holden on the morning the Mackay sisters disappeared.

Lunney said he saw a man who looked "like Mickey Mouse, with big ears that jutted out of his face" driving erratically near Townsville at about 8.15am. Lunney said he tried to pass the car three times, but was nearly run off the road, provoking him to shout furiously at the driver: "How can you be so irresponsible with young children in the car?"

Lunney told the court two girls were sitting next to the driver, with the smaller of the two in the middle, and the older girl leaning forward with her hands on the dashboard. He said the girls appeared relaxed, as though they knew the man who was driving and were comfortable with him.

In 1971 Lunney picked 28-year-old Wayne Francis Gould from a police line-up as a man who closely resembled the driver of the car.

Lunney testified he told police the man "could have been the brother of the man I saw" but did not positively identify him as the driver.

"I will never forget the face - it has haunted me for 26 years," Lunney said.

Retired detective Charles Bopf, who led the investigation into the murders, said during an interview that Wayne Gould was brought back to Townsville from Western Australia where he had "confessed" to the murders after apparently reading a true crime book, but after investigating his movements, police declared Gould could not have killed the sisters.

"I went across personally and brought him back but he didn't fit the bill," Bopf said.

Bopf, who retired in 1982 after 38 years as a police officer, said Neil Lunney was confident at the 1971 line-up that Gould was the man he had seen with the sisters.

"We used Lunney to the fullest of our ability and he picked Gould in the line-up, but he later went cold," Bopf said. "He wasn't as sure in 1971 as he was in court in 1999. People sometimes grow stronger in their beliefs over the years."

Jean Thwaite told the committal hearing a man with two young girls in his car drove into her Ayr service station on the morning the Mackay sisters disappeared. She said the driver was a "fresh-looking, gruff man" in his 30s who was wearing a white shirt that appeared to have been washed with coloured garments.

Thwaite told the court she had been "haunted" by the tearful face of Susan, the youngest child, ever since.

"She was such a pretty little thing. She had been crying and rubbed her eyes, as children do."

Thwaite said she phoned police that evening after recognising Susan on a television news bulletin.

Charles Bopf said Thwaite's sighting was considered high priority information and fully investigated as a serious lead.

"I was out west at the time, but police back in Townsville chartered a light aircraft and spent two days searching the bush for the car Mrs Thwaite described."

Three witnesses told the committal hearing they had been driving together in the early afternoon of 26 August 1970 when they saw a slim man with "woolly dark hair" walking towards a "rounded" early model Holden car parked on the roadside at Antill Creek. They said the man was wearing a white shirt and black, baggy trousers.

Retired cleaner Dorothy Renouf testified she worked with Brown at the Aitkenvale school where the Mackay girls were students. She said Brown was "paranoid" at the prospect of being alone with children, claiming they would "set you up" in compromising situations. She said he refused to work in toilets until she had checked to make certain no children were there, saying "the kids of today will get you hung".

In October 1999 Arthur Brown faced trial in the Townsville Supreme Court for the murders of the Mackay sisters.

At the trial evidence was heard from family members that Brown had mentioned the Mackay murders on many occasions during the 1970s. Valerie Porter, who was married to Brown's stepson, told the court the accused had said to her: "I could have done that."

Crown prosecutor Jim Henry told the jury many witnesses who saw the girls on the day they disappeared described the car they were in as either an EH or EJ Holden - a vehicle similar in shape to Brown's Vauxhall sedan, which had one door a different colour to the rest of the car.

Yvonne Porter told the court Brown confided in her that he had taken the door off his car and buried it in his back yard because he didn't want to be "interviewed or annoyed" by anybody.

But the jury failed to reach a verdict and a retrial was listed for July 2000. Nobody knew it at the time but the case was about to develop into a Pandora's box of legal complexities and ethical arguments over Brown's mental state and his capacity to stand trial.

At the new trial, Brown's legal team challenged the validity of the proceedings on the grounds that, because of his poor mental state, he was unable to mount a proper defence on his own behalf. But a specially-empanelled jury decided otherwise, finding Brown was able to understand proceedings and was fit to stand trial.

In the meantime Brown's wife had taken his case to the Mental Health Tribunal which, after due consideration, found that the accused, because of "progressive dementia" could not properly instruct lawyers for his defence, and he was therefore unfit to stand trial.

But in a see-saw struggle, the Attorney-General appealed the ruling on the basis the tribunal did not have the jurisdiction to make such a decision.

In a 2-1 judgement, the Court of Appeal agreed, finding the tribunal did not have the power to over-rule the jury's lawful decision that Brown should stand trial.

In early 2001 another twist in the bizarre legal wrangle confused the matter even further when the Director of Public Prosecutions Leanne Clare hired an independent psychiatrist to assess Brown's mental condition.

Brown was found by the psychiatrist to have degenerative Alzheimer's disease that was expected to progressively deteriorate. Four other psychiatrists who had previously examined Brown agreed with the diagnosis. As a result, Clare ordered that all charges against him be discontinued. One year later Brown was dead.

Charles Bopf said Brown was never a suspect in the Mackay murders and remained completely unknown to police until 1998 when a family member then living in Perth came forward with allegations that Brown had sexually molested young female relatives in Townsville in the 1970s. The family had kept Brown's alleged sexual activities secret on advice from a now-deceased solicitor who told them a trial and the publicity would be too traumatic for the victims.

"They were advised they shouldn't put themselves through such an ordeal so they didn't and his (Brown's) name never came up," Bopf said. "He had an incredible run of luck, but finally the lady in Perth thought it was time do do something. This lady had a conscience and she gave police very valuable information."

Bopf said his team of detectives had always believed the murderer was somebody known to the children.

"The parents told us the children wouldn't get in a car with a stranger and so we had something to go on," he said. "A male relative working on a station at Winton was an early suspect, but we discovered he hadn't left the area on the day the girls disappeared, so it was quite conclusive that he wasn't the offender."

Another person who raised some degree of suspicion was a local taxi driver who was present when the sisters' bodies were found at Antill Creek.

"Half the population was out searching that day," Bopf said. "The cabbie was out there with three or four others when one of them, a prospector fellow, found the body. We don't know why the cabbie picked that particular area to search, and there were suggestions made, but he had nothing to do with it."

Brown attracted the attention of South Australian police after he was charged with the Mackay murders. He was immediately considered a suspect in the mysterious disappearance of the three Beaumont children from the Adelaide suburb of Glenelg in late January 1966. The children - Jane, 9, Arnna, 7, and four-year-old Grant - were last seen walking from the beach towards a bus stop. A witness also saw them earlier playing with a man at the beach. He was described as slim and athletic, with blond hair and a "rather long face". An identikit picture of the man bears a striking resemblance to Brown.

Police also looked into a possible link between Brown and the August 1973 disappearance of 11-year-old Joanne Ratcliffe, and Kirste Gordon, 4, who vanished during a football match at the Adelaide Oval. Joanne was at the game with her parents and Kirste with her grandmother. The girls went to the toilet together and were last seen talking to a man near the grandstand. A witness reported the three were apparently tring to coax a kitten from beneath the stand.

Despite their suspicions police were unable to gather evidence that Brown was in South Australia at either time and the investigations stalled.

In May 2003 Townsville police re-opened a murder inquiry into the 1972 disappearance of 19-year-old Anita Cunningham, who was hitch-hiking in north Queensland with her friend Robin Hoinville-Bartram, 18, when both young women vanished. Hoinville-Bartram's body was later found in a shallow grave at Sensible Creek, 100 kilometres west of Charters Towers. She had been raped and shot in the head. Cunningham's body was never found.

Following a tip-off from a Melbourne man police excavated the creek bed where Hoinville-Bartram's remains were found. The search unearthed a number of bones but they were later identified as those of an animal.

Police re-investigated the movements of serial killer Ivan Milat at the time the two women disappeared, and were also interested in a possible link between the murders and Arthur Brown, but the case remains unsolved.

Charles Bopf said Brown had not been found guilty of the Mackay murders and was entitled to the presumption of innocence, but he had emerged as a "very strong suspect" as the police case against him "all fell together" in 1998.

"I've seen a lot of weaker cases get convictions, and if he'd been tried again it might have been a different story," Bopf said.

Barrister Jim Henry, who was Crown Prosecutor at Brown's 1999 trial, said the original police investigation may have missed an opportunity to solve the case early by ignoring other vehicles that were similar to eye-witness descriptions of an "EJ-type Holden".

"It was fairly obvious from the early days that detectives wanted to focus on the suspect's car as a Holden, but the police running sheets at the time indicate witnesses could have seen another car," Henry said. "In hindsight, more attention should have been given to similar types of cars.

"The brief suggests he was under their noses the whole time."

Henry said he was not surprised that the jury could not reach a verdict at Brown's trial.

"In all probability the jury was hung because, objectively speaking, the admissible evidence was not overwhelming," he said. "It's a case where the jury could have convicted, but clearly some members were not persuaded to do so."

Henry wouldn't say if he thought Brown was guilty of the Mackay murders, but said during his time as a prosecutor he had never proceeded against an accused person he believed to be innocent.

"This was a bona fide case and I went ahead on that basis."

Arthur Stanley Brown never admitted to the murders, nor to any other crimes attributed to him, and so he died in 2002 an innocent man in the eyes of the law. Whatever terrible secrets he may have harboured about the final hours of Judith and Susan Mackay went with him to his grave.